China's Economic Arrival

Damien Ma
Editor

China's Economic Arrival

Decoding a Disruptive Rise

保尔森基金会
PAULSON INSTITUTE

palgrave
macmillan

Editor
Damien Ma
Paulson Institute
Chicago, IL, USA

ISBN 978-981-15-2274-1 ISBN 978-981-15-2275-8 (eBook)
https://doi.org/10.1007/978-981-15-2275-8

This Palgrave Macmillan imprint is published by the registered company Springer Nature Singapore Pte Ltd.
The registered company address is: 152 Beach Road, #21-01/04 Gateway East, Singapore 189721, Singapore

Acknowledgements

This book would not have been possible without the incredible support of the Paulson Institute. Founded by Henry M. Paulson Jr. in 2011, the nonpartisan and independent institute's focus is dictated by the reality that US–China is the most consequential bilateral relationship in the world. The institute's work ranges from working with financial markets on green lending standards to devising market-based solutions to climate change and conservation.

Yet as debate over the US–China relationship rages on, it is ever more important to produce empirical, balanced, and thoughtful work that dispenses with generalities and grapples with nuance and complexity. At the moment, realistic appraisals of the world's second-largest economy appear to be in short supply—there is simply not enough "China" when it comes to US–China.

This is why our team at MacroPolo, the institute's think tank, has been dedicated to decoding China's political economy with best-in-class analysis and unique research products. And it is the *raison d'etre* of this collection of work from our experts, who combined have decades of practical, analytical, and policy experience with China.

Building a think tank over the last few years has been an enormous challenge, but it is leavened daily by the pleasure of working with one of the best teams in the field today.

All of us owe much gratitude to Evan Feigenbaum for shepherding this enterprise from the very beginning, and to Deborah Lehr for supporting and believing in the importance of what we do day in and day out.

In putting together this collection, my hope was to illuminate to a broader audience why China can no longer remain a distant abstraction but that its reemergence will have significant and practical implications for how we view ourselves and how we interact with the world.

There are no easy answers to how we collectively deal with this epochal and disruptive rise. But understanding its ramifications through this volume is a good place to start.

Whether this book achieves that goal, well, that's up to the readers to decide. For us at MacroPolo, we intend to keep on moving toward that goal.

Chicago
November 2019

Damien Ma

Contents

Politics

US–China

Notes on Contributors

Evan A. Feigenbaum is vice president for studies at the Carnegie Endowment for International Peace, where he oversees research in Washington, Beijing and New Delhi on a dynamic region encompassing both East Asia and South Asia. He is also the 2019–2020 James R. Schlesinger Distinguished Professor at the Miller Center of Public Affairs at the University of Virginia. Initially an academic with a Ph.D. in Chinese politics from Stanford University, Feigenbaum's career has spanned government service, think tanks, the private sector, and three major regions of Asia.

From 2001 to 2009, he served at the U.S. State Department as deputy assistant secretary of state for South Asia (2007–2009), deputy assistant secretary of state for Central Asia (2006–2007), member of the policy planning staff with principal responsibility for East Asia and the Pacific (2001–2006), and an adviser on China to Deputy Secretary of State Robert B. Zoellick, with whom he worked closely in the development of the U.S.-China senior dialogue.

During the intensive final phase of the U.S.-India civil nuclear initiative from July to October 2008, he co-chaired the coordinating team charged with moving the initiative through the International Atomic Energy Agency Board of Governors and the Nuclear Suppliers Group and then to Congress, where it became the U.S.-India Nuclear Cooperation Approval and Nonproliferation Enhancement Act. He negotiated agreements with the governments of Kazakhstan and Turkmenistan and also has extensive policy experience with North and South Korea, Japan, and

Australia. He received three individual and two group superior honor awards from the State Department.

Following government service, Feigenbaum worked in the private and nonprofit sectors: He was vice chairman of the Paulson Institute at the University of Chicago, and the co-founder of MacroPolo, its think tank; head of the Asia practice at Eurasia Group, a global political risk consulting firm; and senior fellow for East, Central, and South Asia at the Council on Foreign Relations. Before government service, he worked at Harvard University (1997–2001) as lecturer on government in the faculty of arts and sciences and as executive director of the Asia-Pacific Security Initiative and program chair of the Chinese Security Studies Program in the John F. Kennedy School of Government. He taught at the U.S. Naval Postgraduate School (1994–1995) as lecturer of national security affairs and was a consultant on China to the RAND Corporation (1993–1994).

He is the author of three books and monographs, including *The United States in the New Asia* (CFR, 2009, co-author) and *China's Techno-Warriors: National Security and Strategic Competition from the Nuclear to the Information Age* (Stanford University Press, 2003), which was selected by *Foreign Affairs* as a best book of 2003 on the Asia-Pacific, as well as numerous articles and essays.

Damien Ma is co-founder and Director of MacroPolo, the Paulson Institute's think tank. He is the author or editor of the books, *In Line Behind a Billion People: How Scarcity Will Define China's Ascent in the Next Decade*; *The Economics of Air Pollution in China* (by Ma Jun); and *China's Economic Arrival: Decoding a Disruptive Rise*. He currently also serves as adjunct faculty at the Kellogg School of Management at Northwestern University.

Previously, Damien was a Senior Analyst at Eurasia Group, the political risk research and advisory firm, where he mainly focused on the China and East Asia markets, including Mongolia. His advisory and analytical work served a range of clients from institutional investors and multinationals to the US, Japanese, and Singaporean governments.

Prior to joining Eurasia Group, he was a manager of publications at the US–China Business Council in Washington, DC, where he was also an adjunct lecturer at Johns Hopkins SAIS. Earlier in his career, he was a manager at public relations firm H-Line Ogilvy in Beijing working with multinational clients.

In addition, Damien has published widely, including in *The Atlantic*, *New York Times*, *Foreign Affairs*, *The New Republic*, *Foreign Policy*, and *Bloomberg*, among others. He has also appeared in a range of broadcast media such as the Charlie Rose Show, BBC, NPR, and CNBC. He has also keynoted or spoken at various industry, investor, and academic conferences, including CLSA and Credit Suisse Latin America.

Damien is a former term member of the Council on Foreign Relations and was named a "99under33" foreign policy leader by the Young Professionals in Foreign Policy. He speaks fluent Mandarin Chinese.

Joy Dantong Ma was formerly an Associate Director of the Paulson Institute's think tank. Her work focused on trade and investment and technology policy, and she co-led projects on China's artificial intelligence industry.

Dinny McMahon is currently Nonresident Associate of the Paulson Institute's think tank and author of the book *China's Great Wall of Debt: Shadow Banks, Ghost Cities, Massive Loans, and the End of the Chinese Miracle*.

Dinny spent 10 years working as a financial journalist in China. Between 2009 and 2015, he was with the *Wall Street Journal* in Beijing where he wrote about China's banking and financial sector, focusing on rising debt levels, urbanization, and the role of the state sector in the economy. Previously Dinny wrote for Dow Jones Newswires in Shanghai where he focused his reporting on the yuan and China's foreign exchange market. He also contributed to the *Far Eastern Economic Review*.

Prior to joining the Paulson Institute, Dinny spent two years as a fellow at the Woodrow Wilson International Center for Scholars in Washington DC.

Dinny has a Bachelor of Commerce and a Bachelor of Arts from the University of New South Wales in Sydney. He also attended the Johns Hopkins SAIS program in Nanjing for Chinese and American Studies.

Matt Sheehan is Fellow at the Paulson Institute's think tank where he leads work on US–China technology issues, with a specialization in artificial intelligence. Matt is the author of *The Transpacific Experiment: How China and California Collaborate and Compete for our Future* (Counterpoint Press, 2019) and co-host and co-producer of "Heartland Mainland: The Iowa China Podcast".

Based in the San Francisco Bay Area, he was formerly the China correspondent for The World Post. From 2010–2016 Matt lived and worked between the Chinese cities of Xi'an and Beijing. In 2016 he moved back to the Bay Area to work as an analyst, consultant, and writer on topics connecting China and California. In 2018, he was selected as a finalist for the Young China Watcher of the Year award.

His work has been published in *The Atlantic, Vice News, Foreign Policy, The WorldPost, The Huffington Post, MIT Technology Review*, and elsewhere. He has been quoted or cited in numerous media outlets, including *The New York Times, The Wall Street Journal, The Financial Times, Reuters, The San Francisco Chronicle, The Diplomat, Dagens Nyheter, The South China Morning Post, 界面, 星岛日报*, and elsewhere.

Houze Song is a Research Fellow at the Paulson Institute's think tank. He previously worked as a researcher at the Columbia Global Center (East Asia). Before that, he worked as a research manager at the Unirule Institute, where he assisted the chairman Mao Yushi with research and project management.

Houze holds an M.A. in quantitative methods and an M.P.A. in international economics, both from Columbia University, and a B.A. in economics from Peking University.

Neil Thomas is a Senior Research Associate at the Paulson Institute's think tank, where he works on Chinese politics, US–China relations, and international political economy. His research for MacroPolo has been featured by publishers such as *The Economist, The Wall Street Journal, The Los Angeles Times, Axios China, The Browser, Sky News*, and the *Sinocism China Newsletter*.

Neil previously worked for the Australian National University, both as a Morrison Scholar at the Australian Centre on China in the World and as a Research Project Officer at the Crawford School of Public Policy. He also spent time at the Carnegie-Tsinghua Center, Danwei Media, and *The Texas Tribune*, and has written for publications including *The Washington Post, Foreign Policy, The Hill, Los Angeles Review of Books (China Channel), East Asia Forum Quarterly*, and the *International Journal of Public Policy*.

Neil holds a Master in Public Policy from the John F. Kennedy School of Government at Harvard University, where he was an IGA Student

Fellow at the Belfer Center for Science and International Affairs, and a Bachelor of Arts in economics and political science from the University of Western Australia, where he was a UWA Fogarty Scholar.

List of Figures

CHAPTER 1

Introduction

Damien Ma

By 2021, China will be set to become a high-income country, the next US administration will take office, and the oldest millennials will turn 40. Disparate as these events may seem, they could shape US–China relations for decades to come.

Even as Beijing graduates into this exclusive club of high-income countries—the World Bank currently puts it at about $12,000 per capita GDP but is adjusted for inflation—the average Chinese will still be less than 20% as rich as Americans. To simply reach parity with the United States' per capita GDP in 2018 (~$60,000), China would need to become an $80 trillion-plus economy, or about the same size as the *entire* global economy today.

Reaching true parity with the United States will have to wait, but that won't prevent perceptions from sprinting impatiently ahead of reality. China's transition into a relatively wealthy country—its first centenary goal of becoming a "moderately prosperous country" 100 years from the founding of the Chinese Communist Party (CCP) in 1921—will likely calcify the Beltway view that this achievement is yet another signpost of the unstoppable march of authoritarian supremacy.

D. Ma (✉)
Paulson Institute, Chicago, IL, USA
e-mail: dma@paulsoninstitute.org

D. Ma (ed.), *China's Economic Arrival*,
https://doi.org/10.1007/978-981-15-2275-8_1

At the same time, however, such a view will be punctuated by pundits swarming cable TV and op-ed pages, predicting the imminent collapse of the Chinese economy. If Chinese power rests on a Potemkin economy, and will fade away like a much larger Japan, then what's the worry?

Policymakers and pundits may never converge on their views of the Chinese economy, but both nonetheless agree on one thing: China poses the greatest challenge to the United States in the twenty-first century. That is indisputable—China's rise is a challenge that is qualitatively different and thornier than any the United States confronted last century.

For one, China's size means that it does not have to reach parity with the United States across all dimensions of power to reshuffle the global order and to contest America's predominance in various theaters. Second, unlike the Soviet Union or Japan, the People's Republic is the only country that has the potential to assume "peer competitor" status with the United States because of its economic might—no other emerging market comes even close. Third, the foci of the competition will cluster largely around economic and technological rivalries rather than military conflicts, at least in the medium term. Fourth, outright ideological warfare isn't likely—Beijing knows that it cannot, nor does it desire to, undo American democracy—but misaligned political values can and will undermine potential cooperation on ostensibly shared interests.

None of this suggests that China is an "existential threat" to the American "way of life"—a hyperbolic claim that isn't grounded in empirical reality. Yet, irrespective of who occupies the White House in 2021, the US assessment of China as a peer competitor is unlikely to change. Viewing China as America's decisive rival may be a foregone conclusion, but reflexively opposing anything China does on the international stage would be an ineffective and even counterproductive strategy to advance US diplomatic, economic, and security interests. In the face of formidable Chinese competition, clearly defining core interests and objectively delineating costs and benefits are vital.

If one such interest is to preserve a global system that maintains peace and generates prosperity, then adjustments are necessary. That's because the scale and speed of China's ascent has already strained an existing system that was not designed to accommodate peer powers.

How that system adapts may be shaped by forces that have been overlooked, in part because we're living amidst the shift in real time. Indeed, beyond the Beltway and policy circles, the fabric of American society is also changing. A generation of millennials, many of whom turn 40 in

2021, will begin to enter positions of power and influence in all fields. This generation's formative experiences could well determine America's approach toward the world, and China specifically, more than is currently recognized.

It is a generation shaped far less by the democratic-capitalist euphoria that followed the collapse of the Soviet Union and much more by the Global Financial Crisis and the Wars on Terror. For instance, a provocative study from Harvard University has shown evidence that just 1 in 3 millennials believe it is "essential" to live in a democracy, compared to more than 60% for baby boomers. And this isn't so much an "age" effect as a "cohort" effect, according to the same study. That is, in 2011, about one-quarter of those born in the 1980s believed that democracy is an inferior form of government, whereas in 1995, only 16% of those born in the 1970s felt the same way.

So it is not necessarily clear that today's millennials are staunchly attached to the US-led system that stitched the world together for 70 years. To be sure, they came of age in a world in which America lost some of its sheen and where China has always been a major player. Millennials, like most Americans, certainly see China as different—more repressive, keen on censorship, and unyielding on free speech—but it is far less foreign and far more a fixture of the global order than the Soviet Union was for previous generations.

What's more, China is much more accessible for this generation—whether it is having the option to take Chinese language classes (some as early as grade school) or spending time in China studying and working. The tangibility of today's China can also be felt in the influx of young Chinese in American schools and colleges.

In fact, numerous polls suggest that concern about China isn't anywhere close to outright hostility. The 2019 public opinion survey from the Chicago Council on Global Affairs shows that the rise of China was only the 11th most pressing issue among the American public. Meanwhile, a recent Pew Research survey reveals that although concerns over China are growing, more than 60% still believe in having strong trade and economic ties with China. Finally, a 2018 Reagan Institute poll showed that 55% of those under 30 believe China to be more of an ally than an enemy, while more than 60% of those over 65 view the country as an enemy.

Of course nothing is preordained, but these results and shifts so far suggest that if great power competition is a generational effort, then it might be difficult to carry the millennial cohort along. Put another way, whatever the new *Washington* consensus is on China, an enduring *American* consensus is unlikely to be forged. Therefore, debates on how to properly handle China's economic and political arrival cannot merely exist in a Beltway silo but will require a national reckoning of what could and should be done.

But such a challenge will be insurmountable without a realistic appraisal of today's China, its political economy, its aspirations, and its capabilities, sound analysis upon which any rational strategy toward China ought to be predicated. Yet empirical and nuanced assessments of what China is—rather than what we wish it to be—are in short supply.

This is especially so in an information environment of accelerated and unrelenting news cycles, political screeds that masquerade as dispassionate analysis, and social media outrage that stirs passions more than revealing truths. Indeed, the democratization of China expertise has made discussions of "the greatest 21st century challenge" both richer and shallower.

So it is my hope that this collection of work from MacroPolo can raise the signal-to-noise ratio and bring value to ongoing discussions about how to manage a more capable Beijing while protecting US interests. This volume is meant to be as accessible as it is substantive, with each chapter focused on unpacking important aspects of China's economy, policymaking, and technological ambition. Each piece in this collection grounds its high-level perspectives in bottom-up analysis, yielding deep insights about contemporary China.

This volume contains eight chapters in addition to the introduction and conclusion, organized under the broad categories of economics, technology, politics, and US–China. Featured authors have not only done extensive work in their respective fields but are also distinguished analysts, practitioners, or former policymaker.

Ultimately, this volume aims to bring more "China" into US–China debates.

Houze Song leads off after the introduction with a chapter that examines China's northeast "rustbelt" to find out why it has fallen behind other regional economies. In examining Liaoning, Song zeroes in on the largest of the three northeastern provinces (the other two being Jilin and Heilongjiang). He uses the case of a failed automotive venture to illustrate broader dynamics that have stifled the local economy, a microcosm of the tangled relationship between state and market. Song argues that restructuring the Chinese economy will require not only surface adjustments but also fundamental institutional changes.

One of those institutional changes is taking place in the financial system. To execute a deleveraging campaign that began around 2016, Beijing created a new "super regulator" for the financial system while relying on an ongoing anti-corruption campaign to overcome resistance to reform. Weighed down by debt after the global financial crisis, China's financial system was in bad shape. But predictions of an imminent catastrophe were always off the mark, in large part because virtually all Chinese debt is internal, walled off by capital controls. In Chapter 3, Dinny McMahon details the methodical and gradualist strategy that Beijing has adopted to "clean up" its financial sector, resulting in progress that has exceeded expectations.

One of the most dynamic elements of the Chinese economy is its technological progress. In Chapter 4, Matt Sheehan examines the disruption of an important aspect of the US–China tech ecosystem: talent. Visas for Chinese high-skilled workers and graduate students may be under threat as the Trump administration has come to believe that Chinese researchers are stealing intellectual property and compromising national security. Yet many of the top Chinese tech talent, particularly in artificial intelligence, appears to want to stay and work in America as part of the global talent pool that underpins innovation in Silicon Valley. How this competition for talent plays out could have significant implications for innovation.

An even fiercer battle is brewing over high-tech industries like semiconductors and 5G. In Chapter 5, Joy Dantong Ma's extensive analysis of Qualcomm's evolution and prospects in the Chinese market elucidates why this competition is so complex. China's success in developing 5G technologies and chips could eat into the market share of a company like Qualcomm, which has dominated the Chinese market in 3G and 4G chips for decades and now depends on it for the majority of the company's revenue. And herein lies the main conundrum: China is both the largest market for semiconductors on the demand side and the biggest potential competitor in producing chips on the supply side. Whether China's success in 5G will come at the expense of US companies makes this one of the thorniest issues to handle.

Technology is also a force for change in Chinese politics, not least in propaganda work. Indeed, "Propaganda in the New Era" under Xi Jinping has gone digital, has a different look and feel, and has been more effective than expected. It is clear that Xi has placed an importance on propaganda not seen since perhaps the Mao Zedong era, elevating much ideological work from state organs to those of the CCP. Propaganda is undercovered in mainstream discussions of Chinese politics, but in Chapter 6, Damien Ma and Neil Thomas analyze the content, the funding, and the effectiveness of propaganda. In the digital age, winning the hearts and minds of domestic audiences has never been more challenging, but the CCP has also learned how to adapt with the times.

Amid significant changes in Chinese elite politics over the past few years, Chapter 7 sheds light on demographic representation in China's highest ruling body, the CCP Central Committee, and the Chinese legislature, the National People's Congress. Relying on an original database of the top 375 Chinese politicians, Damien Ma and Neil Thomas discover interesting patterns in the geographic origins, gender balance, and ethnic diversity of Chinese leaders. China is hardly a paragon of equal representation, but it is surprisingly close to the global average on many metrics.

The last two chapters focus on US–China relations, the key dyad in ongoing reassessments of China. The first is Evan Feigenbaum's "Reluctant Stakeholder," which tackles a key question: is China a revisionist power? How that question is answered matters for shaping an appropriate response to the China challenge. If China is a rule-breaker bent on resetting the global order, its rise would require a very different response than if Beijing simply wants to augment or amend existing rules to better serve its interests. Even if Beijing will never become a full-fledged champion of the US-led order, its leaders seem to recognize how the current system has served its interests, and more so than they like to publicly admit.

Finally, Chapter 9 traces the history in post-Mao China of the American multinational that perhaps best exemplifies the complex and nuanced layers of the US–China relationship: Boeing. The aviation giant is no nation-state, but its evolution in the Chinese market provides a unique window into the forces that have both fortified the bilateral relationship and might now pull it apart. Neil Thomas digs into the historical archives and presents a case study of how Boeing played a starring role both in prying open markets in China and in American debates on China's eventual accession to the World Trade Organization. Both the consequences and rewards of Boeing's operations in China are at the heart of rethinking the US approach to China.

These pieces magnify important dynamics of how the world's second-largest economy has prospered and the challenges it now faces after four decades of relative success. The diversity of subjects should not obscure the unifying theme: China does not exist in a vacuum—it is as shaped by secular forces and affected by macro trends as any other country. The teleology of "Chinese dominance" and that of "Chinese collapse" are both inadequate in capturing extant realities.

In this sense, China is hardly an outlier. What makes the country a true outlier is its scale—no matter what China does today, the ripples are felt far beyond its borders. So far, the world has neither grown accustomed to those ripples nor come to grips with how to make room for a great power that was not party to the current system's creation.

Therefore, grappling with China's arrival must be a collective enterprise comprised of not just American thinkers and doers, but of those from across the world. That belief is reflected in this volume, both in spirit and in substance. I hope these pages can offer readers balanced appraisals of both the constraints and potential of today's China. We do not have all the right answers, but this is our contribution to getting a little closer to them.

Economy

CHAPTER 2

Liaoning: The Smothering Effects of Local Protectionism

Houze Song

When the Liaoning provincial government nationalized Brilliance Auto in 2002, the local private car maker was thought to be one of the most advanced and promising among China's domestic brands. However, the government takeover proved to be the turning point in the company's fortunes, as a once thriving company turned into another struggling and debt-laden state owned firm.

The experience of Brilliance Auto is emblematic of a deeper problem that afflicts local governments throughout China: local protectionism. To be sure, China's auto sector is no stranger to local protectionism—in fact, the industry's notorious fragmentation is largely a result of fierce local competition to crown their own auto champion. Yet most of the local government owned automakers do eventually become viable businesses. The difference in Liaoning is that despite the government's generous support, Brilliance continued to hemorrhage money to the point where its sedan business became insolvent.

H. Song (✉)
Paulson Institute, Chicago, IL, USA
e-mail: hsong@paulsoninstitute.org

D. Ma (ed.), *China's Economic Arrival*,
https://doi.org/10.1007/978-981-15-2275-8_2

The proximate cause of Brilliance's failure can be explained by the Liaoning government's effort to localize the auto supply chain, which ended up hampering the quality of the cars. What happened to Brilliance isn't unique, however. Rather, it reflects a broader trend: the gradual inward turn of the Liaoning economy.

Indeed, since the early 2000s, Liaoning's economy has become more closed—perhaps even tilting toward a mild form of autarky—as indicated by the rising share of local demand and the significant slowdown in export growth. As a result of local protectionism and other distortions, Liaoning's average growth rate has been significantly lower than the national average, while its share of the national economy fell from 6.3 to 2.8% between 1978 and 2018.[1]

More fundamentally, Brilliance's stagnation and the overall deterioration of Liaoning firms' competitiveness can be attributed to a local government-driven investment model that has been practiced for the last 15 years. Allowing a local government that already had strong protectionist tendencies take charge of allocating capital only reinforced local protectionism and harmed the competitiveness of provincial firms. It became a self-fulfilling prophecy: the more the government protected local industry, the less competitive it became, which led the government to further support and protect it. In this environment, it's the politically connected, rather than competitive, firms that become the "winners."

How Protectionism Ruined China's Once Promising Carmaker

Yang Rong, a private entrepreneur, built China Brilliance Auto out of a nearly bankrupt Shenyang state firm he acquired in 1991. Initially, Yang owned Brilliance through a joint venture (JV) with a subsidiary of the People's Bank of China (PBOC), which acted as a passive investor and never exerted any authority over the firm.[2]

Back then, all central government assets were ultimately owned by the National Bureau of State Assets Management (predecessor to the State-owned Assets Supervision and Administration Commission), which was then a Ministry of Finance (MoF) subsidiary. In the late 1990s, Beijing decided to transfer all but the most strategically important central state assets to local governments.[3] Brilliance, too, was destined to be transferred wholesale to the Liaoning government. The only outstanding question was how much Yang would be compensated, as he only directly owned less than 3% of his company.

For the local government, it certainly picked a solid asset to takeover. By 2001, a decade after its founding, Yang's auto venture had grown into a 20 billion yuan ($3.1 billion) business, riding on the rapid expansion of China's auto market. At that time, Brilliance was widely seen as the most advanced and promising domestic carmaker in China. In fact, Yang received enormous validation when Germany's BMW decided to pick Brilliance as a local partner, against the advice of senior Chinese leaders who thought BMW should partner with a state automaker. According to BMW executives, they were impressed by Brilliance's state-of-the-art assembly line and efficient management.[4]

Around the same time, Yang had also formed a JV with the then-struggling British carmaker Rover. That strategy was a technology play aimed at bringing Rover's research and production operations to China and giving Brilliance the technology it needed to produce better quality engines. Up until then, Brilliance had sourced older and unreliable engines from a Shenyang factory run by a JV between Japan's Mitsubishi and a local Chinese partner.

The deal with Rover should have been a coup for Yang. But instead, it marked the unraveling of Brilliance's relationship with the Liaoning government. The key tussle came when Yang wanted to establish a factory to make Rovers in Ningbo, a relatively prosperous port city in Zhejiang province that's close to metropolitan Shanghai. Since Yang was planning to export his Chinese-made Rovers, it made sense to locate in close proximity to China's biggest export hub. Moreover, about 75% of Brilliance's supply chain was concentrated in the Yangtze River Delta, centered on Shanghai.[5]

But the problem was that the Liaoning authorities didn't like Yang's plans. They wanted the new Rover plant in Liaoning.

As construction of Brilliance's Ningbo plant drew closer, the Liaoning government launched what amounted to a hostile takeover, effectively confiscating Yang's shares and taking control of his company. On March 11, 2002, MoF issued a notice to transfer all controlling shares in the Brilliance JV to the Liaoning provincial government. Yang sought to appease the government and cooperated with the process initially, while the authorities allowed him to remain as CEO and board chairman. But a few months later, the Liaoning police launched an investigation into

Yang for "stripping state assets," prompting him to flee to the United States where he has remained ever since.[6]

On paper, the Liaoning government was the undisputed winner. Not only did it now own and control Brilliance, but that control allowed it to consolidate all of the firm's operations and supply chain in Liaoning province. It demanded that the automaker buy its components and materials from local suppliers, which negatively affected Brilliance's own subsidiaries. In the year that Brilliance was nationalized, the company purchased just half as many auto parts as it did previously from its Shanghai subsidiary. After June 2002, Brilliance suspended purchases from the Shanghai subsidiary entirely.

When it came to sourcing inputs, Brilliance never used local steel in the past—despite Liaoning having a sizeable steel sector. But after the government takeover, Brilliance was pressured to buy steel from Benxi Steel, a local state-owned steelmaker. (Notably, Brilliance didn't source from Anshan Steel, which is also based in Liaoning but owned by the central government.)

And unsurprisingly, the Ningbo project also fell apart. As a result, not only did Brilliance eventually have to pay Rover more than 200 million yuan ($30 million) in damages, it was still stuck sourcing lower quality engines without the capability to make its own engines.

The Liaoning government's treatment of Brilliance needs to be understood in the context of a province undergoing a painful economic transition that began in the early 2000s. As part of the transition, thousands of state-owned firms were shut down and millions of jobs were lost. The authorities were desperate to rebuild the local industrial base wherever possible. To that end, they heavily favored Brilliance in government procurement, and the company typically won generous contracts whenever taxis needed to be replaced, police cars upgraded, or garbage truck fleets expanded. And of course, Brilliance also received generous fiscal subsidies every year.

Even with such support, the Liaoning government's embrace spelt disaster for the firm. For instance, China's minibus market has grown by more than 300% since the Liaoning government took control of Brilliance, yet the company sold fewer of its flagship model, the Jinbei minibus, in 2016 than it did in 2001.[7] Meanwhile, Brilliance's domestic brand sedan business has lost so much money since it first entered the market in 2002 that the company's debt now exceeds the value of its assets.[8] What makes that all the more extraordinary is that Brilliance's losses have accumulated even as China's auto market grew sevenfold since 2002.

It is tempting to explain Brilliance's struggle as solely a symptom of state ownership, but it's not that simple. To smooth the ownership transition and ensure the ongoing good management of the firm, the Liaoning government gave Yang's former senior executive team stock options equal to 9.4% of the firm's equity, something unheard of at state firms, even today.[9] Even in public companies in advanced economies, senior management frequently owns less than 10% of the firm. But the fact that the senior management owned part of the firm didn't matter much. The core problem was that their ownership didn't translate into decision-making power and influence over the direction of the company.

How Investment Driven Growth Exacerbated Liaoning's Protectionism Tendencies

The point of highlighting Brilliance's collapse is not that it is unique, but that it is the norm for Liaoning. Indeed, many other industrial firms in the province have seen their share of China's national market decline since 2000 (see Fig. 2.1). In part that's because of protectionism, but specifically it's the combination of protectionism with an economic growth model that relies too heavily on investment, which amplifies the deleterious effects of protectionism.

Between 2002 and 2009, investment had contributed to more than 75% of Liaoning's cumulative economic growth (the ratio is 46% nationally) and it very likely remained the largest driver of economic growth until at least 2013.[10] (2002 is the year Beijing made the revitalization of the northeast a top priority, resulting in a number of plans for increasing investment in Liaoning[11]). In fact, there is strong evidence to suggest that the majority of this investment is driven by the local government. By the end of 2016, the Liaoning government's on-budget debt was 38% of GDP, almost double the national average of 20%.[12]

With plenty of investment projects available, the Liaoning government could deliver growth without worrying about fostering competitive firms. Rather, it coddled local firms, directing government procurement contracts to them, and by farming out fiscal resources to local interests.

This also meant that Liaoning firms didn't have to be competitive with firms from elsewhere in the country and the world, to the detriment of

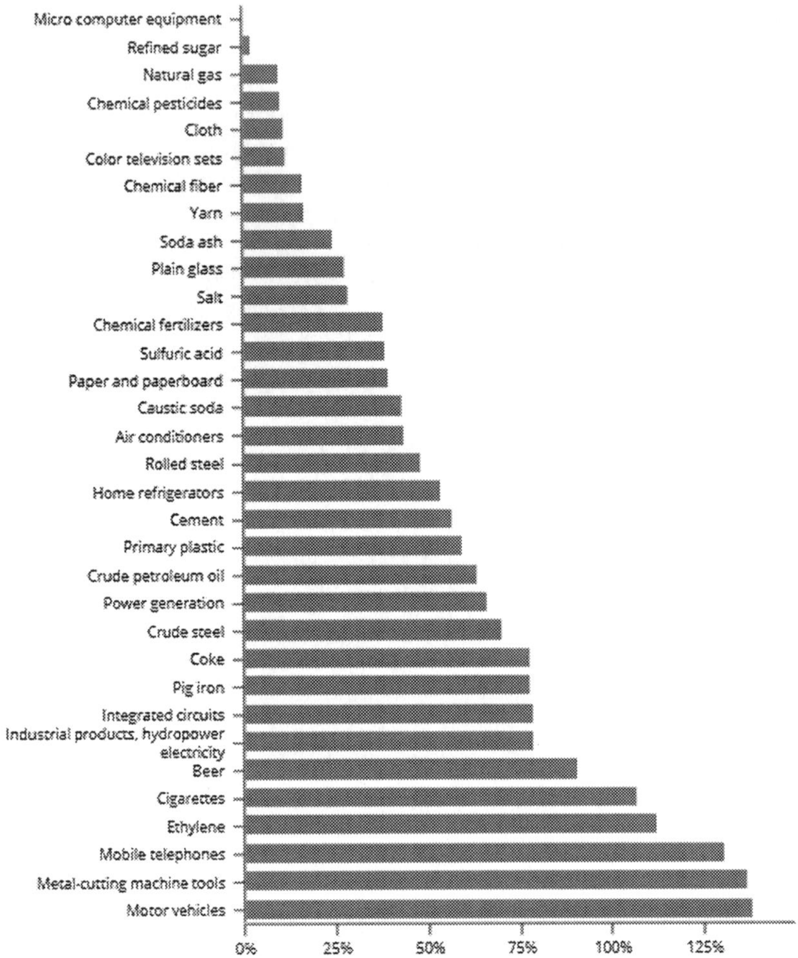

Fig. 2.1 Declining market share of Liaoning's industrial goods (*Note* The figures in the chart are calculated by dividing 2016 market share by 2002 market share. A figure greater than 100% indicates increasing market share. Market share is calculated as Liaoning's production divided by national production. *Source* National Bureau of Statistics)

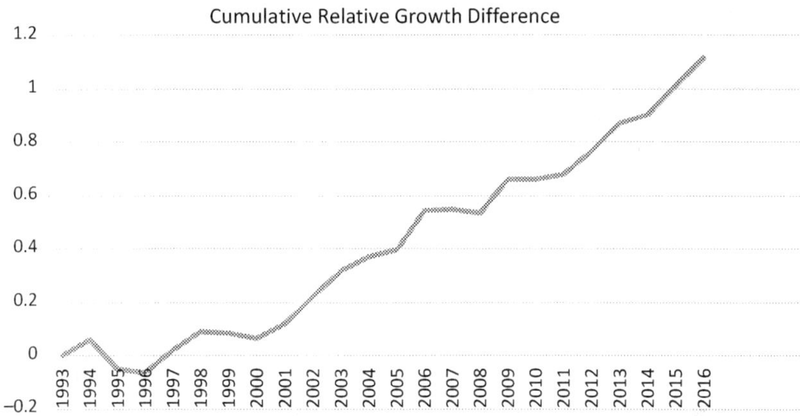

Fig. 2.2 The growth gap between Liaoning exports and national exports has widened after 2001 (*Note* Positive value indicates how much faster national exports grew than Liaoning's exports since 1993. *Source* National Bureau of Statistics)

the local economy. After 2002, Liaoning province's export growth significantly lagged compared to the national average. Between 1993 and 2001, the province's exports cumulatively grew 10% slower than China as a whole (see Fig. 2.2). But between 2002 and 2016, the growth gap widened to more than 100%.[13] Over the course of the last 15 years, the province has experienced a massive shift in the structure of demand.

This decline in the importance of the outside market comes with negative side effects. Selling goods outside your home market requires your goods to be of higher quality and lower cost than your competitors. In other words, even a Liaoning state firm needs to demonstrate its goods are better when it is competing outside of its home court. Exports introduce meritocracy into the local economy, and the declining importance of outside markets meant that Liaoning firms were subject to less market discipline.

Conclusion

Liaoning's economic problems are deep and varied, including an overreliance on investment-led growth, soft budget constraints on state firms, a lack of economic diversification, a disproportionately large role for meddling provincial authorities, and protectionist proclivities.

In the face of this litany of factors, reviving Liaoning's economy will prove particularly challenging. The province's woes have not been lost on Beijing, which has been wracking its brain on how to turn things around. So far, the tactic seems to be injecting new blood into the provincial leadership, in the hopes that new talent can lead the province out of its economic morass. Indeed, since 2013, seven vice-minister and above officials in Liaoning—the most of any province and tied with Shanxi—have been investigated for corruption. Still, without corresponding institutional fixes that can improve government accountability, the impact of such a draconian campaign will likely fade over time.

One modest institutional fix that Beijing is experimenting with is to improve the local judicial system. The central government has installed circuit courts that are directly managed by the Supreme People's Court, to create some distance between local authorities' influence on courts. In 2015, the northeast was chosen as one of two regions to engage in a trial of creating more independent courts. In theory, the introduction of circuit courts can serve as a check on local governments' ability to intervene in judicial decisions that might affect the economy. Given that this is a relatively new experiment, it is still too early to tell how effective these circuit courts will be.

But despite the depth of Liaoning's problems, it's important to bear in mind that Liaoning is not alone. The rest of the northeast region, Jilin and Heilongjiang, also has been heavily reliant on investment to generate growth. Beyond the northeast, other regional economies, too, have been relying on investment. In 2016, 15 out of 31 Chinese regions saw investment as a share of GDP greater than 60%, which is about 15% higher than the national average, in a country already considered to have a high investment rate.[14]

In the past few years, thanks to an easy credit environment, many of these high investment regions managed to sustain, or even double down on, their investment-driven growth model. This resulted in those regions achieving higher growth rates than their peers up until 2017 (see Fig. 2.3).

But as this analysis has demonstrated, this seeming prosperity is misleading. First, the high-growth figures are, in some sense, illusory. As the experience of Dandong, a port city in Liaoning showed, once investment normalizes, GDP growth can virtually collapse overnight.[15] Second, an investment-driven model exacerbates existing distortions in the economy, which leaves lasting negative consequences. As a result, the afflicted

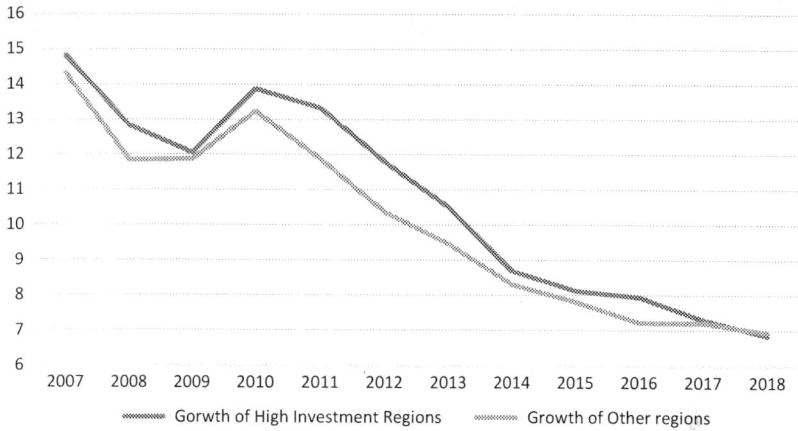

Fig. 2.3 Growth of high investment regions outperform national average (*Note* High investment region is defined as having an average investment share greater than 60% between 2007 and 2017. *Source* National Bureau of Statistics)

region may have to cope with the loss of economic competitiveness for many years after the investment boom ends.

Indeed, since Beijing began to mandate local governments to deleverage and deal with their debt in 2017, the average growth of high-investment regions has declined rapidly and is now below the average growth rate of low-investment regions. Some of these high-investment regions, like Tianjin, have already exhibited signs of repeating Liaoning's economic stagnation. It seems only likely that Liaoning's experience will be replicated elsewhere in China in the coming years.

Notes

1. For other distortions in the Liaoning economy, please see Houze Song, "Provincial Snapshot—Liaoning: How a Rust Belt Province Stagnated and Why It Matters to China," MacroPolo, https://macropolo.org/analysis/provincial-snapshot-liaoning-how-a-rust-belt-province-stagnated-and-why-it-matters-to-china/.
2. "I Helped Yang Rong for Brilliance's IPO in US," *The Economic Observer* (经济观察), July 29, 2002, http://www.eeo.com.cn/zt/jingguan10/2002/wenzhang/2011/04/13/198706.shtml.

3. See 中共中央办公厅、国务院办公厅关于中央党政机关与所办经济实体和管理的直属企业脱钩有关问题的通知 (General Office of the Communist Party of China and General Office of the State Council Notice on Severing Ties Between Central Party and State Organization and their Directly Owned Enterprises), November 8, 1998, http://www.71.cn/2011/0930/633190.shtml.
4. "Why BMW Chooses Brilliance, an Insider Account," *International Finance* (国际金融报), March 28, 2003, http://www.people.com.cn/GB/jinji/32/178/20030328/956431.html.
5. "Yang Rong Explains the Brilliance Myth," *International Finance* (国际金融报), December 13, 2002, http://www.china.com.cn/chinese/jingji/246589.htm.
6. Ibid.
7. See Jinbei Auto (金杯汽车) 2001 Annual Report and "2016 China Commercial Vehicle Market Report," Sohu, http://www.sohu.com/a/128356648_526280.
8. It should be noted that Brilliance's JV with BMW still exists because the deal was struck before the nationalization of Brilliance. The venture is actually profitable, largely because BMW has kept tight control over production. In 2016, BMW contributed almost 90% of the revenue and all the profit to Brilliance.
9. To put this into perspective, in a deal meant to set an example for future state firm reforms, China Unicom recently gave 7855 executives stock options worth less than 3% of the firm. For further explanation on SOE ownership reform, please see Houze Song, "State-Owned Enterprise Reforms: Untangling Ownership, Control, and Corporate Governance," MacroPolo, https://macropolo.org/analysis/state-owned-enterprise-reforms-untangling-ownership-control-corporate-governance/.
10. There is no direct way to determine the investment share in Liaoning post-2010 because during that period, the province's GDP figures are known to be manipulated. But since the central government continued to promulgate policies to bolster the northeast economy in 2009 and 2012, it is reasonable to assume that the investment boom lasted at least until 2013.
11. "16th National Congress of the Communist Party of China Report," November 8, http://www.chinacommercialoffice.org/web/ziliao_674904/zyjh_674906/t10855.shtml.
12. Liaoning has managed to achieve deleveraging since 2016. By the end of 2018, local government on-budget debt/GDP ratio has declined to 34%. In the meantime, according to the author's estimation, Liaoning has also managed to deleverage its off-budget debt. Please see MacroPolo "China's Debt Hangover" for more details on Liaoning's off-budget debt, https://macropolo.org/digital-projects/china-local-debt-hangover-map/.

13. In 2017 and 2018, Liaoning's export growth recovered to above the national export growth, but had dropped again to below national growth by mid-2019.
14. China's provincial economic statistics are known to be significantly exaggerated, and this creates difficulties for estimating the share of investment in local GDP. For example, in 2016, the sum of regional gross fixed capital formation (the technical term for investment in GDP accounting) is nearly 30% larger than the national figure. In the meantime, there is also exaggeration in regional GDP. In 2016, total GDP reported by the provinces added up to 4.5% larger than the national GDP.

    Using the conservative assumption that all regional investment and GDP figures are equally overestimated by the levels cited above, then we should discount local investment share in GDP by 25%. As such, in 2016, only provinces with more than 60% of investment share in GDP are considered more over reliant on investment than the national average.

    Nonetheless, provinces with exaggerated investment figures usually also have exaggerated GDP numbers. Liaoning's GDP figure has been revised down by more than 20%. And if we believe the GDP of over-investment regions are similarly exaggerated as Liaoning's, then the regional investment share is overstated by around 5%, rather than 25%.

    Notably, the 60% threshold excludes many regions, like Tianjin and Chongqing, which are known to rely on investment for growth. Practically speaking, we can say with high confidence that regions with an investment share greater than 55% of GDP as over reliant on investment than the national average. In 2016, 19 provinces met this threshold.
15. For analysis on the economic stagnation of Dandong port, see Houze Song, "Provincial Snapshot—Liaoning: How Government Intervention Crippled China's Only Private Port," MacroPolo, https://macropolo.org/analysis/provincial-snapshot-liaoning-how-government-intervention-crippled-chinas-only-private-port/.

CHAPTER 3

Slow, Steady, Cheap, and Painless: Making Sense of China's Bad Loan Strategy

Dinny McMahon

Summary

In the years following the Global Financial Crisis, China's banking system presided over an expansion in credit of historic proportions. That sustained the Chinese economy's rapid growth but resulted in piles of nonperforming loans (NPLs). Beijing is now pursuing a slow and measured approach to clean up its financial system. The approach is designed to minimize both disruptions to the economy and the cost to the central government.

Central to this approach is opaque NPL data, which gives the authorities greater control over the pace at which banks recognize losses. Beijing has also avoided increasing its own fiscal burden by pushing the cleanup cost onto the banks, private sector, and local governments.

As the economy slows further, Beijing's gradualist approach to NPLs will prove more challenging. But the government remains poised to perpetuate it by experimenting with creative solutions.

D. McMahon (✉)
Paulson Institute, Chicago, IL, USA
e-mail: info@paulsoninstitute.org

D. Ma (ed.), *China's Economic Arrival*,
https://doi.org/10.1007/978-981-15-2275-8_3

Full Text

In the years immediately following the Global Financial Crisis, the Chinese economy underwent what was perhaps the largest, most rapid build-up of debt in economic history. Led by the banks, the financial system directed an incredible flood of lending toward property developers, local governments, and state-owned industrial firms. That allowed China to sail through the crisis relatively unscathed, but it resulted in a huge amount of excess and waste—housing supply with no demand, public works of little utility, and factories producing goods far in excess of what the economy could absorb.

It also created a lot of debt that will never be repaid. And since 2016, China's financial authorities have been quietly pushing the banks to dispose of their bad loans more aggressively. The process has been incremental, but cumulatively meaningful. The measured pace at which Beijing is pursuing its debt cleanup could easily be misconstrued as timidity, a sign that China's political leaders remain either uncommitted to dealing with the risk or unconvinced of the need.

But the pace is deliberate. It is part of a broader, unconventional strategy designed to reduce NPLs in a way that minimizes both disruption to the economy and cost to the central government.

The approach is not without risk. While gradualism helps to avoid the trauma that would accompany a more sudden adjustment, the trade-off is that banks must tolerate a higher level of NPLs for a longer period of time, which affects the banking system's liquidity. That also leaves the banks more vulnerable to economic shocks, which has the potential to lead to far greater economic disruption down the line. That said, Beijing has taken sweeping measures in order to mitigate those risks.

Therefore, making sense of China's gradualist approach to cleaning up its financial system is key to understanding how the economy may perform both in the near and medium terms. In particular, the following analysis outlines the ways in which Beijing's approach is unconventional and what it's trying to achieve. It will then discuss the steps the central government has taken to mitigate the sort of financial instability that could derail the process. And finally, it will look at how worsening economic conditions threaten the sustainability of the approach.

Being Unconventional

Dealing with bad loans is challenging for any government, and ignoring NPLs certainly has its advantages. That's because write-downs of debt reduce GDP,[1] diminish bank profits, and divert capital that might otherwise be used to expand lending. But failing to deal with bad loans in a timely manner can incur steep costs. Ultimately a day of reckoning comes—usually precipitated by some sort of financial crisis—when the accumulated weight of NPLs can no longer be ignored and the government must step in with a bailout.

China is pursuing the third way in addressing its bad loans. First, it has launched the debt cleanup prior to being forced into action by a financial crisis. By getting ahead of the problem, the authorities have been able to dictate the pace of the cleanup. Second, the Chinese government has avoided acknowledging the full extent of bank NPLs. That has frustrated observers trying to gauge the health of China's financial system, but it's part of an approach designed to minimize economic disruption. And finally, to avoid a government bailout—and more broadly to minimize the cost to the central government—Beijing has sought to pass on the cleanup cost either to the banks, the market, or to local governments.

Minimizing Disruption—The Upside of Opacity

In the three years between 2016 and 2018, Chinese banks disposed of 4.4 trillion yuan worth of NPLs, equivalent to 4% of total outstanding loans at the end of 2018 (Fig. 3.1).[2] But it's difficult to know how significant that 4% is as a portion of NPLs, since Beijing hasn't disclosed the total volume of NPLs in the system. The official NPL ratio—1.83% at the end of 2018—is generally regarded as not reflective of reality. In recent years observers have offered estimates of NPL ratios that range from around 4%[3] to as high as 20%.[4] This wide range betrays just how little is known about the extent of the problem.

The official obfuscation serves a purpose. Back in 2013, I asked a senior financial regulator if the official NPL data fairly represented bank asset quality. At the time, the official NPL ratio of 1% seemed incredibly low given the malinvestment that resulted from the 4 trillion yuan stimulus following the global financial crisis. He didn't answer my question directly, but instead asked, "Were China to disclose that it had significantly higher NPL levels, would anyone benefit?"

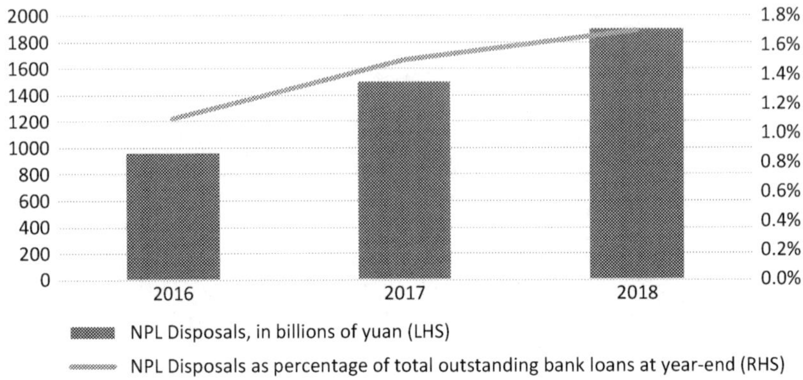

Fig. 3.1 At your disposal (Annual NPLs in billions of yuan, and as percentage of outstanding loans at year-end. *Source* CBIRC, Chinese media)

He went on to explain that in that scenario, the banks would immediately have to raise new capital en masse and at firesale prices and companies would be forced into bankruptcy as banks pursued repayment. However, if the process could be drawn out by not disclosing the true state of NPLs, then much of the trauma could be avoided to buy authorities time to deal with the problem on their own terms and at their own pace.

No doubt he was somewhat overselling the potential trauma. Governments regulate their banks' treatment of NPLs and hence can change capital and loan loss provision requirements to make it less burdensome for banks to recognize and hold bad loans on their books.

However, China's rules for dealing with bad loans are fairly strict. Banks are required to hold provisions equivalent to between 120 and 150% of expected losses on their bad loans (in contrast, European banks had a provisions coverage ratio of 46% at the end of June 2018 and an NPL ratio of 4.4%).[5] In effect, China's banks are forced to provision significantly more than they think they're likely to lose on bad loans, which creates an incentive to dispose of NPLs quickly so they can reclaim the excess as profit.

However, such high provision requirements make it difficult for banks to recognize significantly higher levels of NPLs. Provisions come out of profits, but if profits aren't sufficient then provisions reduce capital—hence the risk of equity firesales the regulator warned of. Of course, Beijing could just change the rules. But significantly weakening defenses against bad loans potentially undermines trust in the system at precisely the wrong moment.

Instead, by maintaining that bad debt levels are significantly lower than is likely the case, regulators and banks can spread out the costs over time and deal with the problem at their own pace. It allows banks to raise fresh capital more slowly and with less urgency, allowing them to stagger their share offerings so as not to flood the market and drive down prices.

Similarly, not recognizing the bad loans all at once allows the banks to dispose of them over time, helping them to extract more value than would be possible if a sudden flood of bad loans were dumped on would-be investors all at once. It means that banks can gradually foreclose on delinquent borrowers and spread out bankruptcies—as well as the attendant job losses—over time. And it means that banks can use the profits they generate over a number of years to write down their bad loans, thereby reducing the need to raise capital.

Minimizing Costs—Passing the Buck

China's central government has long been adept at devising creative ways to avoid using its own fiscal resources to pay for expensive policy measures. For instance, it relied on state banks, rather than its own coffers, to fund the 2008 stimulus. Moreover, it used foreign exchange reserves to recapitalize major banks after the last debt crisis. That creativity is on display once again in Beijing's approach to NPLs as it shifts the costs of the cleanup.

The main cost has been borne by the banks, which have been able to pay for their write-downs of bad loans from profit, something that may not have been possible had banks been forced to recognize NPLs more quickly and in greater volumes. But private-sector savings have also been enlisted in the NPL effort. Platforms such as Taobao, JD.com, as well as dozens of financial asset exchanges, have been auctioning bad loans directly to investors. Securitization—a tool for selling NPLs to risk-averse institutional investors—has also made a small contribution to NPL disposals, with 4% of NPLs disposed of in 2018 packaged into asset-backed securities.

Perhaps the biggest new contributor to NPL disposals has been the creation of more than 50 local AMCs, bad banks that have the right to acquire NPLs from banks in bulk but are limited to operating in one province each. These provincial bad banks have been capitalized by a mix of local governments, state firms, financial institutions, and private companies—and notably not central government resources.

And to the extent that Beijing has been involved in the recapitalization process, it has done so in ways that have mobilized off-balance-sheet resources. In 2018, the National Social Security Fund acquired shares in both China Great Wall Asset Management Co. and China Orient Asset Management Co., two of the four original AMCs. National champions like China Telecom and China Property & Casualty Reinsurance were also mobilized as part of the recapitalization process.

Risks to the Gradualist Approach

While Beijing has so far dealt with NPLs relatively smoothly, its unconventional approach is not without risks. Disposing of NPLs slowly means that banks will likely have to maintain elevated levels of bad loans on their books for long periods of time. Under such circumstances, an economic shock could be potentially more destabilizing, particularly if it results in a sudden spike in NPLs or a sharp deterioration of liquidity conditions. Consequently, the authorities could be forced to abandon their slow, low-impact cleanup.

Beijing recognizes the risks and has engaged in a broad-based effort to rein in financial risk in order to minimize the potential for crises. At the same time, it has augmented its liquidity management tools to ensure it can guarantee bank solvency.

Crisis Prevention

Improving financial stability has been a first-order priority for Beijing since launching its deleveraging campaign in 2016. In fact, the deleveraging campaign is best understood as a de-risking campaign—that is, a broad-based campaign to make China's financial system safer, rather than an effort to reduce the overall debt burden.

Unquestionably, Beijing's long-term goal is to reduce—or at least stabilize—debt levels relative to the size of the economy. However, given that China's economic model is still dependent upon debt-enabled investment to deliver politically acceptable levels of growth, such a reduction is not likely to be feasible in the short term. Hence, the great success of financial reform has been—rather counterintuitively—to make the system

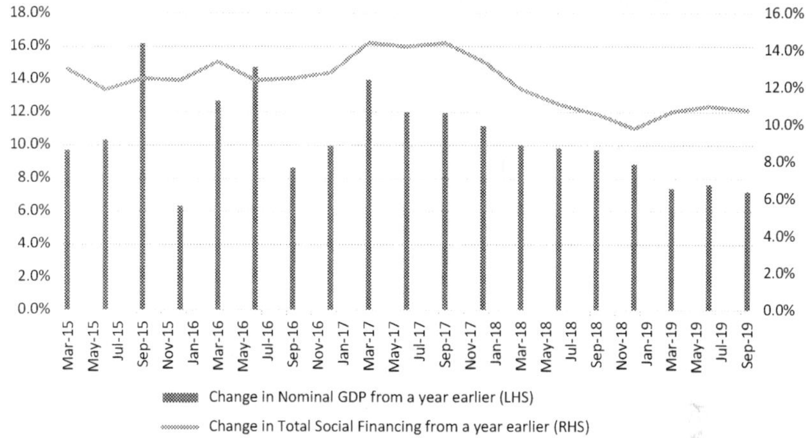

Fig. 3.2 Fast economic growth fueled by even faster debt growth (Change in total social financing from a year earlier, compared with change in nominal GDP. *Source* Wind)

less risky so that it might safely support higher levels of debt, at least for the time being (see Fig. 3.2).

That's not to say the deleveraging campaign has not involved actual deleveraging. Shadow banking has contracted, as has interbank lending, and NPL disposals are themselves a form of deleveraging. But rather than being a goal in itself, deleveraging has been deployed selectively as a tool to support the broader goal of making the financial system safer.

The China Banking and Insurance Regulatory Commission's (CBIRC) de-risking effort has four prongs: reducing banks' NPLs; mitigating the risk of financial contagion by rolling back lending between banks and other financial institutions; preventing the financial system from feeding credit into blatantly speculative activities; and migrating risk from shadow banks back to the formal banking system. All of this has massively reduced the amount of complexity in the system, put the regulators in a better position to manage risk, and generally diminished the likelihood of crisis.

Managing Liquidity

Financial crises are usually caused by a loss of confidence in financial institutions, not a surfeit of NPLs. However, NPLs can help drive that loss of confidence by creating liquidity problems for banks. Banks need the interest payments generated by loans to pay what they owe to depositors and to other funding sources. When loans go bad and those interest payments stop, banks might struggle to meet their obligations.

It's not that the banks are broke. Rather, they likely have plenty of assets—namely, loans made to borrowers—but turning those assets into cash on short notice isn't easy. Hence, banks might find themselves teetering on the edge of insolvency. In such a situation, the central bank can step in and lend to banks in return for collateral, ensuring that banks have sufficient cash to preserve confidence in the system.

China has greater control over market liquidity than other countries. Capital controls mean that the PBOC can print money and it won't drain overseas. Meanwhile, printing money isn't a politically charged issue in the way that it is in other countries, nor is government intervention in the markets. For instance, China's authorities would not have hesitated to prop up Lehman Brothers. The consensus in Beijing is that stability comes before all else. That gives the PBOC the latitude to move more quickly than other central banks, should the situation demand its intervention.

The authorities can also impose solutions on market participants that might not be in their commercial interests. For example, Beijing can force distressed financial institutions into mergers on short notice, or it can demand that big banks keep lending to smaller financial institutions even in the midst of a cash crunch. To complement those advantages, the PBOC has in recent years built up an alphabet soup of lending tools (most notably the Standing Lending Facility and Short-Term Lending Operations) to ensure banks can borrow from the central bank whenever they need to.

What Could Derail the Deleveraging Effort?

Still, the provision of sufficient liquidity is merely a band-aid. It buys time for banks that must then use it to gradually reduce their accumulated NPLs. Despite Beijing's best efforts, two related uncertainties still cloud the approach's long-term viability: the slowing economy and political resolve.

As growth slows, banks could find it more challenging to dispose of sufficient volumes of NPLs without government support or severe economic disruption. Meanwhile, senior leaders' commitment to pursuing financial prudence over stimulating the economy could be seriously tested.

Whittling Down the NPL Stock

For Beijing's gradualist approach to succeed, old NPLs must be disposed of at a faster rate than new ones are created. On one hand, that requires slowing the pace at which new NPLs are created, which has been a key aspect of the deleveraging campaign. But it's somewhat difficult to gauge whether the pace of NPL accumulation is slowing because many NPLs are hidden or disguised as bank assets.

As a group, these "assets"—a product of the shadow banking system—are probably of worse quality than loans, but they don't show up in the NPL data. However, it's likely the case that by reining in shadow banking, the CBIRC has helped curtail the generation of new bad loans.

On the other hand, banks must continue to sell, write down, or otherwise dispose of their existing NPLs at a pace that allows them to reduce the overall burden, or else the whole effort may be futile. Of course, there is no way of knowing whether the banks have been able to realize that goal. Even if they have in the past, it's likely to become more difficult as economic conditions deteriorate.

Slowing growth will likely result in more bad loans as companies that borrowed based on the expectation of continued fast growth will struggle to make loan repayments. Meanwhile, the plunge in the producer price index (PPI)—the measure of change in the prices of industrial and manufacturing inputs—that began in 2018 has increased the real interest rate, therefore making it more difficult for many firms to service their loans (see Fig. 3.3).

And with the economy slowing, banks' profit growth will likely slow as well. Replenishing loan loss provisions has already been eating up a progressively larger chunk of banks' pretax profits in recent years (see Fig. 3.4). For some smaller banks, profits might no longer be sufficient to sustain NPL disposals.

To be sure, banks are expecting NPL pressures to mount. Of those large banks that have published their 2018 earnings, most have disclosed significant increases in impairments against loan losses, in what effectively amounts to preparation for more write-offs to come. And some have been quite vocal in flagging the difficulties ahead.[6]

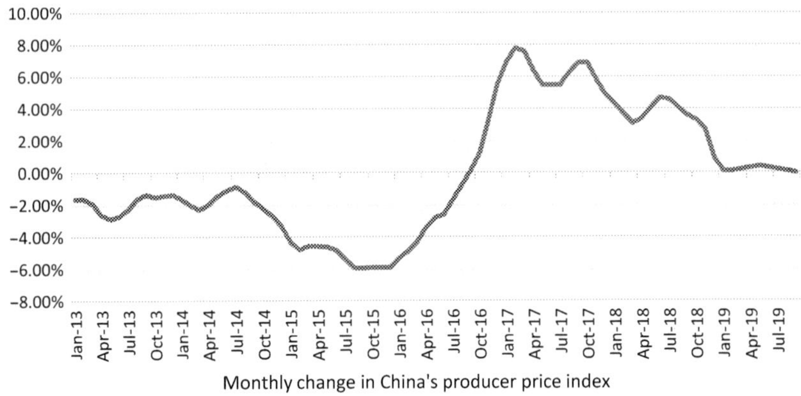

Fig. 3.3 Inflation makes debt repayment easier (Monthly change in China's producer price index. *Source* Wind)

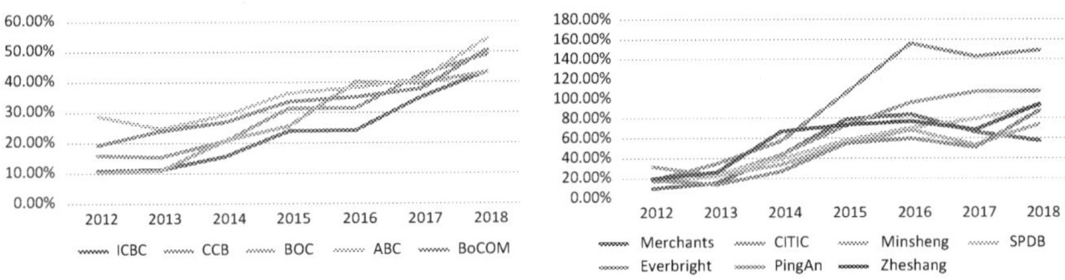

Fig. 3.4 Bank profits have been sufficient to meet NPL write-downs (Increase in loan loss provisions as a share of pretax profits at major banks. *Note* Banks must hold impairments on loan losses against NPLs. Impairments reduce profits. In the above chart, the smaller the percentage, the less impact impairments have on profit. A reading of 100% means that, were it not for impairments, pretax profit would be double. *Source* Banks)

Similarly, the market for buying NPLs might find itself overstretched as well. A bubble in NPL prices popped in early 2018, and since then the pool of domestic NPL buyers has shrunk. Moreover, the local AMCs were relatively lightly capitalized when they were first established, and to maintain their rapid pace of NPL acquisitions they'll likely need to raise more capital.

But the AMCs will likely face competition on raising capital, as analysts expect Chinese banks to raise large amounts of new capital over the next few years in order to maintain capital adequacy levels.[7]

That's not primarily because of NPLs, but because the deleveraging campaign has required banks to rapidly expand lending to compensate for a contraction in shadow banking. This means a tighter capital raising environment, which could make it difficult for the AMCs and could conceivably result in the central government directly recapitalizing the bad banks.

Political Will

Since 2016, Xi Jinping has been willing to accept progressively slower growth in the interest of financial rectitude. The risk is that at some point growth will slow to a level where Xi—or the political consensus that exists around him—loses faith, and the deleveraging campaign is jettisoned. Some argue that Beijing has already pivoted back to stimulus mode with tax cuts, by ramping up local government bond issuance, and by using window guidance to push banks into lending more to small firms.

It would be inaccurate to interpret an increase in the debt level as an abandonment of the deleveraging campaign. In fact, the embrace of a wider range of stimulus tools speaks to Beijing's commitment to cleaning up the financial system. Rather than a free-for-all, where banks and shadow banks are given the freedom to shovel as much credit as possible into the economy—which is broadly the approach to stimulus pursued repeatedly between 2009 and 2016—theses days stimulus is targeted and limited only to banks (that have been chastened since their freewheeling days) and the bond market. The latest efforts to stimulate the economy have been designed specifically to avoid undoing the deleveraging of the last two years.

However, targeted stimulus is showing signs of being insufficient to stabilize growth. If the economy continues to suffer, Xi's political resolve to hold the line on deleveraging could be sapped. If the political consensus around Xi evaporates, then there's a risk that Beijing might again opt for old-style stimulus with the attendant increase in financial risk and bad investment decisions. Although there are no strong signs that this consensus is fraying, political considerations will nonetheless determine the sustainability of Beijing's approach to the debt cleanup.

Getting Creative

In the meantime, it seems likely that regulators will try to maintain their measured approach to dealing with NPLs and will continue to look for creative solutions to keep things moving. On one hand, they could try to make it easier for borrowers to service their loans. This is something recently flagged by Xu Zhong, director-general of the PBOC's research bureau, when he suggested that lower interest rates were needed to help heavily indebted companies.[8] He also suggested that local governments should be able to sell assets to raise the funds necessary to manage their debts. In fact, sales by private companies and state firms of both physical assets and equity in subsidiaries are something that could help with future debt repayments.

On the other hand, the government could make it easier for banks to dispose of their bad loans. It could approve local AMCs to launch IPOs so that they have the capital necessary to acquire greater volumes of NPLs. Or they could allow local AMCs to borrow directly from the interbank lending market, thereby reducing their borrowing costs. The Ministry of Finance could increase the volume of loans to the Big Four AMCs at discount interest rates or even extend that privilege to some of the local AMCs. And it could even mobilize China Development Bank and the other policy banks to play a role in easing the stress on commercial banks.

Whether Beijing will use all the tools at its disposal is uncertain, but it clearly has options. Creativity has been the hallmark of the cleanup process thus far. Provincial AMCs, online NPL auctions, and credit card NPL securitization are all uniquely Chinese approaches to dealing with bad loans—and creativity is likely to remain Beijing's greatest strength.

China is trying to avoid a state-led bailout of the financial system by cleaning up NPLs now, in a way that minimizes both economic disruption and the burden on fiscal resources. So far it has proven to be moderately successful, and may end up being an inspired approach if it indeed achieves the goal of gradually whittling down NPLs.

However, dealing with NPLs represents is only half the battle. At the same time, China needs to reform its economic growth model so that it can deliver sufficiently fast growth with far less debt—in other words, more efficient growth. That's necessary for the long-term health of the financial system, but also to lessen the pain arising from the cleanup. In the meantime, Beijing will continue spreading the costs of dealing with

NPLs around the economy—to the banks, private sector, local government, state firms, and other government entities—while striving to keep its own powder dry as the ultimate backstop.

Notes

1. Michael Pettis, "What Is GDP in China?" Carnegie Endowment for International Peace—China Financial Markets, January 16, 2019, https://carnegieendowment.org/chinafinancialmarkets/78138.
2. Note that the calculation is based on the CBIRC's figure of 110.5 trillion yuan in outstanding loans at the end of 2018.
3. China Orient Asset Management Corp publishes annual surveys of the NPL market in which it asks bankers what they believe is the actual level of NPLs in their area. In 2017 about 60% thought it was between 3% and 8%.
4. Ted Osborn, "Pressure on China's Banks to Report Bad Debt Is Good News for Foreign Investors," *South China Morning Post*, April 2, 2018, https://www.scmp.com/business/banking-finance/article/2139904/pressure-chinas-banks-report-bad-debt-good-news-foreign.
5. "Supervisory Banking Statistics, Second Quarter 2018," European Central Bank, October 2018, https://www.bankingsupervision.europa.eu/ecb/pub/pdf/ssm.supervisorybankingstatistics_second_quarter_2018_201810.en.pdf.
6. Shu Zhang and Julie Zhu, "China's Top Banks Warn of 'Fragile' Bad Loans Scenario as Economy Slows," *Reuters*, March 28, 2019, https://www.reuters.com/article/us-china-banks-results-idUSKCN1RA077.
7. Liang Yu, "Deleveraging While Disseminating: The Task Facing China's Banks," S&P Ratings, October 18, 2018, https://www.spratings.com/documents/20184/0/RatingsDirect_DeleveragingWhileDisseminatingTheTaskFacingChinasBanks_39988427_Oct-19-2018.pdf/d644d494-c43f-29da-44ed-0c0661787142.
8. Xu Zhong, "Xu Zhong: China Should Not Rush to Revamp Local Debt," *Caixin*, January 22, 2019, https://www.caixinglobal.com/2019-01-22/opinion-china-should-not-rush-to-revamp-local-debt-101373076.html.

Technology

CHAPTER 4

Who Loses from Restricting Chinese Student Visas?

Matt Sheehan

Over the course of 2018 and 2019, the Trump Administration's trade war with China steadily expanded to include dozens of peripheral sectors, including visas for Chinese students studying in the United States.

In May of 2018, US embassies and consulates reportedly received instructions to tighten visa restrictions on Chinese students attending US graduate programs in technical fields such as robotics, aviation, and high-tech manufacturing.[1] Those are all industries singled out for government support in "Made in China 2025," the Chinese industrial policy at the center of US–China tensions.

Later that year, the *Financial Times* revealed that the May 2018 restrictions paled in comparison to the actions President Trump had been considering just a few months prior: an outright ban on student visas for all Chinese nationals.[2]

That focus on higher education—particularly graduate students in technical fields—highlighted the way technological competition sits at the heart of the Trump Administration's "trade" war. The United States runs

M. Sheehan (✉)
Paulson Institute, Chicago, IL, USA
e-mail: msheehan@paulsoninstitute.org

D. Ma (ed.), *China's Economic Arrival*,
https://doi.org/10.1007/978-981-15-2275-8_4

a major trade *surplus* with China in higher education, but stunting China's technological prowess through severing education ties is seen as far more important than any marginal impact on trade.

Though an outright ban on Chinese students appears unlikely for the time being, the impact of the more narrowly tailored restrictions are already being felt. Many Chinese Ph.D. students report waiting three to four months to renew their visas and reenter the United States each year, and professors at leading California research universities also describe new difficulties in recruiting and retaining top Chinese students.[3]

"Great Move" or "The End of US Tech Supremacy"?

Reactions to the new restrictions were polarized. Senator Marco Rubio hailed the May 2018 restrictions as "another great move!" on Twitter, describing Chinese student visas as "weapons" in China's campaign to "cheat and steal" its way to world dominance.[4] On the opposite end, former Mexican ambassador to China Jorge Guarjado's predicted the restrictions will end up hurting the United States.[5] He argued that Chinese innovators would take their talents elsewhere, and warned that the new restrictions marked the "beginning of the end of US tech supremacy."

Rubio's reaction reflected a highly politicized DC climate, while Guarjado's take channeled the Silicon Valley orthodoxy that openness is a prerequisite for innovation. But both of these views are off the mark.

The vast majority of Chinese graduate students are neither "cheating" nor "stealing" for their home country—they're trying to learn and contribute at the cutting edge of their fields globally. But the orthodoxy that equates innovation with absolute openness also doesn't appear to be on solid ground any longer. If the rise of the Chinese internet giants has taught us anything, it's that technological upgrading is as much about gathering a critical mass of engineers, entrepreneurs, and money as it is about cultural norms like openness.

With that in mind, which country stands to gain more—or lose less—from restrictions on Chinese students? It's a question that reflects the zero-sum approach of the Trump Administration to international relations, and its concerted efforts to slow down China's technological catch-up. There are a number of issues with that zero-sum approach: US and

Chinese technology ecosystems are deeply intertwined and interdependent, and protecting national security in an age of highly autonomous systems will require scientific engagement on issues of safety.

But as a matter of understanding the actions of policymakers, it's worth asking the same zero-sum question that appears to guide their thinking: who "loses" when the United States takes in fewer Chinese graduate students?

Answering that question requires moving beyond hyperbolic assertions and looking at actual data on the types of Chinese students that come to the United States, as well as what they end up doing after graduation.

Should I Stay or Should I Go: 2004 Edition

Looking at the data from fifteen years ago, the answer to the above question would have been clear: the United States would lose from restricting the number of Chinese graduate students. At that time, China was sending an unprecedented number of its best and brightest students to the United States for graduate studies, and very few of them were returning to China.

Of Chinese students who earned PhDs in the United States in 2002–2004, 86% of them were still in the United States in 2013.[6] That was tied with India for the highest stay-rate of any country, and nearly triple the 32% stay-rate of South Korean doctorate recipients. Even among Chinese nationals who had earned PhDs during the height of the US financial crisis of 2007–2009, five-year stay rates remained at 84%.

This seems like an unqualified win for the United States: America attracted the brightest young minds from China, trained them at US universities, and benefited from their skills (and tax dollars) in the domestic economy for decades to come.

Should I Stay or Should I Go: 2019 Edition

Today, the picture is murkier. The United States remains a top destination for the best and brightest graduates of Chinese undergraduate programs, hosting roughly 130,000 Chinese graduate students during the 2017–2018 academic year.[7] At large public institutions such as the University of California, roughly one-quarter of all engineering and computer science graduate students are from China.[8]

But what these students intend to do after graduation is much more split. There isn't comprehensive data on the return rates of recent graduates, but a mix of broader indicators and anecdotal evidence point to substantial growth in the number of Chinese-born, US-educated students who choose to return home after earning advanced degrees.

According to China's Ministry of Human Resources and Social Security, 2017 saw a record-setting 480,000 Chinese students who had studied around the world return home.[9] China's Ministry of Education estimated that by 2016, around 70–80% of Chinese students abroad eventually returned to live in China.[10]

While those government estimates should be taken with a large grain of salt, they roughly line up with a 2018 Purdue University survey of Chinese students' post-graduation plans: 51.5% planned to spend some time in the United States before returning to China, 14.4% said they planned to return to China immediately, and only 9.7% said they hoped to stay in the United States indefinitely (24.4% said they didn't know their plans).[11]

Students, Technology, and Silicon Valley

This shift in the post-graduation plans has been especially pronounced among graduates in technical fields, particularly those working in Silicon Valley. There isn't data specifically capturing the return rates of Chinese technologists, but interviews with dozens of Chinese engineers and researchers in both China and America suggests a major change.

Ten years ago, it was rare to find a Chinese engineer who had given up a plush job at Google or Facebook to return to China. But in the past five years, the tide appears to have turned. Top Beijing startups are now frequently founded and staffed by entrepreneurs and engineers who graduated from elite US computer science programs, worked several years in Silicon Valley or Seattle, and then chose to return to China.

The higher return rates reflect both a pull (back to China) and a push (away from the United States). Many recent graduates are "pulled" home by the energy and the opportunities in the Chinese technology ecosystem: the explosion of new products and business models, the boom in venture capital funding for startups, and the opportunity to take on leadership roles that many believe are harder for Asian immigrants to find in Silicon Valley.

Digging deeper, the pull of returning to China does not appear to act equally on all graduates in technical fields. While Chinese technology *entrepreneurs* are often drawn back to China by business opportunities there, preliminary evidence suggests that Chinese *cutting-edge researchers* appear more likely to remain in the United States.

A recent MacroPolo study of one of the world's top artificial intelligence (AI) conference, NeurIPS 2019, found that the vast majority of Chinese-born scientists publishing upper-tier AI research were currently working or studying at US institutions.[12] When looking specifically at the subset of Chinese-born AI researchers who have already finished their studies in the United States and gone on to work, a full 78% of them were currently affiliated with US institutions.

These studies draw on a small and highly specific sample population: Chinese-born AI researchers publishing at a top conference. But they suggest a trend reflected in qualitative observations and interviews—for technical researchers who work at the global frontier of a field like AI, the labs of US companies and universities remain the most attractive destination.

The Push Back to China

But for those Chinese students who do intend to work in America, there remains a formidable "push" back to China: increasingly restrictive federal policies on both student and work visas. In April of 2017, President Trump signed the "Buy American and Hire American" executive order, which pledged to "protect the interests of United States workers in the administration of our immigration system, including through the prevention of fraud or abuse." In practice, that meant a dramatic rise in rejections for H-1B visa applications, the most popular visa for high-skilled foreign citizens who have been hired by a US company.

Between 2015 and the first quarter of 2019, the initial rejection rates for H-1B applicants shot up from under 5% to nearly 25%.[13] The US Citizenship and Immigration Services also nearly tripled the percentage (22.3–60%) of applicants whose eligibility it challenged through a "request for evidence." This is a demand on the applicant's US employer to submit more documentation to prove that the worker does, in fact, have necessary specialized skills that cannot be performed by a US worker. The new restrictions and mounting rejections prompted one rejected Chinese applicant—an entrepreneur with law degrees from China and Oxford, and an MBA from Stanford—to ask in a *New York Times* op-ed, "Is Anyone Good Enough for an H-1B Visa?"[14]

These tightening restrictions around student and work visas are still evolving, and it will take time for them to fully manifest in data on five- and ten-year stay-rates for graduates. But industry observers say the restrictions are already taking a bite, one that they believe will grow with time. Rick Sun came to the United States for a Ph.D. in computer science, worked at Google for six years, and now runs a company that helps Chinese graduates of US universities find jobs in Silicon Valley.

"Gradually, I think a lot of Chinese families and parents will actually be affected—already, I think," Sun said in an interview. "'OK. Since it's so hard to stay in the US, why bother? Come back to China when you graduate.'"

The Biggest Loser?

Now, returning to the central question: which country would lose more from declining Chinese student enrollment in the United States?

The answer to that question, especially given the new reality of rising return rates of Chinese after graduation, comes down to weighing two counterbalancing impacts on Chinese technological innovation. Will China lose more from missing out on the knowledge its returning PhDs would have gained from training in the United States? Or will China gain more by holding onto its most promising PhDs, who now won't go to the United States in the first place?

On the one hand, keeping China's best minds locked up in their home country just isn't as limiting on them as it used to be. If the United States had implemented the visa restrictions ten years ago—when the country admitted many Chinese PhDs who would stay, but far fewer who would return home—it's entirely possible that would have slowed China's technological catch-up in fields like AI.

But today, universities like Tsinghua and Peking are often ranked among the top five institutions in the world for AI research.[15] Chinese researchers have become so important to the field that major conferences have been rescheduled so they don't conflict with Chinese New Year. In addition, academic researchers' commitment to publishing their results—often instantly and openly online—is dramatically shrinking the international knowledge gap in technical fields.

And yet, there's a good reason why so many of China's brightest minds still choose to study at US universities: they believe America is the best place for them to develop world-class skills. In this sense, Chinese students continue to "vote with their feet," both in choosing to attend American schools and, for some of them, in heading back to China to continue their careers.

There's no clear answer yet to which of the above forces will dominate. While this author leans toward the idea that China holding onto its top graduates will, on balance, accelerate its technological progress, this is far from a settled question.

Stapling Diplomas

The current approach of restricting visas works entirely through incurring relative losses: keeping out Chinese engineering PhDs will hurt some US companies, but the hope is that it will hurt China more.

But there is a different approach that has been proposed, one that was in fact endorsed by former presidential candidates Mitt Romney, Hillary Clinton, and many lawmakers on both sides of the aisle. That is, making it easier for highly skilled Chinese workers to remain in the United States by "stapling a green card" to the diploma of every Ph.D. in a STEM (science, technology, engineering, math) field.

Staple-a-green-card is a policy with its heart in the right place (and a nice piece of political imagery), but in this particular instance, such an approach could prove counterproductive. The prospect of one day receiving a green card is a major incentive for foreign nationals to continue living and working in the United States. In interviews, multiple Chinese PhDs working in Silicon Valley have said that they stayed in the United States *until* they got a green card. Once they had the security of knowing they could return to the United States any time for the next ten years, they headed back home to pursue new opportunities. Given these incentives, stapling green cards could actually backfire.

But there might be a policy tweak that would work: the United States government could "staple an H-1B" to new STEM PhDs, allowing foreign graduate students to skip the suspense of the H-1B application process. That would give them permission to work in the United States and also an incentive to do so for several years (the path from an H-1B to a green card is often around six years for a Chinese citizen).

Policies like those described above could moderate the "push" felt by Chinese graduates, allowing the United States to compete for talent on its own strengths: cleaner air, a gentler education system for the kids, a more creative and critical thinking pedagogy, and greater personal liberties and legal protections. Still, eliminating the "push" would only solve half of the problem, doing nothing to weaken the "pull" exerted by China's own vibrant technology ecosystem.

In a world where the United States no longer has a monopoly on high-tech innovation or talent, that may be the most optimal outcome policy-makers can hope for.

Notes

1. Josh Lederman and Ted Bridis, "AP Sources: US to Impose Limits on Some Chinese Visas," *The Associated Press*, May 29, 2018, https://apnews.com/82a98fecee074bfb83731760bfbce515.
2. Demetri Sevastopulo and Tom Mitchell, "US Considered Ban on Student Visas for Chinese Nationals," *The Financial Times*, October 2, 2018, https://www.ft.com/content/fc413158-c5f1-11e8-82bf-ab93d0a9b321.
3. Author conversations with STEM Ph.D. students and professors at three leading research universities in the state of California.
4. Marco Rubio, Twitter Post, May 30, 2018, 3:59 a.m. //twitter.com/marcorubio/status/1001780008124387328.
5. Jorge Guarjado, Twitter Post, May 30, 2018, 6:05 a.m. //twitter.com/marcorubio/status/1001780008124387328.
6. Michael G. Finn and Leigh Ann Pennington, "Stay Rates of Foreign Doctorate Recipients from U.S. Universities, 2013," Oak Ridge Institute for Science and Education, January 2018, https://orise.orau.gov/stem/reports/stay-rates-foreign-doctorate-recipients-2013.pdf.
7. "2018 Fact Sheet: China," *Open Doors 2018: Report on International Educational Exchange*, Institute for International Education.
8. "Fall Enrollment at a Glance," The University of California, https://www.universityofcalifornia.edu/infocenter/fall-enrollment-glance.
9. 叶昊鸣. "2017 年度我国各类留学回国人员总数达 48.09 万人" 新华网, April 17, 2018, http://www.xinhuanet.com/2018-04/17/c_1122697495.htm.
10. "A Record Number of Chinese Students Abroad in 2015 but Growth Is Slowing." ICEF Monitor, April 6, 2016, https://monitor.icef.com/2016/04/a-record-number-of-chinese-students-abroad-in-2015-but-growth-is-slowing/.

11. "2018 Purdue Survey of Chinese Students and Scholars in the United States: A General Report." Center on Religion and Chinese Society, Purdue University, October 17, 2018, https://www.purdue.edu/crcs/wp-content/uploads/2018/10/2018-Purdue-Survey-Report_Rev.pdf.
12. Matt Sheehan, "Chinese AI Talent in Six Charts," MacroPolo, May 28, 2019, https://macropolo.org/china-ai-research-talent-data/.
13. Melissa Manna, " USCIS Data Confirms Increase in RFEs and Denials, Especially for H-1Bs." Ogletree Deakins, February 27, 2019, https://ogletree.com/insights/2019-02-27/uscis-data-confirms-increase-in-rfes-and-denials-especially-for-h-1bs/.
14. Frida Yu, "Is Anyone Good Enough for an H-1B Visa?" *New York Times*, November 23, 2017, https://www.nytimes.com/2017/11/23/opinion/immigration-visa-h1b-trump-.html.
15. Emery D. Berger, "CSRankings: Computer Science Rankings," http://csrankings.org/#/fromyear/2018/toyear/2019/index?ai&vision&mlmining&nlp&ir&world. CSRankings provides a tool for generating rankings of top computer science programs, filtering for different time periods and areas within computer science. The ranking cited was generated by filtering for all areas under "AI," and looking at publications from 2018 to 2019.

CHAPTER 5

From Windfalls to Pitfalls: Qualcomm's China Conundrum

Joy Dantong Ma

Introduction

For many multinational businesses, the launch of China's Reform and Opening forty years ago seemed nothing short of an opportunity of the century. The potential to tap a market of nearly one billion customers was mind-boggling. For many first movers, the bet on Chinese consumers paid off handsomely.[1] Yet for other multinationals, the opportunity turned out to have numerous strings attached, particularly in the realm of technology.

China's fixation on gaining technological leadership is embedded in the design of the Reform and Opening policy. As early as 1987, a concerned US Congress had demanded extensive studies on China's technology transfer practices in attracting foreign investment.[2] To some extent, it was viewed by US multinationals as the cost of accessing China's market. What has changed in the past decade is China's own growing capabilities and its technological ambitions. Not only are Chinese companies now capable of developing their own leading technologies, they are also increasingly demanding the crown jewels of foreign technology firms.

J. D. Ma (✉)
Chicago, IL, USA

D. Ma (ed.), *China's Economic Arrival*,
https://doi.org/10.1007/978-981-15-2275-8_5

This has certainly not sat well with governments from the United States to Europe. For instance, when the United States Trade Representative Office (USTR) in August 2017 launched a year-long investigation into China's practices in technology transfer and intellectual property (IP) theft, it ended up launching the US–China trade war. Even though headlines have been dominated by tit-for-tat tariffs, the Trump administration ultimately aims to get Beijing to modify its behavior on technology transfers.

American multinationals, however, are caught in a bind. On the one hand, transferring critical technology is tantamount to creating your own future competitors and no company is going to do that willingly. On the other hand, these longstanding concerns have not obscured the vast opportunities China's market afforded US multinationals.

This is especially true for technology companies. For them, it wasn't simply about the revenue potential of selling to a market that was a quarter of humanity. They also saw China as a unique opportunity to cement their technology standards to dominate global market share. These companies were playing a long game, with China being the focal point of the strategy.

One American technology giant that's emblematic of both the enormous windfalls and eventual pitfalls of operating in China is Qualcomm. In the early days, Qualcomm had pushed its products, technologies, and standards into the Chinese market, at times against the government's economic agenda. Its efforts yielded tremendous commercial success and allowed the company to gain dominance in global telecommunication standards for decades.

Qualcomm's very success, however, was also partly responsible for its own loss of momentum in the Chinese market. It is tempting to blame Qualcomm's recent troubles—from fighting off a hostile takeover[3] from Singapore-based Broadcom to scrapping its attempted acquisition of NXP because the Chinese authority blocked it[4]—on collateral damage from the US–China trade war. But that would be overly simplistic and skirts the company's storied and complicated tenure in the Chinese market.

Beijing's blocking of the NXP bid was bound to happen, irrespective of the trade war. At its core, this isn't about any single deal, but is a logical outcome of a brewing battle—between Qualcomm and China's rising technological ambitions—over the future of international telecom standards and market leadership. Indeed, Qualcomm's meteoric rise and gradual descent in China is emblematic of the country's transformation from a market that passively accepted Western companies' standards to a contender in the global technology race.

Qualcomm's 2G Windfall in China

In March 1999, Zhu Rongji, China's firebrand premier, issued a direct guidance to China Unicom and ordered the company to adopt Qualcomm's CDMA standard.[5] This marked a major victory for Qualcomm's seven-year push since 1992 to get a firm foothold in the Chinese market, giving the company a significant edge in the global competition for second-generation (2G) cellular standards. To understand why that's important, a brief detour into the development of 2G standards is warranted.

CDMA vs. GSM

The 1980s was a period in which global telecom standards were transitioning from analog to 2G. In the analog age, each user's cell phone call was assigned a channel in which a single call could be transported. Since spectrum is a finite resource, the number of calls that can be made at the same time is limited. To put it differently, a highway is only so wide, which means only a certain number of cars can simultaneously fit across it before space runs out. Much like physical infrastructure, the constraints imposed by analog infrastructure meant that it could not accommodate huge volumes of calls and data.

The breakthrough in 2G technologies was that it allowed for multiple calls on the same channel, thereby overcoming the constraints of limited spectrum space. At the time, most of the world focused on a radio transmission technology called Time Division Multiple Access (TDMA).[6] This technology improved spectrum usage efficiency by dividing the channel into multiple time slots and assigning them to different calls on the same radio channel. It was a solution to maximize the usage of channel space that was often wasted or under-utilized during a phone call. It is essentially the equivalent of allowing multiple cars to run on different schedules in the same lane on the highway, except it's for multiple radio transmissions over a digital highway.

Qualcomm, founded in 1985 by UC San Diego professor Irwin Jacobs, pioneered another method that came to be known as Code Division Multiple Access (CDMA). This technology assigned each call with a code, and that call is then disassembled, transmitted, and then reassembled at the receiver's end by using the code. Because of the code identifier, the call is no longer limited to stay in one channel but can hop on other channels as needed. Therefore, multiple users can speak at the same time. To use the highway analogy again, cars no longer need to stay in a single lane and can now also use other lanes whenever there is availability, allowing for more efficient use of all radio frequencies (see Fig. 5.1).

CDMA might be more technologically fitting for cellular communication than TDMA, but it was too late to the party. By the time Jacobs successfully prototyped the standard in 1989, the telecom industry had already sunk millions of dollars into TDMA infrastructure and incorporated it into a Global System for Mobile Communications (GSM). Moreover, since GSM was developed through a collaborative effort by multiple European telecom companies, there was more buy-in of the standard from industry stakeholders.

According to the International Telecommunication Union's report, by the end of 1998, roughly 130 million phones around the world were running on the GSM standard.[7] Almost 90% of mobile phones in Europe, 35% in Asia, and 88% in Africa subscribed to the GSM standard. In contrast, Qualcomm's 2G standard, which came to be called cdmaOne, had only 20 million subscribers with a minimal footprint on every continent in the world except for North America.

Just as the world was becoming more connected through mobile phones, Qualcomm appeared to be on the losing end of the standards competition. This is why seizing the Chinese market was so integral to Qualcomm's strategy. At the time, China was a market that had very low

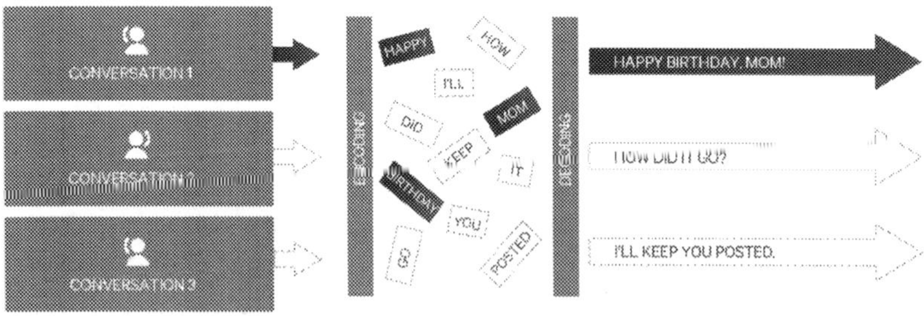

Fig. 5.1 How CDMA works (*Source* Qualcomm)

mobile penetration, and if hundreds of millions of Chinese started adopting devices with Qualcomm hardware, that would turn the tables on the 2G competition. In the standards race, the name of the game is market share.

Qualcomm CEO Jacobs reached the same conclusion when he visited China for the first time in 1992,[8] the year Deng Xiaoping embarked on his "Southern Tour" to revive flagging economic reforms. Jacobs immediately set about finding ways to enter the Chinese market. But Qualcomm's initial overtures met resistance from a Chinese government that had already set its sights on the GSM standard.

The reason was simple. Beijing preferred GSM because it didn't have to pay hefty royalties. Since GSM was a product of joint development among different countries, it had to be open source to enable collaboration. In contrast, the cdmaOne standard was developed virtually exclusively by Qualcomm, which meant it alone held numerous critical patents. Any manufacturer of CDMA-enabled mobile phones or network equipment had to pay for Qualcomm's IP.

So in 1994, when the Chinese government decided the country needed to advance from analog to 2G standards like the rest of the world, it studied both GSM and cdmaOne as potential candidates and eventually decided to go with GSM for commercial applications.

Even so, that didn't stop Qualcomm from testing the waters. The company recognized early on that it needed to enlist a key domestic constituency in China to support its efforts. It found an unconventional partner: the People's Liberation Army (PLA). Although China had selected the GSM standard for commercial use, the PLA at the time was searching for a radio transmission technology that would be secure for military communication. Because Qualcomm's CDMA technology was based on coded radio transmissions, it seemed like a good fit for what the PLA wanted.[9]

While such a partnership would be unthinkable and forbidden today, the 1990s was a period in which the PLA had more latitude to engage in commercial activities that ranged from automobile manufacturing to pharmaceuticals and hotels.

In the Qualcomm case, the Ministry of Post and Communication (MoPC), the predecessor to the powerful Ministry of Industry and Information Technology (MIIT), ordered its local bureaus to set up a joint venture (JV) with local PLA divisions called "Great Wall." The JV was granted a civil–military dual-use license to experiment with cellular networks with the cdmaOne standard on the 800 MHz spectrum in four major cities: Beijing, Shanghai, Xi'an, and Guangzhou.[10] By 1997, Qualcomm's 2G networks for both commercial and military applications in these cities were up and running, with the potential to expand into other Chinese cities.

But the JV collapsed almost as soon as it was formed. Just a year after the 2G network went live, Chinese President Jiang Zemin issued an order that forbid the PLA from engaging in any commercial activities.[11] The experimental CDMA network remained in place, however, though it never grew to cover more than half a million users, all of whom were later transferred to other networks.

The timing of this episode was peculiar. Some observers even suspected that the MoPC was anticipating this outcome all along and was setting up the JV to fail just to kill the CDMA standard in its infancy.[12] In fact, while granting the CDMA dual-use license to Great Wall, the MoPC simultaneously accelerated the approval of a national GSM license on the 900 MHz band to China Telecom, one of the national champions.[13] MoPC's true motivations will never be known, but one thing was clear enough to Qualcomm's Jacobs, who said on the record that because the MoPC fully owned the 900 MHz band used for GSM, the ministry favored GSM.[14]

These early setbacks didn't dissuade Qualcomm from continuing its pursuit of the Chinese market. The environment was different in 1999, when Beijing was wrapped up in intense negotiations to enter the World Trade Organization (WTO), which required winning Washington's acceptance. Qualcomm, like many companies at the time, saw an opportunity to ramp up the pressure on China to open its market. From the Chinese vantage point, liberalizing the telecom sector could go a long way toward mollifying the United States and securing its support for WTO entry. And so, Premier Zhu inked his support for Qualcomm on March 2, 1999 as detailed above and gave his promise to the US delegation, led by Commerce Secretary Bill Daley, that was soon to arrive in Beijing.

Even with Zhu's blessing, negotiations were far from over. That's because MoPC's head at the time Wu Jichuan, a major proponent of China's decision to adopt the GSM standard in 1994, was a hard-nosed negotiator. Wu wasn't about to give in until Qualcomm met three demands: develop a new mobile phone model that can run on both CDMA and GSM networks; lower the royalty fees; and share the design of Qualcomm's CDMA chipset.[15] In other words, Wu wanted options to abandon

CDMA at will, use the technology cheaply, and own the IP so that China can make its own chipsets.

Wu's demands were of course a nonstarter, and he probably knew it but wanted to play hardball anyway. These demands were viewed by the US government as China's disingenuous attitude toward WTO entry. Daley raised the issue multiple times during broader talks with Chinese leaders. While underscoring the White House's determination to push through key trade legislation that will support Beijing's WTO entry, Daley also made it very clear that Qualcomm was a high priority among America's commercial interests.[16]

With US government support and intensive efforts, Qualcomm finally secured an in-person meeting with Premier Zhu. On October 6, 2000, Jacobs, Wu, Brent Scowcroft (former National Security Advisor who heads the consultancy The Scowcroft Group), and Yang Xiaozu (Chairman of China Unicom) all met in a conference room at Tsinghua University. Zhu was there to broker a compromise among the competing interests. He demanded all the parties present to write down a list of demands and disagreements and to "sort it out."[17]

At this critical juncture, China's quest to enter the WTO was the priority, which meant Wu's ambitious demands had to take a back seat for the time being. The impasse was broken: Qualcomm was allowed in the Chinese market. In March 2002, a decade after Jacob's first trip to China, China Unicom announced its commitment to deliver CDMA services to more than 350 cities.[18]

When Success Comes Back to Bite

In the decade after Zhu lent his support to Qualcomm on the ledge of a memo, the American tech giant's revenue stream from China grew from virtually nil to \$2.4 billion, more than twice the amount from its home market and accounting for one-fifth of its global revenue (see Fig. 5.2).[19] Yet that very success led to two unintended consequences that would eventually turn the tables on Qualcomm: (1) It prompted China to nurse a grudge against the company, particularly toward its fee structure; (2) It clarified for Beijing that it needed to raise its game in global standards-setting or else accept ponying up licensing fees in perpetuity.

But Qualcomm wasn't done with profiting from 2G. It was hoping to extend its windfall in China to the 3G era, which officially commenced in January 2009 when Li Yizhong, the head of MIIT, announced China's

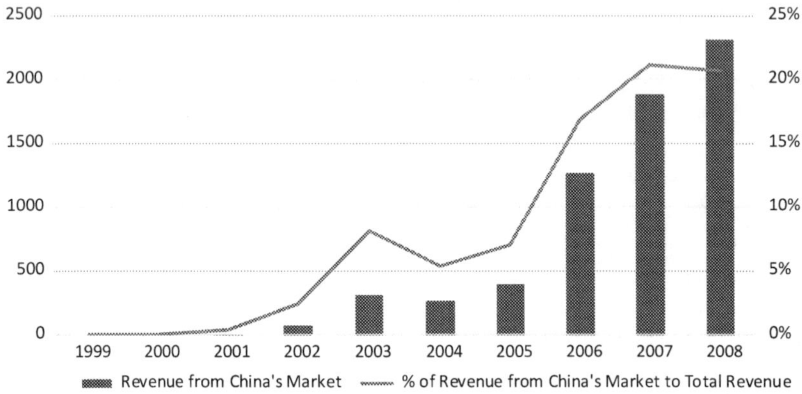

Fig. 5.2 Qualcomm's revenue stream from China (*Source* Qualcomm's annual reports [1999–2008]; author calculations)

transition from 2G to 3G.[20] In the months leading up to this announcement, MIIT had already been laying the groundwork by consolidating the state telecom industry from six major carriers to just three: China Mobile, China Unicom, and China Telecom. This "big three" competitive landscape, much like China's state oil industry, is the one that endures today.

One of the rationales behind the industry restructuring was that each state giant would be awarded one of three competing 3G standards: WCDMA that evolved from GSM (license granted to China Unicom); CDMA2000 that evolved from Qualcomm's own cdmaOne (license granted to China Telecom, which took over China Unicom's CDMA network for $16 billion during the restructuring),[21] and China's homegrown Time Division Synchronous Code Division Multiple Access (TD-SCDMA) (license granted to China Mobile).

The "Double Dipping" Fee Structure

However you sliced it, this 3G standards landscape would significantly benefit Qualcomm. That's because with anything that had the acronym "CDMA" in it, chances are Qualcomm owned some of the core IP since it was the original developer of the CDMA technology. According to Qualcomm's 2009 financial report, both the WCDMA and CDMA2000 technologies were derived from CDMA and were covered by the company's patents. The company also claimed to hold critical patents for the TD-SCDMA standard.

With a firm grip on the core IP of the 3G era, Qualcomm made money by both licensing the IP and directly selling its own 3G-enabled chips to mobile phone vendors, who would still need to pay a royalty. Selling its own 3G chips may have been a larger contributor to the company's revenue stream, but Qualcomm's real profits were made from its licensing fees. By amassing hundreds of thousands of patents in cellular communication standards, Qualcomm's fingerprints were virtually everywhere in the telecom industry. For years, the telecom industry had a running joke that while death and taxes are two certainties in life, paying royalties to Qualcomm was another certainty in the wireless industry.[22]

Maintaining what amounted to a patent monopoly on 3G standards enabled Qualcomm to leverage a unique and highly lucrative licensing fee structure that is still largely in place today. It basically works like this: mobile phone manufacturers license Qualcomm's technologies and pay the company royalties that are as much as 5% of the final sale price of the phone.[23] This means the royalties increase with the phone price, even if Qualcomm's technology inside the phone remains unchanged. In contrast, other telecom companies, such as Ericsson and Nokia, charge a flat fee for the specific technologies that licensees actually use.[24]

To illustrate, if a basic mobile phone costs $400, then Qualcomm gets 5% of that in royalties, or $20 per phone. If the manufacturer decides to add a high-resolution camera, a bigger screen, or a sleeker case to soup up the phone, the price doubles to $800. Now the manufacturer has to pay $40 in royalties to Qualcomm even though the technologies licensed have not changed.

On top of paying royalties, as a 3G mobile phone manufacturer, you would either need to make your own 3G chips or buy from other chip makers. More likely than not, manufacturers end up buying chips from Qualcomm, so they have to pay the company again. This fee structure came to be known as "double dipping" and, needless to say, has irked many manufacturers.[25]

This pricing strategy was also applied to the Chinese market. But initially, it was foreign manufacturers that felt the brunt of Qualcomm's fee structure. That's because when the company entered China in 1999, the country was still a technological backwater incapable of producing quality mobile phones. Major carriers like China Unicom had to sign contracts with foreign manufacturers, such as Nokia and Ericsson, to import the

Time	Carrier	Standard	Standard Set by	Equipment
1994 - 2002	China Mobile	GSM	Foreign	Buy foreign
	China Unicom	GSM, CDMA	Foreign	Buy foreign
2002 - 2008	China Mobile	GSM	Foreign	Buy local, reduce foreign
	China Unicom	GSM, CDMA	Foreign	Buy local, reduce foreign
2008 - 2014	China Mobile	TD-SCDMA	Local	Buy local
	China Unicom	WCDMA	Foreign	Mostly local
	China Telecom	CDMA2000	Foreign	Mostly local

Fig. 5.3 Evolution of China's mobile standards adoption (1994–2014) (*Source* Jefferies Equity Research)

phones. (Those manufacturers also relied on Qualcomm chips and IP, so were paying the company.)

It would take about another decade for Chinese manufacturers to acquire the capability to produce low end to "good enough" 3G mobile phones (see Fig. 5.3). And that was when Chinese producers started to directly feel the pinch of Qualcomm's double-dipping strategy. Since Qualcomm held patents for all three 3G standards in China, manufacturers had little choice but to pay licensing fees. In addition, few Chinese manufacturers had the ability to make their own 3G chips, so they had to rely on foreign imports, including Qualcomm's.

Demand for 3G mobile phones skyrocketed in China after 2009, and has grown 15 times in the 15 years since Qualcomm's official entry into the Chinese market (see Fig. 5.4).[26] This led to another windfall for Qualcomm. By 2010, Qualcomm's revenue from China reached $3 billion, surpassing that of South Korea.[27] Just four years later, the company's Chinese market revenue for the first time exceeded combined revenue from the rest of the world, including the United States.[28]

Yet as Qualcomm's profit margins widened, Chinese mobile phone makers' margins were being squeezed. Domestic original equipment manufacturers (OEMs) already had to keep prices low because of fierce competition that often resulted in price wars. Meanwhile, as Chinese manufacturers started to make more expensive phones with better displays and high-end cameras, they discovered that Qualcomm's licensing fee kept on increasing, even though they were using the same IP.

Unsurprisingly, this did not sit well with Chinese OEMs nor with the Chinese government. What's more, it wasn't exclusive to China. The fee

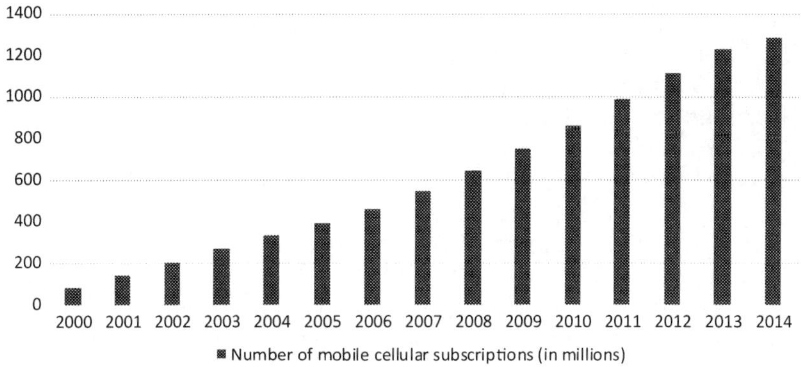

Fig. 5.4 Mobile phone's growth in China, 2000–2014 (in millions) (*Source* Statista)

structure irritated many global mobile phone makers, especially as they were under the pressure of product cycles to constantly deliver new and more expensive features such as larger and better displays and fancier cameras. The price of their products went up, and like Chinese manufacturers, they also suddenly found themselves paying Qualcomm double or even triple the royalties for licensing essentially the same technologies.

In subsequent years, Qualcomm's double-dipping strategy would become a major source of conflict, not only in the Chinese market but also in the broader telecom industry. Qualcomm has long argued since the 1990s that no matter what went into the phones, it was their technology that enabled them all. But this argument gained less traction in the 2000s. In the eyes of Qualcomm's customers, the company's technology was contributing less value to mobile phones yet the licensing fees kept on rising.

By 2015, Qualcomm was embroiled in controversies or being fined by regulators in Taiwan ($773 million), South Korea ($1.23 billion), and Europe ($853 million). Even Apple jumped on the bandwagon and fought multiyear legal battles with Qualcomm over this issue, arguing that it was engaged in "illegal practices." By mid-2018, Apple announced that it would manufacture its own chips for the iPhone, completely moving away from Qualcomm's chips.[29]

It didn't help matters that Qualcomm, at times, may have rubbed salt in the wound. In its 2014 annual financial report, the company noted several licensing disputes in China, including underreporting royalties and delaying tactics in entering licensing agreements.[30] While some Chinese manufacturers certainly found ways to circumvent royalty payments, Qualcomm still had all the chips in its corner.

Complaints in China grew louder and became harder to ignore for Chinese regulators. So they sprang into action. In November 2013, months before the issuance of 4G licenses, the National Development and Reform Commission (NDRC) initiated an investigation into whether Qualcomm's licensing practices violated China's Anti-Monopoly Law, which took effect in 2007. As the investigation proceeded, Qualcomm was preparing for a fine of 1–10% of its previous year's revenue and other remedies.[31]

After the 14-month investigation concluded, Chinese regulators slapped a $975 million fine,[32] equivalent to 3.7% of the company's 2014 revenue, the largest fine ever in China for monopolistic practices. On top of the fine, Qualcomm agreed to lower its royalty rates on 3G devices to 5% and 3.5% for 4G devices, using a royalty base of 65% of the final sale price as opposed to 100%. So the company effectively lowered its royalty rates to 3.3% and 2.3%, respectively, on 3G and 4G devices, lower than in other foreign markets including India. In response, Qualcomm's annual dividend saw a $0.60 cents per share reduction.

China's First Failed Attempt on Standards Setting

What resulted was beyond Qualcomm's expectations, but such an outcome should not have been a surprise. The writing was already on the wall four years before the investigation when MIIT in 2009 unveiled its grand designs on promoting 3G standards.

The lack of domestically developed IP in mobile standards has clearly frustrated Chinese regulators to no end. They learned first-hand from Qualcomm how having a near monopoly on core technology patents is directly linked to market position and profits. From Beijing's perspective, why should China passively accept standards when it had the market size to come up with competing standards to Qualcomm's?

MIIT's answer to that question was to order the China Academy of Telecommunications Technology (CATT) to collaborate with Germany's Siemens to develop a new 3G standard that would come to be known as TD-SCDMA. In 2001, backed by all three Chinese carriers, TD-SCDMA was approved to join the global 3G standards governing body, the 3G Partnership Project (3GPP).[33] However, it was China Mobile that was

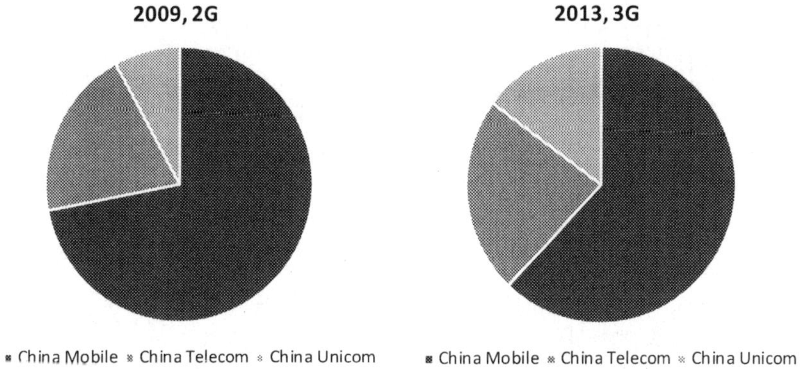

Fig. 5.5 China mobile lost market share from 2G to 3G (*Source* Caixin)

granted the TD-SCDMA license. Of the three state carriers, China Mobile was MIIT's favorite and had dominated the 2G market (see Fig. 5.5).[34] But being the favorite also meant that China Mobile had the unenviable task of ensuring that the indigenous but commercially unproven 3G standard becomes a success.

Except the opposite happened. TD-SCDMA turned out to be far less developed than the prevailing 3G standards WCDMA or CDMA2000, both of which had proven to be commercially viable for years. No carrier outside of China ever used TD-SCDMA and even Chinese carriers, including China Mobile itself, sought to disassociate themselves with it.[35]

But MIIT didn't want to give up hope and ordered China Mobile to develop an entire 3G network based on TD-SCDMA. This was ostensibly a last-ditch effort to bolster the homegrown technology. But instead, China Mobile lost 10% of its market share over the four years it was being forced to support the weaker standard. From the perspective of Chinese telecom industry experts, TD-SCDMA was not a viable technology at the time and led China's telecom companies to deviate from the global standard.[36]

China's effort to introduce a domestic 3G standard ended in failure, but its appetite for reducing dependence on foreign core technologies remained as strong as ever. The Chinese government had learned a hard lesson but did not exactly hide its ambition to have another go at setting standards. It bided its time and largely went with the flow as the world moved to 4G standards.

But even then, two Chinese companies, Huawei and ZTE, had started to make some waves. According to Jefferies equity analysis, ZTE held 6% and Huawei 1% of all patents in 4G standards.[37] That would change quickly as Huawei matured and trained its sights directly on Qualcomm. If Huawei succeeds in leading on global 5G standards, it will prove disruptive for Qualcomm's business in China.

The 5G Race Is On

On July 26, 2018, China's telecom giant Huawei presented a medal to Dr. Erdal Arikan, a Turkish expert in polar coding theory.[38] The medal was designed and crafted by Monnaie de Paris with a Baccarat crystal. As extravagant as the medal was, its value was negligible compared to the royalties Huawei was about to collect by developing its own IP based on Arikan's theory.

Huawei had been quietly pouring 15% of its annual revenue, or more than $61 billion, over the past decade to develop technologies that have the potential to become global 5G telecom standards.[39] One such technology is based on Arikan's polar coding theory. To understand why that's important, a brief explanation of 5G standard development is needed.

Just like in the 2G and 3G eras, delegates from the world's major telecom operators, networks, terminals and chipset vendors, and internet companies regularly met at 3GPP, the international governing body of telecom standards, to pitch technical solutions to various 5G challenges. One of the main problems that needed to be solved was reducing data transmission errors as the volume of data grew exponentially. More errors have crept into large volumes of data due to noise, interference, and fading.

A method called channel coding—which is basically repeating a piece of data to reduce errors—was developed to overcome the problem. To oversimplify, channel coding according to MIT basically works like this: if you were trying to transmit a message with only three bits, like 001, you could send it three times "001001001". If an error crept in, and 001011001 was received instead, you could be reasonably sure that the correct string was 001.[40]

Arikan's polar coding theory is one such channel coding method that could be applied to improve data accuracy. So Huawei decided to back polar coding and invested billions into its commercialization. Within the course of eight years, this relatively new theory had become a viable solution in practice, surprising even Arikan.

The direct competitor to polar coding technology is, no surprise, Qualcomm's low-density parity-check (LDPC) technology. Compared to polar coding, LDPC has a much longer track record of commercial viability. The theory of LDPC was first introduced in 1963, 45 years earlier than polar coding.[41] In subsequent decades, Qualcomm pioneered LDPC's commercial application and developed critical patents.[42] By the time polar coding was introduced in 2008, LDPC applications had already been deployed in the real world.

The contest over whether LDPC or polar coding would become the global 5G standard for channel coding erupted on November 14, 2016 in Nevada, where 3GPP held meetings to vote on accepting a channel coding solution.

Debate was intense at the meeting, with companies picking sides. Western companies, led by Qualcomm, largely fell in line behind LDPC while numerous Asian manufacturers favored Huawei-backed polar coding. In an interview in the *Wall Street Journal*, an expert who was at the meeting recalled it was apparent that Chinese companies viewed it as an extremely critical opportunity, which resulted in one of the biggest political battles at 3GPP.[43]

Eventually, the two sides reached a compromise: both polar coding and LDPC would be adopted as part of the channel coding standard. This was a victory for Huawei as it gained a critical patent in the 5G global standard.

More such battles have been fought, and Chinese telecom companies have made considerable strides in establishing a foothold in 5G standards. According to technology research firm LexInnova, Huawei and ZTE today hold about 10% of critical 5G patents, compared to 15% for Qualcomm (see Fig. 5.6).[44]

To some extent, the global standards race is a zero-sum game in that only one technology will be ultimately suited to addressing one critical technical challenge. And the incentives are such that, like Qualcomm, each company is aiming for market dominance, not just market share. Therefore, the very nature of this competition means that Qualcomm increasingly finds its own dominance being chipped away by the emergence of formidable rivals—some of which are Chinese manufacturers who were once Qualcomm's customers but are now using what they learned to compete with it.

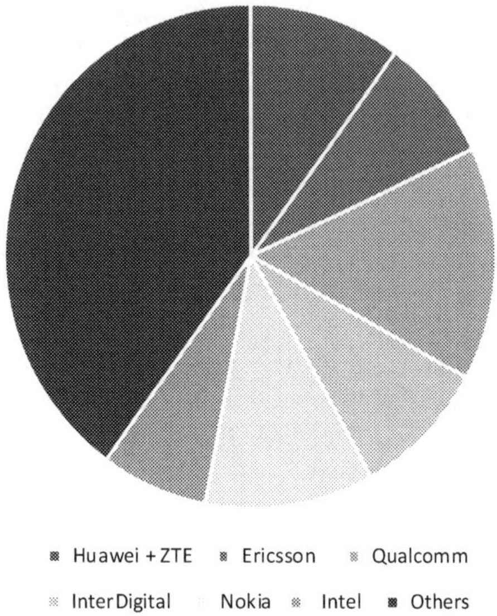

Fig. 5.6 Shares of critical 5G patents by company (*Source* LexInnova)

As if fending off new competitors isn't tough enough, Qualcomm also had to face pressure from the Chinese government to transfer its knowledge to Chinese companies. Although the government has long dangled the carrot of market access to get foreign companies to share certain technologies, the difference today is that the relative leverage has shifted.

Qualcomm still carries a lot of weight, but it is no longer the only player in town. Beijing has choices now, and if Qualcomm isn't willing to play ball, the market share will go to a competing European firm or better yet, a rising Chinese company. This makes the trade-off challenging for Qualcomm: lose market share to Western tech giants today or lose market share to Chinese upstarts tomorrow.

Competition is also taking place in the area of hardware, namely advanced chipsets that are capable of supporting 5G data processing speeds. In fact, Moore's Law's famous prediction of computing speed doubling every two years was predicated on fitting ever more microscopic transistors on a chip. That's because computing power is positively correlated with the number of transistors that can be piled onto a chip. The current generation of advanced mobile chipsets use 14-nanometer transistors.

But few Chinese companies have the ability to manufacture such chips. So eight months after NDRC slapped the fine on Qualcomm, the company agreed to form a JV with Huawei and China's Semiconductor Manufacturing International Corp. (SMIC) to develop 14 nm chips. This move was widely interpreted as a way to patch up relationships with the Chinese government, with little upside for Qualcomm otherwise.[45]

These chips, however, quickly became obsolete. A true 5G network would enable users to download a full movie in 15 seconds, compared to 6 minutes in 4G. This means that the data processing capacity required for a 5G chip is much higher than that of 4G. The chips need to fit even more transistors, which means their size had to be reduced to at least 10 nm.

Even global giants like Intel struggle with developing 10 nm chips,[46] let alone Chinese semiconductor fabricators. But Qualcomm in 2017 again decided to help SMIC's subsidiary SJSemi to start the qualification of wafer bumping, a technique in chip manufacturing, to produce 10 nm chips. This made SJSemi the first ever chip manufacturer in mainland China to enter the 10 nm arena. Qualcomm at the time said that such collaboration "shows our commitment to support the upgrade of China's local IC manufacturing industry and to better serve our Chinese customers."

Currently, Samsung, Huawei, and Qualcomm are leading the pack in developing 5G chipsets. Huawei started its R&D efforts into 7 nm processors in 2015 and has invested over $300 million in developing a prototype.[47] On August 15, 2018, Samsung launched the first 10 nm 5G chipset that's fully compliant with 3GPP standards.[48] Huawei immediately responded by announcing that it would launch its own 7 nm 5G chipset Kirin 980 on August 31.[49] Qualcomm, however, quietly launched its own 7 nm Snapdragon chip ahead of Huawei on August 22.

New Battles on the Horizon

Qualcomm brought CDMA to China in the early days of Reform and Opening, even as the Chinese government had already decided to go in a different direction. But the American tech giant persisted, using various leverage points like negotiations over China's WTO entry to get into a market that was crucial to its long-term strategy.

Qualcomm's persistence paid off handsomely: Beyond the billions of profits, without the Chinese market, it would not have been able to dominate two generations of telecom standards. By having China adopt the 2G and 3G CDMA standards, Qualcomm's market position in global telecom standards was cemented.

The American company's success, however, left lasting impressions on the Chinese government and companies about the importance of leading in global telecom standards primarily through the development of indigenous IP. Qualcomm also didn't help itself by alienating Chinese manufacturers and the telecom industry writ large with its lucrative fee structure that many viewed as unfair. In fact, China's effort to set its own 3G standard with TD-SCDMA, albeit one that ended in failure, was a response to widespread domestic frustration over not having any influence in global standards.

After a stellar run of 15 years in the Chinese market, Qualcomm's rise may be interrupted. As China's telecom firms and mobile phone manufacturers have matured, and having absorbed the previous lessons of failure, they appear ready to challenge the industry leaders. For Chinese companies, Qualcomm's experience taught them that if you win the patents battle, you win the standards war. This is reflected in a Chinese company like Huawei, which has taken chapters from the Qualcomm playbook and has been obsessively filing patents (see Fig. 5.7).

Qualcomm's future prospect is arguably more uncertain than it has been in decades. It is stuck in a paradoxical position: the market that today contributes more than 60% of Qualcomm's global revenue also happens

Fig. 5.7 Huawei vs. Qualcomm Patent Wall (*Source* Qualcomm and Damien Ma)

to be the market that is most likely to challenge its dominant position. To make matters worse, this is coming at a crucial period of transition to the next-gen 5G standards in which no clear winner has been crowned.

This race is set to intensify, and so will the politics around it because technology is the main source of current US–China tensions. But ultimately, this is a competition between multinational companies—they are both proxies of respective national ambitions and potential collateral in the escalating conflict between their home countries. For Qualcomm, the battles it has already fought and won in the Chinese market appear to pale in comparison to the new battles on the horizon.

Notes

1. "How KFC Changed China and How China Changed KFC," MacroPolo, August 3, 2018, https://macropolo.org/analysis/how-kfc-changed-china-and-how-china-changed-kfc/.
2. "Technology Transfer to China," U.S. Congress, Office of Technology Assessment, July 1987, https://www.princeton.edu/~ota/disk2/1987/8729/8729.PDF.
3. "U.S. Sees National Security Risk from Broadcom's Qualcomm Deal," *Reuters*, March 6, 2018, https://www.reuters.com/article/us-qualcomm-m-a-broadcom/u-s-sees-national-security-risk-from-broadcoms-qualcomm-deal-idUSKCN1GI1S8.
4. "Qualcomm Scraps $44 Billion NXP Deal After China Inaction," *New York Times*, July 25, 2018, https://www.nytimes.com/2018/07/25/technology/qualcomm-nxp-china-deadline.html.
5. "China Has Beckoned to Qualcomm, Only to Hang Up the Phone—Twice," *The Wall Street Journal*, July 13, 2000, https://www.wsj.com/articles/SB963441151473349382.
6. Qualcomm company website, https://www.qualcomm.com/invention/stories/world-changing-technology.
7. "World Telecommunication Development Report 1999," International Telecommunication Union, October 1999, https://www.itu.int/ITU-D/ict/publications/wtdr_99/material/wtdr99s.pdf.
8. Dave Mock, *The Qualcomm Equation: How a Fledgling Telecom Company Forged a New Path to Big Profits and Market Dominance* (NewYork: AMACOM, March 4, 2005), pp. 193–194.

9. James Mulvenon and Thomas Bickford, "The PLA and the Telecommunications Industry in China," in *The People's Liberation Army in the Information Age*, eds. James C. Mulvenon and Richard H. Yang (Santa Monica, CA: RAND, 1999), pp. 245–257.
10. "联通 CDMA: 5000 亿市场浮出水面," *People's Daily*, September 30, 2001, http://www.people.com.cn/GB/it/306/2071/3000/20010930/573822.html.
11. "1998 年江泽民宣布 "军队不再经商" 震惊世界," *Phoenix New Media*, June 20, 2013, http://news.ifeng.com/history/zhongguoxiandaishi/detail_2013_06/20/26597774_0.shtml.
12. "Qualcomm's Long March," *Newsweek*, June 24, 2001, https://www.newsweek.com/qualcomms-long-march-153441.
13. "中国移动通信产业 20 年大事记," *Sohu*, May 18, 2007, http://it.sohu.com/20070518/n250100497.shtml.
14. "China Has Beckoned to Qualcomm, Only to Hang Up the Phone—Twice," *The Wall Street Journal*, July 13, 2000, https://www.wsj.com/articles/SB963441151473349382.
15. "Qualcomm Convinces China's Unicom to Enlarge CDMA-Reliant Network," *The Wall Street Journal*, October 20, 2000, https://www.wsj.com/articles/SB971982171585036281.
16. "Qualcomm's Long March," *Newsweek*, June 24, 2001, https://www.newsweek.com/qualcomms-long-march-153441.
17. Ibid.
18. "Qualcomm Announces Availability of the R-UIM/UTK Software for CDMA MSM Chipsets," Qualcomm, March 11, 2002, https://www.qualcomm.com/news/releases/2002/03/11/qualcomm-announces-availability-r-uimutk-software-cdma-msm-chipsets.
19. Qualcomm company website, https://investor.qualcomm.com/annual-reports.
20. "中国发放 3 张第三代移动通信经营牌照," *Xinhua News*, January 7, 2009, http://it.people.com.cn/GB/1068/42905/8640030.html.
21. "China's $40 Billion Deals Kick off Telecoms Shake-Up," *Reuters*, June 1, 2008, https://www.reuters.com/article/us-chinaunicom/chinas-40-billion-deals-kick-off-telecoms-shake-up-idUSHKG24678720080602.
22. "Does Apple Enjoy a Licensing Loophole on iPhone?" *The Wall Street Journal*, November 20, 2009, https://blogs.wsj.com/digits/2009/11/20/does-apple-enjoy-a-licensing-loophole-on-iphone/.
23. "Apple and Qualcomm's Billion-Dollar War over an $18 Part," *Bloomberg*, October 4, 2017, https://www.bloomberg.com/news/features/2017-10-04/apple-and-qualcomm-s-billion-dollar-war-over-an-18-part.
24. "Qualcomm to Charge Up to $16.25 in Royalties for Every 5G Phone, More Than Ericsson's $5/Phone," Fierce Wireless, November

28, 2017, https://www.fiercewireless.com/5g/qualcomm-to-charge-up-to-16-25-royalties-for-every-5g-phone-more-than-ericsson-s-5-phone.
25. "Apple Lawsuit Accuses Qualcomm of Operating Illegal Business Model," *ZDNet*, June 20, 2017, https://www.zdnet.com/article/apple-lawsuit-accuses-qualcomm-of-operating-illegal-business-model/.
26. "Number of Mobile Cellular Subscriptions in China from 2000 to 2018 (in Millions)," Statista, September 2019, https://www.statista.com/statistics/667798/number-of-mobile-cellular-subscriptions-in-china/.
27. Qualcomm company website, https://investor.qualcomm.com/annual-reports.
28. Ibid.
29. "Qualcomm: Apple Won't Use Our Chips in the Next iPhone," *CNN*, July 25, 2018, https://money.cnn.com/2018/07/25/technology/qualcomm-intel-apple-chips/index.html.
30. Qualcomm company website, https://investor.qualcomm.com/annual-reports.
31. Ibid.
32. "Qualcomm to Pay $975 Million to Resolve China Antitrust Dispute," *Reuters*, February 9, 2015, https://www.reuters.com/article/us-china-qualcomm/qualcomm-to-pay-975-million-to-resolve-china-antitrust-dispute-idUSKBN0LD2EL20150210.
33. "TD-SCDMA Forum Welcomed into 3GPP Standards Body," *EE Times*, June 26, 2003, https://www.eetimes.com/document.asp?doc_id=1189713.
34. "TD 式创新," *Caixin*, December 8, 2014, http://weekly.caixin.com/2014-12-05/100759605.html?p0#page2.
35. "TD 标准何以'霸王硬上弓'," *Caixin*, December 9, 2014, http://opinion.caixin.com/2014-12-09/100760671.html.
36. "TD 式创新," *Caixin*, December 8, 2014, http://weekly.caixin.com/2014-12-05/100759605.html?p0#page2.
37. "Telecom Services—The Geopolitics of 5G and IoT," Jefferies Equity Research Global, September 14, 2017, https://www.jefferies.com/CMSFiles/Jefferies.com/files/Insights/TelecomServ.pdf.
38. "Huawei Recognizes Dr. Erdal Arikan, the Father of Polar Codes, for His Dedication to Basic Research and Exploration," Huawei company website, July 26, 2018, https://www.huawei.com/en/press-events/news/2018/7/Huawei-Dr-Erdal-Arikan-Polar-Codes.
39. "5G Ecosystem: Huawei's Growing Role in 5G Technology Standardization," Counter Point Research, August 20, 2018, https://www.counterpointresearch.com/huaweis-role-5g-standardization/.
40. "Explained: The Shannon limit," *MIT News*, January 19, 2010, http://news.mit.edu/2010/explained-shannon-0115.

41. Robert G. Gallager, "Low-Density Parity-Check Codes," *IRE Transactions on Information Theory*, Vol. 8, 1962, 21–28.
42. "Five Wireless Inventions That Define 5G NR—The Global 5G Standard," Qualcomm blog, December 18, 2017, https://www.qualcomm.com/news/onq/2017/12/18/five-wireless-inventions-define-5g-nr-global-5g-standard.
43. "The 5G Race: China and U.S. Battle to Control World's Fastest Wireless Internet," *The Wall Street Journal*, September 9, 2018, https://www.wsj.com/articles/the-5g-race-china-and-u-s-battle-to-control-worlds-fastest-wireless-internet-1536516373.
44. "Testimony of Doug Brake Director of Telecommunications Policy Information Technology and Innovation Foundation Before the U.S.-China Economic and Security Review Commission," Information Technology & Innovation Foundation, March 8, 2018, http://www2.itif.org/2018-testimony-china-5g.pdf.
45. "China's SMIC-Qualcomm 28-nm Deal: Why Now?" *EE Times*, July 3, 2014, https://www.eetimes.com/document.asp?doc_id=1322988&page_number=1.
46. "Intel Outlines Its Struggles with 10-nm Chip Production," The Tech Report, April 30, 2018, https://techreport.com/review/33579/intel-outlines-its-struggles-with-10-nm-chip-production/.
47. "5G 移动芯片"首发"之争 高通"截胡"华为," *Sina News*, August 23, 2018, http://tech.sina.com.cn/it/2018-08-23/doc-ihhzsnec4638684.shtml.
48. "Samsung Announces Exynos Modem 5100, Industry's First 5G Modem Fully Compliant with 3GPP Standards," *Wireless One News*, August 15, 2018, http://wirelessone.news/10-r/1124-samsung-2018-complete-5g-chipset.
49. "Huawei's 7nm Kirin 980 Chip Could Give Qualcomm Reason to Worry," *Endgadget*, August 31, 2018, https://www.engadget.com/2018/08/31/huawei-kirin-980-mobile-chip-7nm/.

Politics

CHAPTER 6

In Xi We Trust: How Propaganda Might Be Working in the New Era

Damien Ma and Neil Thomas

On November 29, 2012, the newly selected Chinese Communist Party (CCP) General Secretary Xi Jinping visited the "Road to Rejuvenation" exhibit at the National Museum in Beijing. With the Politburo Standing Committee (PBSC) in tow, Xi unveiled his vision of the "Chinese Dream" (中国梦)—the simple idea that the CCP's collective mission to rejuvenate the nation also advances the myriad individual ambitions of Chinese citizens. Political theater aside, Xi used the occasion to clearly articulate what amounts to a mission statement: under his leadership, the CCP will lead China's return as a global power.[1]

Many foreign observers at the time dismissed the Chinese Dream as unoriginal, a lifting of a distinctively American idea to capture a similar sentiment among upwardly mobile middle-class Chinese. But such analyses mostly missed the point. Xi's speech, in fact, marked the start of a major campaign to reorient domestic policy and to overhaul propaganda

D. Ma (✉) · N. Thomas
Paulson Institute, Chicago, IL, USA
e-mail: dma@paulsoninstitute.org

N. Thomas
e-mail: nthomas@paulsoninstitute.org

D. Ma (ed.), *China's Economic Arrival*,
https://doi.org/10.1007/978-981-15-2275-8_6

work to support this new agenda. That Xi chose to launch a conceptual idea, rather than economic targets or policies, in his first important speech as General Secretary is significant. Not only did it distinguish him from previous leaders, it also spoke volumes about the problem Xi inherited.

That problem was the CCP itself. Most Chinese were well aware that the Party had drifted toward crony capitalism, as corruption swelled within its rank-and-file. The CCP brand reached its nadir when the Bo Xilai crisis—in which the populist and ambitious leader of Chongqing was purged and jailed after his wife murdered a British national—exploded in early 2012, reinforcing the growing cynicism the Chinese public held toward its government.[2]

The crisis shook the CCP just before Xi took the reins of the world's largest political party. Xi's urgent task, then, which likely had consensus approval from other senior leaders, was to strengthen a weakened Party through a massive anti-corruption campaign and a reimagined Party narrative to win the hearts and minds of Chinese people.[3]

These twin efforts were of equal importance to Xi's goals and were mutually reinforcing in their implementation. From the CCP's vantage point, faltering public trust was as much an existential threat to its legitimacy as a potential economic collapse. The Party understood that it must stand for something beyond perpetuating its own power and its cadres' self-enrichment. Indeed, the CCP had to fill its platform with more compelling ideas—or face a credibility crisis of monumental proportions. In this context, Xi's Chinese Dream set the stage for the elevation of ideological work to a level perhaps not seen since the Mao era.

Propaganda often gets short shrift in mainstream coverage of Chinese politics, possibly because the propaganda apparatus is frustratingly opaque and its effectiveness hard to measure. But the CCP, as a Leninist ruling party that demands political unity among its 89 million members and public compliance with its dictates from nearly 1.4 billion Chinese citizens, invests enormous resources in the promulgation of official ideologies, media management, and public opinion guidance.[4]

Propaganda work is so instrumental to the political system that the Central Propaganda Department (CPD), established in 1924, is almost as old as the CCP itself, which was founded three years earlier in 1921.[5] Since 1992, the propaganda system has been overseen by a PBSC member, who heads the Central Leading Small Group on Propaganda and

Thought Work (CLSGPTW). This system is responsible for all Party publicity and for the supervision of all information domains in China and, to the extent possible, abroad.[6]

That it was so important for Xi to be the first top leader since Deng Xiaoping to enshrine his name in the Party Constitution—under the aegis of "Xi Jinping Thought on Socialism with Chinese Characteristics"—is a testament to the tight control and crucial role of political expression under CCP rule.[7]

This analysis seeks to make sense of what may be termed "Propaganda in the New Era," by examining what has changed (or not) during Xi's tenure across several dimensions: bureaucracy, funding, content, and effectiveness. The focus is mainly on propaganda work aimed at domestic audiences rather than on efforts to project China's soft power externally.

Combining a range of data and qualitative approaches, this analysis assesses how CCP propaganda under Xi (1) has been increasingly controlled by Party rather than state bureaucracies; (2) has received increased funding; (3) has markedly improved content quality; and (4) has shown effectiveness in raising levels of public trust in the Chinese government.

The Organizational Backbone of China's Hearts and Minds

Some specialists have observed that "the more things change, the more they stay the same" with regard to Xi's propaganda work compared to that of his predecessors, Hu Jintao (2002–2012) and Jiang Zemin (1989–2002).[8] That is true, to an extent: after all, the propaganda system is still led by the CLSGPTW; the agency that manages propaganda work is still the ministerial-level CPD directly under the all-powerful CCP Central Committee; and the Party still controls the media and censors political debate. But since the 19th Party Congress in October 2017, Xi has overseen an important shakeup of China's propaganda apparatus (see Fig. 6.1).

The General Secretary has appointed his political allies to leadership positions in the propaganda bureaucracy, but more significant is Xi's reassertion of Party control over aspects of propaganda work that had been under state administration for decades. The practical consequences of these reforms have manifested in the various changes to messaging, content, and technology adoption. But it likely also had an effect on tightening the discipline and padding the budgets of Party propaganda organs,

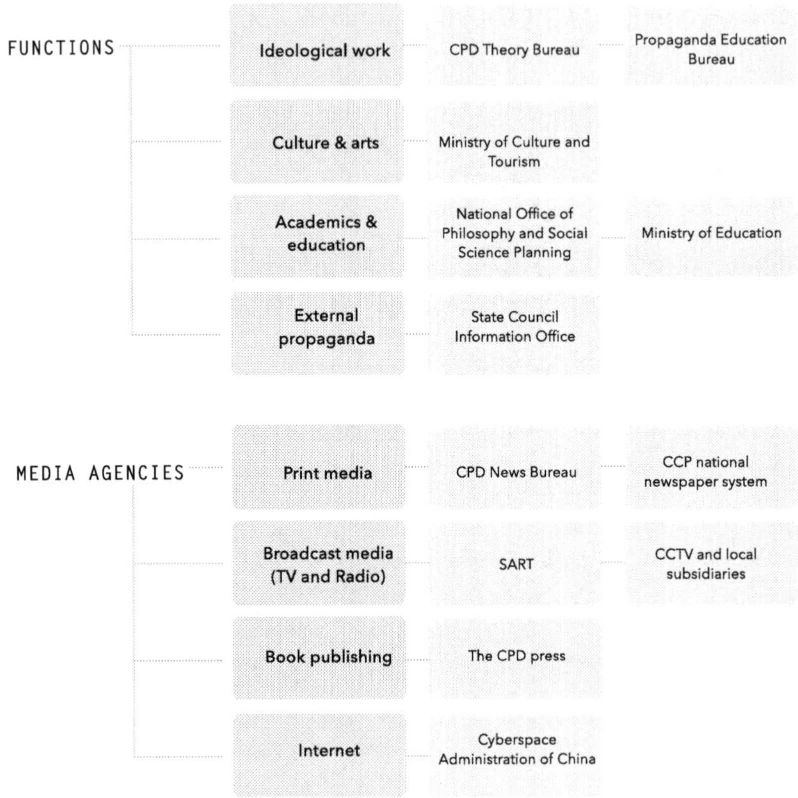

Fig. 6.1 Snapshot of Central Propaganda Department ecosystem (*Source* The Initium)

which would be necessary to better control messaging and produce high-value documentaries like *Amazing China* (see the section below on propaganda content improvements).

Personnel Changes Important but Expected

The swift launch of the Chinese Dream concept signaled that gaining control of the propaganda system was an early priority for Xi. In August 2013, Xi laid out his vision for elevating propaganda work in a speech to the quinquennial National Propaganda and Thought Work Conference, where he said the CCP should "do propaganda work better" and relevant agencies must "maintain a high degree of unanimity with the Party's Central Committee."[9]

Sources later told the *South China Morning Post* that Xi's speech was actually "far stronger" than the summary that appeared in state media. He had apparently urged the Party to be "combative" online and "wage a war to win over public opinion" by forming a "strong internet army to seize the ground of new media."[10]

That same meeting had established, for the first time, that the CPD should treat online public opinion work as its "highest priority" (重中之重).[11] Against this backdrop, Xi moved quickly to establish and chair a Central Leading Small Group on Internet Security and Informatization (CLSGISI, which was upgraded to the Central Cyberspace Affairs Commission in March 2018). The leading group is meant to coordinate the Party's work to censor China's vibrant online discourse, improve digital propaganda, set global internet standards, and become a tech superpower.[12] Given that Tencent's WeChat can have 1 billion-plus monthly active users, it is no surprise that Xi's team has prioritized managing the digital domain.

As has been common under his rule, Xi prefers to concentrate authority in Party leading groups rather than distribute power to the State Council, which is nominally China's government. To ensure the loyalty of those under his authority, Xi also had to clean out political detritus in the propaganda system. He did so by sending anti-corruption inspectors into the CPD and purging the head of the Cyberspace Administration of China (CAC), Lu Wei, who was relieved of that position in June 2016.[13]

Lu was replaced by Xu Lin, a CPD Deputy Director who served as an aide to Xi when he ran Shanghai, and who in August 2018 became head of the State Council Information Office, a CPD-controlled agency responsible for external propaganda.[14] That same month, Zhuang Rongwen, another CPD Deputy Director, who worked under Xi in Fujian province, replaced Xu at CAC.[15]

Placing loyalists in the government apparatus is a tried and true way for China's top leaders to consolidate control over policymaking. And Xi also won major personnel placements at the 19th Party Congress in October 2017 when Wang Huning, widely credited with shaping Xi's populist image and being the originator of the Chinese Dream concept, was himself elevated to the PBSC and to chair the CLSGPTW. The new Director of the CPD, Huang Kunming, who worked with Xi for over two decades in Fujian and Zhejiang provinces, enjoyed an accelerated promotion from an alternate member of the 18th Central Committee to full membership of the 19th Central Committee and a seat on the powerful 25-member Politburo.

But just how indicative are personnel reshuffles of wider changes to China's propaganda system? This is hard to determine precisely. Having loyal subordinates will certainly help Xi execute his propaganda agenda, but it is normal for China's paramount leader to install close allies to leadership positions, particularly for jobs like propaganda work that require a high level of trust. Instead, what likely has had a bigger impact on propaganda work is the reconfiguration of the bureaucracy. In this area Xi has been unusually active.

Significant Propaganda Powers Revert to the Party

At the conclusion of the annual National People's Congress (NPC) in March 2018, the Central Committee published a far-reaching "Plan for Deepening Reform of Party and State Institutions." The main outcome of this reorganization for the propaganda machinery is that the Party now exerts more direct control over propaganda work than it has in decades.[16]

The plan dissolved the State Administration of Press, Publication, Radio, Film and Television (SAPPRFT) and essentially separated broadcast industries like radio and television from the print and film industries. Management of radio and television was parsed out to the new State Administration of Radio and Television (SART), a ministerial-level government agency under the State Council. SART is led by Nie Chenxi, a Central Committee member and CPD Deputy Director.[17]

In addition to the separation, the main state radio and television stations—China National Radio, China Radio International, and China Central Television (CCTV), including its international branch, China Global Television Network (CGTN)—were merged into a new China Media Group (CMG) that will be known as "Voice of China" overseas. While CCTV used to be a vice-ministerial unit that answered to SAPPRFT, CMG is a ministerial-level institution located under the State Council but now under the direct leadership of the CPD. CMG is headed by Shen Haixiong, a Central Committee alternate member and CPD Deputy Director.[18]

The most significant element of the plan, however, was that responsibility for film, press, and publications moved out of the governmental State Council apparatus and into direct Party control under a National Film Bureau and a National Office of Press and Publication (NOPP) within the CPD. These two new divisions are led at the CPD Deputy Director level: the former is headed by Wang Xiaohui (a Central Committee member) while the latter awaits a new leader after ex-head Zhuang Rongwen moved to the CAC.

State, rather than Party, agencies had overseen the press and publishing industries since 1970 and the film industry since 1949. So, Xi's administrative reshuffle suggests that he places greater emphasis on the importance of the written word and the silver screen, as well as the Internet, for propaganda work (although SART retains responsibility for online video content) (see Fig. 6.2).

Since the 2018 NPC, the Party has continued to siphon responsibilities for media regulation from state organs. In September 2018, for instance, the NOPP gained oversight of the registration and licensing of online games from SART and the Ministry of Culture and Tourism. The Party organ will "implement controls on the total number of online video games, control the number of new online video games, explore an age-appropriate rating system in line with China's national conditions, and limit the amount of time minors [spend playing games]."[19]

Hasn't the Party Always Controlled Propaganda?

Of course, it is true that the Party always wielded decisive control over China's propaganda activities, even those that were administratively under the State Council's auspices. Still, Xi's reforms are significant because the Party and the administrative state are formally separate entities. The Party holds ultimate political power but can only exercise that power within state institutions through the supervision of Party committees within these agencies and through its appointment of bureaucratic personnel, most of whom are Party members and therefore subject to Party discipline if they disobey its orders. Party-state separation still matters because it gives the state bureaucracies agency to advance parochial policy agendas via the selective application and interpretation of Party directives.[20]

But the Party's cannibalization of the propaganda system likely means there will be less internal debate over the interpretation of high-level directives, less bureaucratic resistance to central policy preferences, and

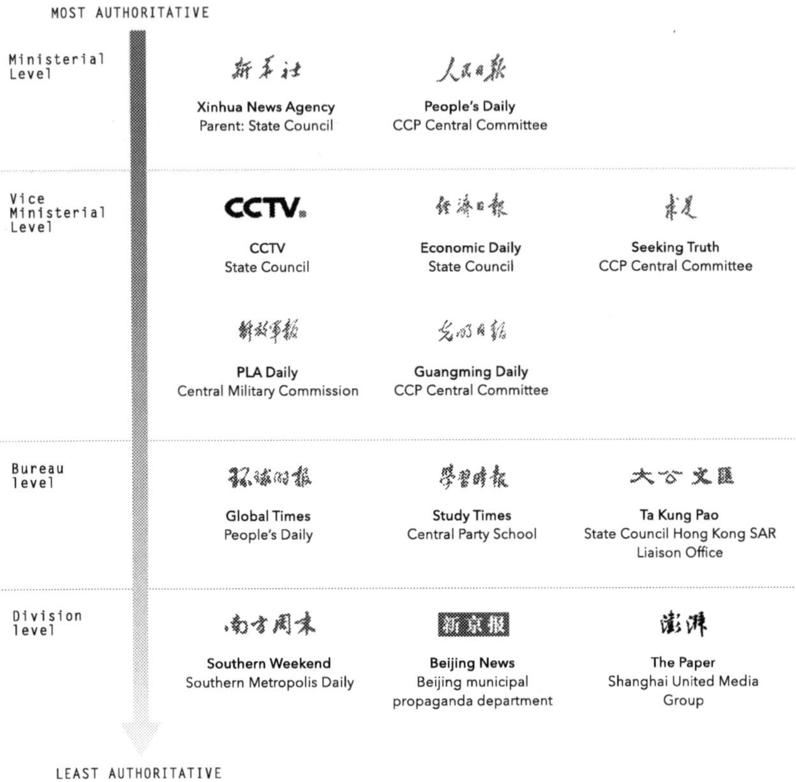

Fig. 6.2 The official hierarchy of Party-state media (*Source* The Initium)

easier recourse to shut down publications and silence troublemakers. Xi's reforms aim to create a more disciplined and reliable messaging machine in service of the goal to "strengthen the Party's unified leadership of news and public opinion work."[21]

Another effect of shifting direct control from the state to the Party is that press, publication, and film work are no longer subject to the *State Council Open Government Information Ordinance*, in effect since 2008, which requires a degree of information disclosure by state agencies both on their own initiative and in response to citizen requests. The CPD, however, has no website and is not compelled to publish information about its activities. Chinese citizens have also lost the right to lodge information requests regarding government decisions in these sectors. In short, propaganda work has become even more opaque.[22]

The prospective bifurcation between Party and state bureaucracies can become especially salient when there exists internecine contention over propaganda-related questions. One particularly relevant example was the release in late February 2015 of Chai Jing's hard-hitting anti-pollution documentary *Under the Dome*.[23] Widely compared to Al Gore's *An Inconvenient Truth*, Chai's film criticized China's urban smog and blamed it on heavy industry. The movie went viral and garnered hundreds of millions of views within days. But, following outcry from powerful vested interests, particularly the oil industry, and a rising number of citizens openly expressing their discontent at China's pollution, the Party soon removed Chai's documentary from the Chinese internet.

One interpretation of how *Under the Dome* came to be released is that lower-level officials ushered the film through approval procedures without explicit top-level authorization.[24] With the centralization of propaganda decision-making power, Xi probably hopes to avoid these kinds of decision-making discrepancies in the future.

But with greater power comes greater responsibility—as well as risk. For the Party, this means that if "mistakes" are made in the formulation or implementation of propaganda work, those Party leaders in charge will have a harder time shifting the blame onto the government bureaucracy. In other words, there is more pressure for propaganda officials, such as Wang Huning and Huang Kunming, to perform well and avoid mistakes, or else risk Xi's wrath.

Show Me the Money

One way to judge the priority of propaganda work under Xi is to look at the finances of agencies within the propaganda ecosystem. Unfortunately, CPD finances are notoriously opaque because it is a Party organ, meaning it does not have to publicize its activities, release a budget, or disclose performance metrics. However, there exist some proxy indicators that suggest the propaganda budget may have seen sizable increases under Xi.

According to the only public report to our knowledge on the CPD's budget, its 2015 funding skyrocketed by some 433% from the year before to 2.5 billion yuan ($357 million).[25] The ostensible reason for this enormous growth is reportedly the reclassification of funds for "cultural construction" from state budgets. This shift aligns with the pattern of transferring decision-making responsibility from the state to the Party. Although these figures cannot be independently verified, comparing the 2.5 billion yuan figure against other indicators does imply that such a CPD budget is credible (even if a 433% jump seems less likely).

For instance, based on the 2015 official audit of government budgets, which for an unknown reason included some Party departments (it has not done so since), the CPD failed to spend about 716 million yuan ($102 million) in that fiscal year—equivalent to about 25% of a 2.5 billion yuan budget—with the surplus being rolled over into 2016.[26]

What's more, since the Shanghai municipal government operates something of a "gold standard" freedom of information regime in China, it publishes a budget for the local CCP propaganda department. These disclosures show that Shanghai's municipal propaganda budget rose dramatically from 2.5 billion yuan in 2017 to 3.6 billion yuan ($514 million) in 2018 and to 4.03 billion yuan in 2019 ($576 million), an increase of over 70% in two years (see Fig. 6.3).[27] Because Shanghai is a large and important market for propaganda, and provincial- and lower-level governments are responsible for actually implementing CPD directives, it makes sense that its propaganda budget could exceed the central CPD budget.

It's also possible to get a glimpse of how Shanghai spends its propaganda funds. Of Shanghai's 3.6 billion yuan propaganda budget in 2018, nearly 90% (3.2 billion yuan) was slated for propaganda activities in "culture, sports, and media." Of this 3.2 billion yuan in spending, 25.5 million yuan ($3.6 million) were for "artistic performance venues," 503 million yuan ($71.9 million) for "artistic performance groups," and the remaining billions were designated as "other," which includes spending on newspapers, news websites, radio and television, and development of creative industries (see Fig. 6.4).

State entities, unlike Party entities, do publish their finances. SAPPRFT, the short-lived SART precursor, which filed budgets from 2013 to 2017, spent a massive 36.7 billion yuan ($5.24 billion) on "media, culture, and sports" (including radio, television, film, and publishing) in 2017. However, this represented only a modest increase from the 34.8 billion yuan ($4.97 billion) it spent in 2013, a 5.7% increase over five years. (SART, in its first year of operation in 2018, spent 32.1 billion yuan [$4.59 billion] on the same.)

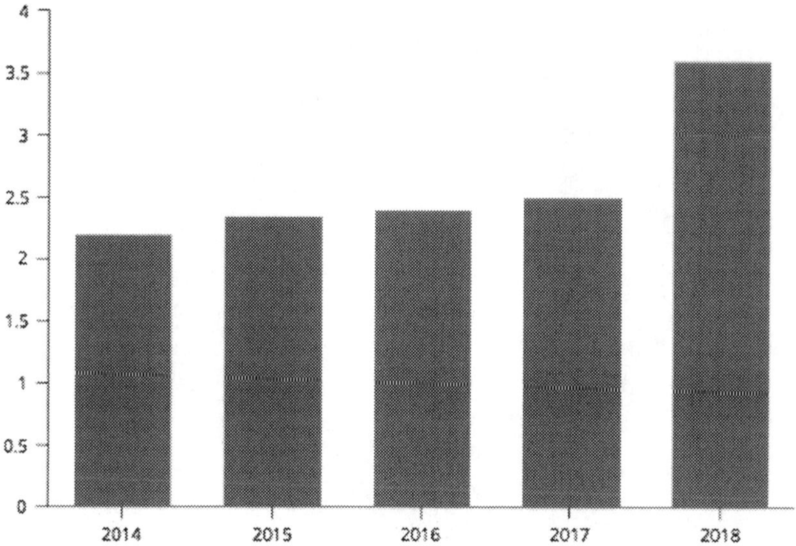

Fig. 6.3 Shanghai's propaganda budget jumped in 2018 (in billion yuan) (*Source* Shanghai Municipal Propaganda Department)

Xinhua's spending on its core business, however, increased by over 18% from 2013 to 2017, rising from 4.9 billion yuan ($700 million) to 5.8 billion yuan ($829 million), but then falling to 5.5 billion yuan in 2018 ($786 million). These dips in spending seem to align with the latest moves of shifting propaganda functions from the state to the Party, where the money disappears from public records.[28]

Even with these budgets, it's difficult to ascertain exactly how the CPD uses its money and on what sort of activities. Only a partial picture can be formed based on the above data, which certainly do not encapsulate the totality of public spending on the propaganda ecosystem, much of which may come from Party sources.

Another proxy measure, as proposed by the political scientist Elizabeth Perry, is to take total state expenditure on "cultural undertakings" (文化事业) as a gauge for general trends in propaganda spending.[29] Data from the Ministry of Culture and Tourism show that this figure has risen steadily as a proportion of total government outlays. This type of spending reached a low of 0.36% under Hu Jintao in 2010 and 2011 and has risen

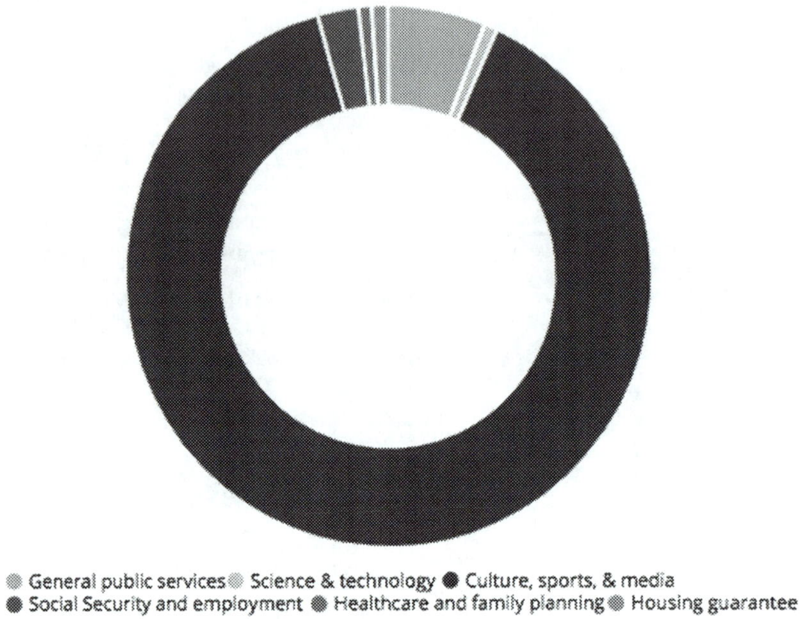

Fig. 6.4 Shanghai propaganda spending breakdown, 2018 (*Source* Shanghai Municipal Propaganda Department)

to a two-decade high of 0.42% under Xi in 2018, when China spent 92.8 billion yuan ($13.3 billion) on cultural undertakings.[30]

Increased spending and tighter control in the propaganda apparatus can only go so far to persuade citizens to buy into the Chinese Dream. Perhaps the most important outcome of these developments, though, is that more resources and stricter management of propaganda has seemingly elevated its production value and sophistication. This has been done through adopting new technologies, borrowing leading film techniques, and cultivating younger talent to make propaganda that the Chinese public actually wants to watch and can perhaps even enjoy. In other words, more money appears to be buying increasingly creative efforts to target audiences on new media platforms.

New Era, New Oeuvre

To the many job titles Xi has accumulated, one can add that of "Storyteller-in-Chief." He has repeatedly exhorted the Party "to tell the China story well."[31] And this insistence on crafting a compelling narrative is, at its core, about connecting China's past, present, and future to the CCP's right to rule indefinitely. This requires beating back public cynicism and strengthening belief in the Party's capacity to lead the country.

One reason for this emphasis is that a key conclusion of numerous CCP internal studies on the reasons for the Soviet Union's collapse was a loss of ideological belief among Soviet citizens. It was a process, according to the CCP's telling, precipitated by leaders like Nikita Khrushchev and Mikhail Gorbachev who chose to criticize their party's history and even let ordinary people do the same.[32] Speaking at a Central Committee study session in early 2013, Xi said as much:

> Why did the Soviet Union collapse? Why did the Soviet Communist Party lose power? A major reason was intense struggles in the ideological sphere, which comprehensively negated the history of the Soviet Union and the Soviet Communist Party, negated Lenin, negated Stalin, brought about historical nihilism, confused thinking, rendered useless Party organizations at every level, and caused the military to no longer be under Party leadership. In the end, a Party as big as the Soviet Communist Party scattered like birds and beasts, a socialist country as big as the Soviet Union collapsed and fell apart—we must learn from the mistakes of our predecessors![33]

Xi's emphasis on ideological work is also attributable to events more recent than the Soviet collapse: the digital-media-driven revolutions of the Arab Spring in 2011. It was perhaps then the Party realized the potential for social media to, as Mao Zedong put it, spark a political prairie fire. The Arab Spring put the Party on high alert that it must take the initiative to upgrade its propaganda—both in content and delivery—for the twenty-first century.

In fact, the Arab Spring likely had a similarly catalytic effect in revolutionizing the Party's approach to propaganda as the first Gulf War in 1990–91 did in jump-starting a renewed emphasis on technological adoption in China's military. That short war, televised 24/7 on CNN, demonstrated America's technological superiority in modern combat. It spurred Beijing to pursue an ambitious agenda of high-tech military modernization starting in the late 1990s—meaning an emphasis on advanced weapons, integrated systems, and civil–military integration to support defense-related modernization. Both of these events served to shine a spotlight on deficiencies that Beijing needed to remedy.

An inevitable aspect of Xi's ideological initiative is the need to delegitimize alternative ideas and values in order to elevate domestic propaganda and champion the CCP's views. This has meant tightening controls on the media and, in particular, stifling key elements of Western liberalism like democracy and information freedom. In other words, Xi has sought to crowd out competing ideas in order to maintain a near monopoly for the CCP's offerings. In April 2013, the Office of the Central Committee circulated an internal "Communiqué on the Current State of the Ideological Sphere" that prohibited discussion of the core tenets of liberal democracy.[34]

To consolidate the CCP's near-monopoly in the realm of ideas, Xi and his propaganda team appear to have understood that they had to improve and adapt to new audiences and new market trends. Which is why one of the more striking features of Propaganda in the New Era is its noticeably improved quality. Gone are the days of Jiang Zemin's tepid "Three Represents" and Hu Jintao's bland "Harmonious Society"—instead, the Chinese Dream is relatable and uplifting and aims to spread Xi's trademark "positive energy" (正能量). This more attractive concept has been accompanied by qualitative improvements in the Party's propaganda, and even significant upgrades in production value.

It is worth illustrating the changing nature of propaganda work with a couple of brief case studies, namely the *Amazing China* (厉害了，我的国) documentary and the recent output from the Road to Rejuvenation Studio (复兴路上工作室). These cases show the Party's new focus on nontraditional propaganda—both in content and delivery—that blurs the line between pure propaganda and what Westerners might consider political advocacy campaigns.

Propaganda in High Definition

The immediate difference from previous propaganda that one notices about *Amazing China*, released in Chinese theaters in March 2018, is its Hollywood-ification. The 90-minute film, which became the highest grossing domestic documentary ever, is replete with grandiose panoramic shots, sharp high-definition frames, and even a soaring score—cinematic techniques typical of a sleek Hollywood blockbuster.[35] Mastery of such tricks of the movie trade makes this state-sponsored documentary a far cry from the staid and soporific propaganda productions of the past. And whether or not one approves of the content, the sheer sleekness of the film can make its substance more "watchable"—so the medium is at least half the message.

The enormous publicity surrounding *Amazing China* obscured its origin: it began as a six-part CPD miniseries that aired a year earlier in the lead-up to the 19th Party Congress.[36] Called *Splendid China* (辉煌中国), the miniseries not only employed sophisticated techniques, its production was expansive in scope. Official media proudly touted that shooting the miniseries required eight film crews to traverse 31 provinces and regions over three months, capturing some 3200 hours of hi-def film, 300-plus hours of aerial footage, and 108 interviews.[37] These kinds of efforts are usually reserved for a David Attenborough mega-production like *Planet Earth*, not a Chinese propaganda flick.

Beyond the high production value, there is little doubt that *Splendid China* is full-on propaganda. The six episodes—spanning China's technological and engineering feats to environmental stewardship, global integration, and military prowess—all fall under the rubric of the Chinese Dream. The key political message continues to link Xi's "new era," and by extension the CCP's, to China's past, present, and future in a cohesive and uninterrupted narrative. The nationalism peddled by Xi's propaganda is increasingly sophisticated. *Splendid China* and *Amazing China* are not particularly anti-foreign but rather decidedly pro-China.

Many Chinese seem to have found *Amazing China* appealing. On Maoyan, a Chinese equivalent of IMDB, the documentary has a rating of 9.6/10 from around 117,000 votes as of September 2019. While many of these votes may come from "bots" or paid commenters, the individual review comments appear to be organic and suggest the main theme of "Chinese pride" is about as compelling a message as the CCP has ever conveyed to stir the public imagination. Naturally, the CCP has decreed that the documentary be used as teaching material in colleges across China.[38]

Digital Shorts and "Explainers"

Just weeks before the Third Plenum of the 18th Party Congress in October 2013, an animated "explainer" video popped up on Youku, the Chinese YouTube. It was titled "How Leaders Are Made" and it compared the political leadership selection process in the United States, the United Kingdom, and China. While it playfully explained complex political subjects, the digital short contained an underlying message: compared to Western democracies, Chinese leaders are tested more rigorously than an American president or British prime minister. It was produced by an outfit called the "Road to Rejuvenation Studio."

This digital short went viral in China, but the background of its creator remained a mystery.[39] Many suspected that this was a new initiative from within the propaganda system. According to one *People's Daily* investigation, the studio is in fact on Rejuvenation Road (复兴路) in Beijing, where both CCTV and the then-SAPPRFT had offices, and is staffed by a young team from diverse disciplines.[40] (*The Wall Street Journal* reported, however, that the studio was run out of the Party's International Liaison Department, which handles the CCP's relations with foreign political parties.)[41] Interestingly, the team hires foreigners to help develop content for their digital products—perhaps most aptly captured in an English-language explainer video on the 13th Five-Year Plan, which was released by CGTN America's official YouTube channel.

The studio's products have won accolades from the Chinese government and viewers alike, particularly for a follow-up effort called "The CCP Walks Alongside You." Although it is clearly aligned with Xi's agenda and the Chinese Dream, the studio's content and delivery are far from that typically associated with traditional propaganda—it is, in fact, closer to the work of a corporate public relations division and is clearly targeted at millennials. According to the public opinion monitoring office of the state-owned *China Youth Daily* newspaper, 70% of netizens who saw "The CCP Walks Alongside You" liked the video, with at least a quarter of their comments commending the improvement in propaganda content.[42]

The apparent resonance of this type of slick digital persuasion seems to comport with the popular idiom of the Chinese Dream, which topped numerous lists of China's online "word of the year" as far back as 2013, according to the *China Youth Daily*.[43] But more than resonating with a younger demographic, the studio's success seems to have influenced the overall sensibility and tech-savviness of propaganda content.

Propaganda on the Silver Screen

Cinema has become a new propaganda priority, as reflected in the bureaucratic restructuring that put the film industry more firmly under Party control. The CPD's National Film Bureau, China's first dedicated movie bureau since 1986, now has responsibility for the administration, guidance, monitoring, distribution, screening, and censorship of Chinese films, as well as the management of national film events, Sino-foreign coproductions, and film imports and exports.

The Party's latest emphasis on elevating the role of movies in both propaganda work and entertainment culture is likely also due to its recognition of market trends. That is, like the Internet, film is a growth market in China. The country now boasts the world's second largest film market, with total ticket sales of $8.6 billion in 2017,[44] and is on course to overtake North America as the top market in a few years.

Film is undoubtedly a powerful mass medium, as the smashing success of the patriotic and jingoistic blockbuster "Wolf Warrior 2" demonstrated in 2017.[45] Making over $870 million worldwide, it became the highest grossing Chinese made film ever.[46] Most of these ticket sales were domestic, indicating the movie's enormous popularity with the Chinese public. Indeed, the Public Sentiment Monitoring team of *People's Daily* hailed Wolf Warrior 2 as a model for how Chinese films could "tell the China story well" by "rooting individual destiny in national destiny."[47] And, in the vein of *Amazing China*, the core nationalistic sentiment of Wolf Warrior 2 is at least as much pro-China as it is anti-foreign.

The unexpected success of Wolf Warrior 2 reinforced the Party's longstanding focus on turning China from a "big film country" (电影大国) into a "powerful film country" (电影强国) with global influence. In fact, China has been trying to establish an influential film industry since at least 2010,[48] when authorities wondered if China could make a global blockbuster like *Avatar*.[49] In April, Propaganda chief Huang Kunming chaired a unique Symposium on Research and Investigation into Film Production that doubled down on this goal by introducing a national film evaluation system and calling for the development of "red and expert" film talent.[50]

These techniques are now widely applied across the Chinese bureaucracy, as infographics and animated explainers have proliferated. According to a July 2018 study of the government's social media presence, 80% of the ministries under the State Council have a WeChat account and 66% have a Weibo account, many of which are avid infographic generators. The foreign ministry led in the number of Weibo followers, at 7.5 million, but even the more staid state assets management agency rounds out the top five with 4.6 million followers (see Fig. 6.5).

In the last few years, it seems almost standard practice for a major policy document or announcement to be accompanied by an infographic that breaks down its key messages for audiences on social media platforms such as WeChat. Some of these infographics come from agencies themselves but, more often, they are made by *Xinhua* or the *People's Daily* as part of their standard reporting. For instance, one of the most useful and dynamic infographics came from the *People's Daily* official WeChat account, when it disseminated a comprehensive explainer of the bureaucratic reorganization approved by the NPC in March 2018.[51]

While Propaganda in the New Era is better at responding to market demands for more attractive content, the Party remains uncompromising in controlling the substance of its message. In September 2016, the Central Committee General Office issued an "opinion" that demanded state-owned cultural enterprises put "social effect" before economic profits—including incorporating performance metrics that weigh the former over the latter—which means that toeing the correct political line is prioritized over the corporate bottom line.[52]

Agency	Weibo Followers
Ministry of Foreign Affairs	7.52 million
Ministry of Education	7 million
Ministry of Commerce	6.22 million
Ministry of Defense	5.87 million
State-owned Assets Supervision and Administration Commission	4.59 million
Ministry of Civil Affairs	4.34 million
Ministry of Industry and Information Technology	4.12 million
People's Bank of China	3.13 million
National Health Commission	2.41 million
National Bureau of Statistics	2.41 million

Fig. 6.5 Top 10 State Council agencies with the most Weibo followers (July 2018) (*Source* Horizon Consulting)

Does New Era Propaganda Work?

Have higher quality and more appealing content, as well as more robust budgets, translated into greater effectiveness for Propaganda in the New Era? Examining shifts in public opinion is a good way to gain insights on effectiveness, but it is difficult to identify precise causal factors behind such shifts. This is in part because public opinion research is not as developed in China as it is in liberal democracies like the United States. Still, certain polling data can shed light on whether public trust in the CCP as an institution has increased and whether the idea of Chinese exceptionalism is taking hold, both of which are broad goals for the CCP's propaganda efforts.

The CCP does not allow pollsters to assign it an approval rating, although multinational public opinion surveys tend to record relatively high levels of regime support in China.[53] Most of these surveys have not yet published data from the Xi era, but the Pew Research Center is a notable exception. When asked whether they had "confidence" in their president in 2011, 2012, and 2014, Chinese respondents gave former President Hu Jintao an 86% confidence rating in 2011 and 82% in 2012. When asked the same question of Xi in 2014, respondents gave him a 92% confidence rating, 10 percentage points higher than Hu on the eve of his retirement.[54]

Of course, these quasi "approval ratings" could well shift for Xi in the future, as he may stay in office for another two terms, and especially as disagreement over some of his policies seems to have surfaced. But at least during his first term, the Chinese public's confidence in their leader seemed to have improved, which surely owed something to the different nature and broader appeal of his early propaganda efforts.

Pew has also surveyed Chinese on questions of general life satisfaction that point indirectly (yet not definitively) to the possible influence of propaganda under Xi's tenure. In 2015, 96% of Chinese said their standard of living was "better than their parents," more than three quarters said they were "better off financially" than five years ago, and over 70% said their own economic situation was "good."[55]

From 2013 to 2016, more than 80% of Chinese polled believed their children today would "be better off financially than their parents."[56] In 2014, the last time Pew posed the question in China, 87% of Chinese respondents said they were "satisfied" with their country's overall direction.[57] Such satisfaction may not be an entirely sound metric to determine whether people trust the CCP more but, as a proxy, it suggests there probably isn't a crisis of confidence either.

Some of these conclusions appear to be corroborated by a 2016 joint study on American and Chinese public opinion by the Chicago Council on Global Affairs and Horizon Consulting, China's leading private–public opinion surveyor. About 39% of American respondents said their parents were better off than they were, compared to only 27% of Chinese who said the same. Chinese respondents were also far more optimistic about the future than Americans. Nearly two-thirds believed their children will be economically better off, while only 11% of Americans believed the same. Perhaps in another indication of the effectiveness of domestic propaganda, the majority of Chinese respondents believed that China is both economically and militarily stronger than the United States, aligning with Xi's emphasis on "becoming strong."[58]

When it comes to measuring trust specifically, Edelman, the American public relations firm, has released an annual "Edelman Trust Barometer" since 2001. In the 2019 edition, China topped a 26-market ranking of average public trust in institutions.[59] In 2018, Chinese people's trust in their government reached the barometer's "highest recorded levels"—84% of the general public and 89% of the "informed public" trusted China's government. What's more, 68% of Chinese believed that, compared to business, media, or NGOs, the government is the institution "most likely to lead to a better future" (see Fig. 6.6).[60]

Edelman called these 2018 results "unprecedented in the history of the study" and "a genuine reflection of the general population's confidence in reaction to both economic and social achievements in China."[61] If these 18 years of data are any guide, Xi's propaganda seems to be succeeding in rekindling some trust between the Party and the governed.

Conclusion

After the rumor mill ran hot with stories of dissension within Xi's ranks over summer 2018, the General Secretary returned to Zhongnanhai seemingly emboldened to double down on his agenda.[62] That was manifest in one of his first orders of business, which was to chair the National Propaganda and Thought Work Conference on August 21–22, 2018.[63] His speech at the conference amounted to a ringing endorsement of the

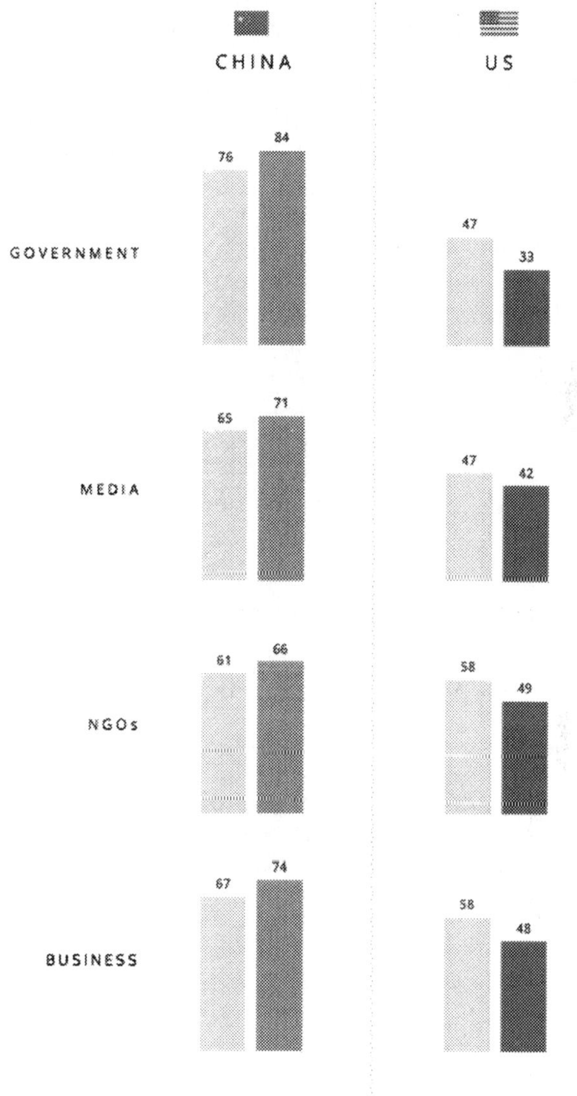

Fig. 6.6 Chinese and American trust in institutions: 2017 vs. 2018 (*Source* 2018 Edelman Trust Barometer)

Party's propaganda work under his leadership and of the performance of Wang Huning and Huang Kunming, both of whom also spoke at the event.[64]

Xi said that "Since the 18th Party Congress, we have placed propaganda and thought work in an important position in our overall work" and "practice has proved that the Party center's propaganda policies and ideological work are completely correct, and the broad masses of officials on the propaganda and ideological front are completely trustworthy."[65]

Whether there was in fact serious elite dissent, Xi did not mince his words when he declared that his propaganda work was effective in winning over the Chinese public.[66] A course change does not appear to be on the horizon, which means more creative content, more disciplined messaging, higher production values, increased Party control, and greater focus on the Internet and new media will continue to be the defining features of Propaganda in the New Era.

For state-sponsored works such as *Amazing China*, sequels should be expected. And like *The Godfather*, the sequel may turn out to be better than the original.

Notes

1. "习近平: 承前启后 继往开来 继续朝着中华民族伟大复兴目标奋勇前进," *Xinhua*, November 29, 2012, http://www.xinhuanet.com/politics/2012-11/29/c_113852724.htm.
2. Cheng Li, "The Bo Xilai Crisis: A Curse or Blessing for China," Brookings Institution, April 18, 2012, https://www.brookings.edu/on-the-record/the-bo-xilai-crisis-a-curse-or-a-blessing-for-china/.
3. Alice Miller, "The 18th Central Committee Leadership with Comrade Xi Jinping as General Secretary," *China Leadership Monitor*, Vol. 48, Fall 2015, https://www.hoover.org/publications/china-leadership-monitor/fall-2015-issue-48.
4. Anne-Marie Brady, *Marketing Dictatorship: Propaganda and Thought Work in Contemporary China* (Lanham: Rowman & Littlefield, 2007).
5. "主要职能," CCP Official News Website, https://web.archive.org/web/20190511143601/http://cpc.people.com.cn/GB/64114/75332/5230610.html.
6. Brady, *Marketing Dictatorship*, Chs. 2, 5.
7. Chris Buckley, "China Enshrines 'Xi Jinping Thought,' Elevating Leader to Mao-Like Status," *The New York Times*, October 24, 2017, https://www.nytimes.com/2017/10/24/world/asia/china-xi-jinping-communist-party.html.

8. Anne-Marie Brady, “Plus Ça Change? Media Control Under Xi Jinping,” *Problems of Post-Communism*, Vol. 64, Issue 3–4, 2017, pp. 128–140.
9. “习近平：胸怀大局把握大势着眼大事 努力把宣传思想工作做得更好,” *People’s Daily*, August 21, 2013, http://cpc.people.com.cn/n/2013/0821/c64094-22636876.html; “学习贯彻习近平在全国宣传思想工作会议上重要讲话精神,” Special Topic Page, *Xinhua*, 2013, http://www.xinhuanet.com/politics/szxzt/qgxcsxgzhy/index.htm.
10. Cary Huang and Keith Zhai, “Xi Jinping Rallies Party for Propaganda War on Internet,” *South China Morning Post*, September 4, 2013, https://www.scmp.com/news/china/article/1302857/xi-jinping-rallies-party-propaganda-war-internet.
11. Wang Xianfu, “把网上舆论工作作为宣传思想工作的重中之重,” *People’s Daily Online*, October 31, 2013, http://theory.people.com.cn/n/2013/1031/c40537-23387807.html.
12. Oiwan Lam, “The Fall of Chinese Internet Czar Lu Wei,” *Hong Kong Free Press*, December 12, 2017, https://www.hongkongfp.com/2017/12/12/fall-chinese-internet-czar-lu-wei/.
13. “中央第一巡视组向中央宣传部反馈专项巡视情况,” Supervision Bureau of the Central Commission for Discipline Inspection, June 8, 2016, http://www.ccdi.gov.cn/special/zyxszt/djlxs_zyxs/fkqk_18jzydjl_zyxs/201606/t20160613_80397.html; “中央宣传部原副部长、中央网信办原主任鲁炜严重违纪被开除党籍和公职,” *Xinhua*, February 13, 2018, http://www.xinhuanet.com/2018-02/13/c_1122415612.htm.
14. Zhou Xin, Choi Chi-yuk and Nectar Gan, “Xi Jinping to Shake Up Propaganda, Censorship Chiefs as China’s Image Abroad Suffers,” *South China Morning Post*, July 26, 2018, https://www.scmp.com/news/china/policies-politics/article/2156921/china-reshuffles-propaganda-cyber-administration-chiefs.
15. Zhou Xin and Choi Chi-yuk, “Beijing Names New Internet Watchdog as China Keeps Door Closed to Global Tech Giants,” *South China Morning Post*, August 1, 2018, https://www.scmp.com/news/china/policies-politics/article/2157762/beijing-names-new-internet-watchdog-china-keeps-door.
16. “中共中央印发《深化党和国家机构改革方案》,” *Xinhua*, March 21, 2018, http://www.xinhuanet.com/politics/2018-03/21/c_1122570517.htm.
17. Ibid.
18. “中央广播电视总台正式揭牌亮相!,” *CCTV*, April 19, 2018, http://m.news.cctv.com/2018/04/19/ARTInAFNw1HW6nZ2P4xpjWDY180419.shtml.
19. Zhou Xin and Zheping Huang, “China’s Gaming Boom Hit by Freeze in Licensing as Propaganda Body Takes Charge,” *South China Morning Post*, September 7, 2018, https://www.scmp.com/news/china/china-ec

onomy/article/2163308/chinas-gaming-boom-hit-freeze-licensing-propaganda-body.

20. Neil Thomas, "China's 'Toilet Revolution' Shows Us That Politics Still Matters in the Xi Era," MacroPolo, July 31, 2018, https://macropolo.org/chinas-toilet-revolution/.
21. Ng Yik-tung, Yeung Mak and Yang Fan, "China's Central Propaganda Department Takes Over Regulation of All Media," *Radio Free Asia*, March 21, 2018, https://www.rfa.org/english/news/china/china-propaganda-03212018140841.html.
22. Xiao Tian, "欢迎进入广电总局的新时代," *China Digital Times*, March 23, 2018, https://chinadigitaltimes.net/chinese/2018/03/ngocn-%E6%AC%A2%E8%BF%8E%E8%BF%9B%E5%85%A5%E5%B9%BF%E7%94%B5%E6%80%BB%E5%B1%80%E7%9A%84%E6%96%B0%E6%97%B6%E4%BB%A3/.
23. Matthew D. Johnson, "Institutionalizing Independence: Security, Culture, and Unofficial Documentary Filmmaking Under the Xi Jinping Government," *Problems of Post-Communism*, Vol. 64, Issue 3–4, 2017, pp. 152–166.
24. Ma Tianjie, "January: A Moment of Reflection," *Chublic Opinion*, January 19, 2016, https://chublicopinion.com/2016/01/19/january-a-moment-of-reflection/.
25. Yang Zhijin, "学习党部预算: 五部门公共预算支出 37.68 亿," *21st Century Business Herald*, March 18, 2015, https://m.21jingji.com/article/20150318/herald/f4056081dbc6b15ea9cd9878ad4b4325.html.
26. National Audit Office of the People's Republic of China, "2016 年第 5 号公告: 中央部门单位 2015 年度预算执行等情况审计结果," June 29, 2016, http://www.audit.gov.cn/n5/n25/c84845/content.html.
27. Most Recent: Shanghai Municipal Government, "上海市 2019 年市级部门预算: 中国共产党上海市委员会宣传部," February 2019, http://www.tianshunsc.com/Attach/Attaches/201902/201902180451544555.pdf.
28. Ministry of Finance of the People's Republic of China, "Central Budget and Final Accounts Public Platform," http://www.mof.gov.cn/zyyjsgkpt/zybmyjs/bmjs/index.html.
29. Elizabeth J. Perry, "Cultural Governance in Contemporary China: 'Re-Orienting' Party Propaganda," in *To Govern China: Evolving Practices of Power*, eds. Vivienne Shue and Patricia M. Thornton (Cambridge: Cambridge University Press, 2017), Ch. 1, pp. 29–55.
30. Ministry of Culture and Tourism of the People's Republic of China, "中华人民共和国文化和旅游部 2018 年文化和旅游发展统计公报," May 2019, http://zwgk.mct.gov.cn/auto255/201905/t20190530_844003.html.
31. Central Commission for Discipline Inspection of the Chinese Communist Party, "关于讲好中国故事, 习近平总书记这样说," November 17, 2017, http://www.ccdi.gov.cn/toutiao/201711/t20171113_126275.html.

32. David Shambaugh, *China's Communist Party: Atrophy and Adaptation* (Berkeley: University of California Press, 2008), Chs. 4–7.
33. Zhang Shuhua, "苏共垮台、苏联解体与历史虚无主义," *Chinese Academy of Social Sciences Online*, January 14, 2018, http://www.cssn.cn/lsx/lishixuezhuanti/bwcxljsm/zjpx/201801/t20180114_3814303.shtml.
34. "Document 9: A ChinaFile Translation," *ChinaFile*, November 8, 2013, http://www.chinafile.com/document-9-chinafile-translation.
35. Zheping Huang, "China's Top-Grossing Documentary of All Time Is About How Great Xi Jinping Is," *Quartz*, March 15, 2018, https://qz.com/1229834/amazing-china-chinas-top-grossing-documentary-of-all-time-is-about-how-great-xi-jinping-is/.
36. "辉煌中国," *CCTV*, http://jingji.cctv.com/special/hhzg/index.shtml.
37. Shi Jingnan, "六集电视纪录片《辉煌中国》全景展现党的十八大以来经济社会发展成就," *Xinhua*, September 16, 2017, http://www.xinhuanet.com//politics/2017-09/16/c_1121675078.htm.
38. "《厉害了，我的国》免费进各大校园: 兰州财经大学四场连映," *The Paper*, April 22, 2018, https://www.thepaper.cn/newsDetail_forward_2089741.
39. Fu Shan, "习近平博鳌动画视频: 复兴路上工作室又一力作，更短更轻更萌," *The Paper*, March 25, 2015, https://www.thepaper.cn/newsDetail_forward_1314791.
40. Chai Yifei, "'十三五之歌' 引海内外关注——走进 '复兴路上工作室'," *People's Daily Online*, November 5, 2015, http://cpc.people.com.cn/n/2015/1105/c83083-27780525.html.
41. Chun Han Wong, "Chinse President Xi Jinping's Extreme Makeover," *The Wall Street Journal*, May 12, 2016, https://www.wsj.com/articles/xi-jinpings-extreme-makeover-1463069291.
42. Jiang Tao, "复兴路上工作室再推中共宣传片 讲述百姓梦想获点赞," *China News Service*, January 2, 2014, http://www.chinanews.com/gn/2014/01-02/5691442.shtml.
43. Wang Mengjie, "2013 年官媒发声 '渐入佳境'," *China Youth Daily*, January 6, 2014, http://zqb.cyol.com/html/2014-01/06/nw.D110000zgqnb_20140106_1-06.htm.
44. Patrick Brzeski, "China Box Office Returns to Robust Growth in 2017, Hitting $8.6B," *Hollywood Reporter*, January 2, 2018, https://www.hollywoodreporter.com/news/china-box-office-returns-robust-growth-2017-hitting-86b-1070895.
45. Chris Buckley, "In China, an Action Hero Beats Box Office Records (and Arrogant Westerners)," *New York Times*, August 16, 2017, https://www.nytimes.com/2017/08/16/world/asia/china-wolf-warrior-2-film.html.
46. Box Office Mojo data, https://www.boxofficemojo.com/movies/?id=wolfwarrior2.htm.

47. Liu Yuyao and Lu Ziyao, "Amid Danger, China Comes to the Rescue! What Does the Box Office Success of Wolf Warrior 2 Say about the Patriotic Spirit?" *People's Daily*, August 10, 2017, http://yuqing.people.com.cn/n1/2017/0810/c209043-29463411.html.
48. Liu Yang, "Moving from 'Big Film Country' To 'Strong Film Country'," *People's Daily*, January 30, 2010, http://media.people.com.cn/GB/120837/10881195.html.
49. "The 'Strong Film Country' Dream: When Chinese Blockbusters Can Make Foreign Countries Rename Their Mountains," *People's Daily*, January 28, 2010, http://media.people.com.cn/GB/40606/10861131.html.
50. "Huang Kunming: Study Hard Xi Jinping's Thought on Culture and the Arts, Strive to Build a 'Strong Film Country'," *People's Daily*, April 13, 2018, http://cpc.people.com.cn/n1/2018/0413/c64094-29925626.html.
51. "一目了然! 深化党和国家机构改革方案动态图," People's Daily WeChat Official Account, March 21, 2018, https://mp.weixin.qq.com/s/saJu1f4glUajSfyTr9aufg.
52. "授权发布：中共中央办公厅、国务院办公厅印发《关于推动国有文化企业把社会效益放在首位、实现社会效益和经济效益相统一的指导意见》," *Xinhua*, September 14, 2015, http://www.xinhuanet.com/politics/2015-09/14/c_1116559409.htm.
53. Wenfang Tang, "The 'Surprise' of Authoritarian Resilience in China," *American Affairs*, Vol. 2, No. 1, Spring 2018, https://americanaffairsjournal.org/2018/02/surprise-authoritarian-resilience-china/.
54. Pew Research Center, "Confidence in the Chinese President," Global Indicators Database, https://www.pewresearch.org/global/database/indicator/69/country/cn/.
55. Pew Research Center, "Chinese Happy with Economic Situation," September 28, 2015, https://www.pewresearch.org/global/2015/09/24/corruption-pollution-inequality-are-top-concerns-in-china/china-report-10/.
56. Pew Research Center, "Children's Financial Future," Global Indicators Database, https://www.pewresearch.org/global/database/indicator/74/country/CN/.
57. Pew Research Center, "Satisfaction with Country's Direction," Global Indicators Database, https://www.pewresearch.org/global/database/indicator/3/country/cn/.
58. Karl Friedhoff and Craig Kafura, "Views From the G2: Public Opinion in the US & China," The Chicago Council on Global Affairs, November 30, 2016, https://www.thechicagocouncil.org/sites/default/files/us-china-survey-report_161130.pdf.

59. "2019 Edelman Trust Barometer: Global Report," Edelman, January 2019, https://www.edelman.com/sites/g/files/aatuss191/files/2019-02/2019_Edelman_Trust_Barometer_Global_Report.pdf.
60. "2018 Edelman Trust Barometer: Global Report," Edelman, January 2018, https://www.edelman.com/sites/g/files/aatuss191/files/2018-10/2018_Edelman_Trust_Barometer_Global_Report_FEB.pdf.
61. Jeffrey Yu, "China: High Trust, But Skepticism Toward Business," Edelman, April 11, 2018, https://www.edelman.com/post/china-high-trust-skepticism-towards-business.
62. "How to Read Summer Grumbles About China's Swaggering Leader," *The Economist*, August 9, 2018, https://www.economist.com/china/2018/08/09/how-to-read-summer-grumbles-about-chinas-swaggering-leader.
63. "习近平在全国宣传思想工作会议上强调举旗帜聚民心育新人兴文化展形象更好完成新形势下宣传思想工作使命任务," *CCTV*, August 22, 2018, http://tv.cctv.com/2018/08/22/VIDE21Xdv2a2RNqPkwoN1PhT180822.shtml.
64. Qian Gang, "Signals from Xi's Speech on Ideology," *China Media Project*, August 23, 2018, http://chinamediaproject.org/2018/08/23/signals-from-xis-speech-on-ideology/.
65. "China's Xi Says Ideology Work 'Absolutely Correct' Amid Trade Row Criticism," *Reuters*, August 22, 2018, https://www.reuters.com/article/us-china-politics/chinas-xi-says-internet-must-be-clean-and-righteous-idUSKCN1L71CG.
66. Geremie R. Barmé, "Imminent Fears, Immediate Hopes—A Beijing Jeremiad," *China Heritage*, August 1, 2018, http://chinaheritage.net/journal/imminent-fears-immediate-hopes-a-beijing-jeremiad/.

CHAPTER 7

Who Rules China? Comparing Representation on the NPC and Central Committee

Damien Ma and Neil Thomas

March Madness for China-watchers is the "Two Sessions," the annual meetings of the National People's Congress (NPC) and the national committee of the Chinese People's Political Consultative Conference (CPPCC). Yet, from scripted press conferences[1] to rubber-stamp approvals,[2] these two institutions are often dismissed as political pageantry of little significance.

Recent scholarship suggests otherwise. Rory Truex argues persuasively that the rote proceedings and staged appearance of the Two Sessions belie the real political significance of the NPC.[3] In fact, the Chinese Communist Party (CCP) rewards NPC delegates who, throughout the year, make suggestions that transmit citizen preferences on nonsensitive political issues, such as environmental protection, to central policymakers.

D. Ma (✉) · N. Thomas
Paulson Institute, Chicago, IL, USA
e-mail: dma@paulsoninstitute.org

N. Thomas
e-mail: nthomas@paulsoninstitute.org

D. Ma (ed.), *China's Economic Arrival*,
https://doi.org/10.1007/978-981-15-2275-8_7

In short, the NPC serves as an information feedback mechanism that allows the CCP to better "serve the people," placate anti-government sentiment at the grassroots, and address grievances from various constituencies. For instance, the Xi Jinping administration this year was focused on mollifying two interests: the domestic business community (cutting their entitlement contributions)[4] and the foreign business community (passing the new Foreign Investment Law).[5] Thus, the NPC achieves what Truex calls "representation within bounds."

But who does the NPC actually represent? Who are the 2975 NPC delegates who descended on Beijing in March 2019? The conclusion of this year's a better sense of their identities emerges by comparing several demographic characteristics of NPC "representatives," as compiled by NPC Observer,[6] with those of the 375 "policymakers" with full or alternate membership of the CCP Central Committee (CC), based on the MacroPolo database.[7]

Examined below are several different types of representation: geographic, ethnic, gender, and generational.

Geographic Representation[8]

How much does where you're from affect how far you go in Chinese politics? The CC, formally the highest body in Chinese politics, and the NPC, formally the highest organ of state authority, have quotas that ensure some degree of equality in the representation of officials who serve in each province. But many senior officials are not from the provinces in which they work, so the geographic backgrounds of officials are not necessarily equally represented.

For every CC and NPC member, the government publicizes their "place of ancestry" (*jiguan*), which official regulations[9] define as being "the long-term residence of one's paternal grandfather."[10] It turns out that some jiguan are significantly over-represented or under-represented in the NPC and the CC. This finding suggests that people whose families are from certain provinces are more likely to reach the highest echelons of political power in China (Fig. 7.1).[11]

CC members whose paternal ancestors hail from the wealthy coastal provinces of Zhejiang, Jiangsu, Shandong, and Beijing are over-represented by at least 50% relative to their provincial populations.[12] For instance, Shandong, China's second-most populous province, enjoys jiguan representation almost double that relative to its population size.

Province	CC Members	% of 375	Resident Population (End 2017)	% of 1388340000	CC Representation Index	NPC Delegates	% of 2975	NPC Representation Index
Tibet	2	0.533333333	3370000	0.242735929	2.197175074	14	0.470588235	1.938683889
Shandong	52	13.86666667	100060000	7.207168273	1.924010394	321	10.78991597	1.497108928
Zhejiang	28	7.466666667	56570000	4.074650302	1.832468093	152	5.109243697	1.253909739
Jiangsu	35	9.333333333	80290000	5.783165507	1.613879686	228	7.663865546	1.325202527
Beijing	9	2.4	21710000	1.563737989	1.534783971	32	1.075630252	0.687858362
Liaoning	18	4.8	43690000	3.146923664	1.525299153	141	4.739495798	1.506072693
Shanghai	9	2.4	24180000	1.741548299	1.378004963	25	0.840336134	0.482494735
Hebei	27	7.2	75200000	5.416540617	1.329261702	185	6.218487395	1.148055158
Shaanxi	13	3.466666667	38350000	2.762291658	1.25499661	84	2.823529412	1.022169185
Qinghai	2	0.533333333	5980000	0.430730225	1.238207358	14	0.470588235	1.092535904
Hubei	19	5.066666667	59020000	4.251120043	1.191842765	158	5.31092437	1.249300024
Jilin	8	2.133333333	27170000	1.957013412	1.09009643	68	2.285714286	1.167960461
Ningxia	2	0.533333333	6820000	0.491234136	1.08570088	12	0.403361345	0.821118312
Henan	26	6.933333333	95590000	6.885201031	1.006990689	194	6.521008403	0.947105012
Heilongjiang	10	2.666666667	37890000	2.729158563	0.977102138	63	2.117647059	0.775934051
Fujian	10	2.666666667	39110000	2.817033292	0.946622347	64	2.151260504	0.763661725
Hunan	17	4.533333333	68600000	4.941152744	0.917464723	152	5.109243697	1.034018571
Inner Mongolia	6	1.6	25290000	1.821599896	0.878348754	51	1.714285714	0.941087951
Gansu	6	1.6	26260000	1.891467508	0.845904037	50	1.680672269	0.88855466
Chongqing	6	1.6	30750000	2.214875319	0.722388293	56	1.882352941	0.84986858
Jiangxi	9	2.4	46220000	3.329155682	0.720903505	81	2.722689076	0.817831707
Tianjin	3	0.8	15570000	1.121548321	0.71334104	15	0.504201681	0.449584689
Shanxi	7	1.866666667	37020000	2.666493798	0.700045381	90	3.025210084	1.134527328
Anhui	11	2.933333333	62550000	4.505380526	0.651073381	166	5.579831933	1.238481833
Xinjiang	4	1.066666667	24450000	1.761099985	0.605683436	39	1.31092437	0.744379853
Yunnan	6	1.6	48010000	3.458086636	0.462683608	76	2.554621849	0.738738533
Guangxi	6	1.6	48850000	3.518590547	0.454727533	75	2.521008403	0.716482458
Sichuan	10	2.666666667	83020000	5.979803218	0.445945555	150	5.042016807	0.843174369
Guizhou	4	1.066666667	35800000	2.578651307	0.413658101	51	1.714285714	0.664807662
Guangdong	5	1.333333333	111690000	8.044859828	0.165737309	95	3.193277311	0.39693389
Hainan	0	0	9260000	0.666983592	0	10	0.336134454	0.503962103

Fig. 7.1 Politicians from wealthy coastal provinces are over-represented while poorer southwest provinces are under-represented (*Note* The representation index compares the proportion of CC or NPC representatives claiming a *jiguan* in that province with the proportion of the national population residing in that province. E.g., A score of 1 connotes perfect representation, a score of 2 connotes double representation, and a score of 0.5 connotes half representation. *Source* MacroPolo, National Bureau of Statistics, and NPC Observer)

Other provinces that are generously over-represented include Tibet, Liaoning, Shanghai, and Hebei. Shaanxi, the provincial *jiguan* of President Xi, is over-represented by 25%.

The most under-represented jiguans on the CC are provinces in the south and southwest—Guizhou, Yunnan, Guangxi, and Sichuan have at least 50% fewer members with a local *jiguan* than should be expected based on their population size. Guangdong, however, is an outlier. It is a relatively wealthy coastal province that is under-represented by over 80%. Despite being China's most populous province, only five CC members trace their origins to Guangdong. No CC member has a *jiguan* in Hainan province, the island off the southern coast of China.

The pattern of *jiguan* representation on the NPC is broadly similar to that in the CC, although representation in the NPC is on average somewhat more equal than in the CC. For example, there are 10 NPC delegates whose *jiguan* is in Hainan. However, some patterns are reversed in the NPC: politicians with ancestry in Beijing, Shanghai, and Tianjin are significantly under-represented as compared to the CC, whereas there is much better representation of those from Anhui, Shanxi, and Sichuan.

Ethnic Representation[13]

When it comes to minority representation, each of China's 55 officially recognized ethnic minorities, which together constitute 8.5% of the national population,[14] has at least one representative in the NPC. Even the three ethnicities with fewer than 5000 people—the Tatars, Lhoba, and Gaoshan—each have an NPC delegate. When it comes to the CC, however, a full 38 of the 55 ethnic minorities are not represented at all. This number includes the Tujia people, who with 8.35 million members are the largest ethnic group excluded from the CC (Fig. 7.2).

If one considers the representation of ethnic groups on the CC compared to their proportion of China's population, the picture is mixed for different minorities. Of those 18 ethnicities with CC members, some are still under-represented relative to their size, such as the Miao, Manchu, Yi, and Zhuang peoples—whose numbers range from 8.71 million to 16.9 million.

Minorities in western China, such as Tibetans, Uyghurs, Mongols, and Hui, are actually over-represented on the CC. Such appointments, however, are probably intended to co-opt local elites, as those regions' allegiance to Beijing is a perennial preoccupation of the CCP. As Han

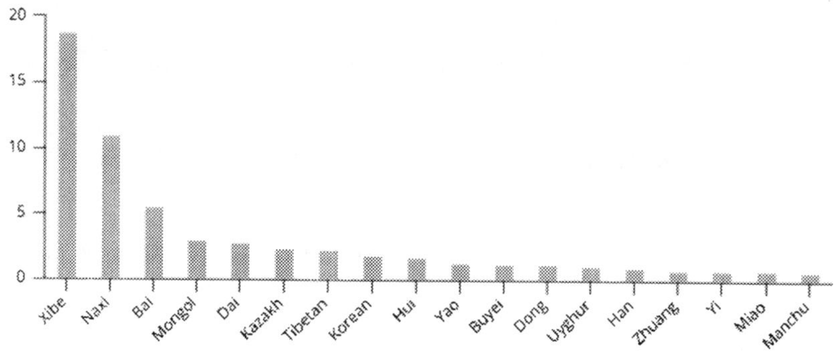

Fig. 7.2 Only 1/3 of China's minorities are represented on the Central Committee (*Note* The graph shows a representation index that compares the proportion of CC members of a particular ethnicity with the proportion of the national population of that ethnicity. E.g., A score of 1 connotes perfect representation. *Source* MacroPolo and National Bureau of Statistics)

Chinese make up only 85.3% of NPC delegates, relative to 91.5% of the national population, their under representation means that almost every minority is over-represented on the NPC.

Gender Representation

Gender representation cuts across ethnicities. It is well known that Chinese female politicians tend to hit a "glass ceiling" and are significantly under-represented in the CC. According to previous MacroPolo analysis, the CC is only 8% female, with women comprising less than 5% of full members.[15] But the NPC helps to correct some of this imbalance female membership is almost 25%, still well short of equality but three times better than on the CC. Female representation on the NPC actually narrowly beats the global average for women[16] in parliament and does just better than the US Congress (Fig. 7.3).[17]

Generational Representation[18]

Chinese politics is also ageist, in the sense that experience and seniority are often prerequisites for advancement up the political hierarchy. The

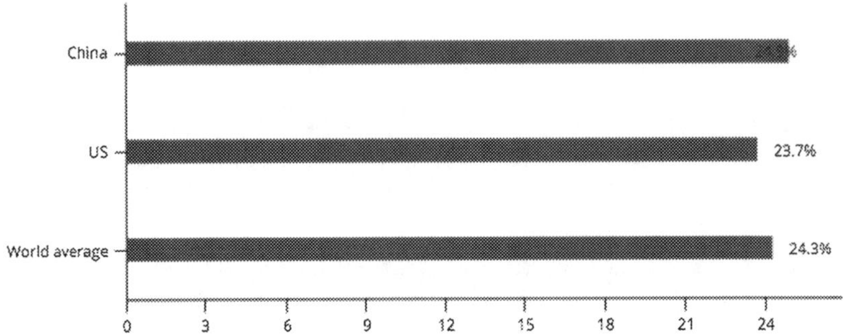

Fig. 7.3 Female representation in Chinese legislature aligns with world average (*Source* NPC Observer and Inter-Parliamentary Union)

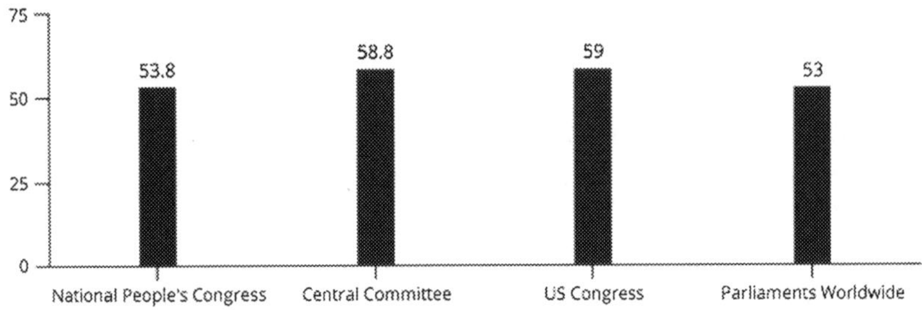

Fig. 7.4 Average age of Chinese politicians similar to elsewhere (*Source* MacroPolo, NPC Observer, Quorum, UNDP)

average age of CC members is 58.8—it's 59 for US congressional representatives[19]—while for full members it is slightly higher at 61.2. NPC delegates have an average age of 53.8, a full five years younger than CC members, and in line with the global average age for parliamentarians of 53.[20] Still, the median age in China is 37, so young people are significantly underrepresented, a fact common around the world (Fig. 7.4).

Conclusion

What do these data tell us? The NPC is younger, more female, and far more ethnically diverse than the CC—although both bodies fall short of achieving equal representation for women and young people. It seems nearly impossible for ethnic minorities and women to reach the uppermost rung of Chinese politics. In addition, the greater demographic diversity found in the NPC seems to support Truex's theory that the NPC is an institution that the CCP uses, in the absence of free elections and widespread polling, to collect valuable information about its performance from a much wider cross-section of society.

Perhaps a more fundamental finding is that there may be significant inequality of political opportunity for Chinese whose ancestors come from different parts of China. In both the NPC and the CC, there are proportionately far more members who trace their lineage to the wealthy coast than to the poorer southern provinces.

So, the person that you're most likely to see in the halls of Chinese political power is a fifty-something Han Chinese man who has familial ties to the east coast.

Notes

1. Stephen McDonell, "China's National People's Congress: Eye Rolls and Tame Questions," *BBC*, March 13, 2018, https://www.bbc.com/news/blogs-china-blog-43382141.
2. Tony Saich, "The National People's Congress: Functions and Member ship," Harvard Kennedy School, November 2015, https://ash.harvard.edu/files/ash/files/the_national_peoples_congress.pdf.
3. Rory Truex, *Making Autocracy Work: Representation and Responsiveness in Modern China* (New York: Cambridge University Press, 2016).
4. Houze Song, "GDP Target and Beyond: Things to Watch at This Year's NPC," MacroPolo, March 1, 2019, https://macropolo.org/china-2019-npc-two-sessions-what-to-watch/.
5. Full text and translation of the "Foreign Investment Law of the People's Republic of China" found at NPC Observer, https://npcobserver.com/lawlist/foreign-investment-law/, accessed September 25, 2019.
6. The NPC Observer database collected and analyzed the demographic characteristics of the 2980 delegates who attended the annual NPC meeting in 2018. In the year since, nine delegates were removed, and four new delegates were added, so this database is slightly out-of-date. Nevertheless, the difference between the 2018 and 2019 delegates is not significant enough to affect our analytical conclusions. We also use 2019 statistics for the ethnicity and gender of NPC delegates. The analysis is found here: https://npcobserver.com/2018/03/10/exclusive-demographics-of-the-13th-npc/, accessed September 25, 2019.

7. The Committee database, which can now capture interesting but overlooked patterns and trends with the latest biographical data and enhanced search functions, can be accessed here: https://macropolo.org/digital-projects/the-committee/.
8. We could not find this data for four alternate members of the CC. We do not include these members in the analysis but we do calculate the representation index for each province of ancestry as a proportion of the 375 total members of the Central Committee. Additionally, one alternate member of the CC claims Taiwan as their place of ancestry, and we have not represented this situation.
9. "How to Fill in Your Jiguan?" The Beijing Daxing District Communist Party Committee Organization Department, June 15, 2007, http://dxdj.bjdx.gov.cn/web/dj/djzs/jbzs/64710.htm.
10. There are many Chinese terms that describe different places of personal belonging, such as laojia, zuji, yuanji, etc. We use jiguan because this is the data that is the most reliable and accessible for government officials, while many other similar data are often not provided by official sources and are thus not as reliable.
11. The term "province" is used to refer to all provincial-level administrations in mainland China. Beijing, Chongqing, Shanghai, and Tianjin are actually provincial-level municipalities. Guangxi, Inner Mongolia, Ningxia, Xinjiang, and Tibet are provincial-level autonomous regions.
12. The resident populations of provinces have of course changed over the years, as a result of continued population flows from rural to urban China. But issues of data reliability, changing administrative boundaries, and the impossibility of selecting a perfect historical year for comparison mean that we relied on the latest available population data in 2017.
13. We could not find this data for five alternate members of the CC. For the purpose of this analysis, we assume that they are members of the Han majority. Population data are from the 2010 national census.
14. "The Sixth National Population Census (2010)," National Bureau of Statistics, April 28, 2011, http://www.stats.gov.cn/tjsj/tjgb/rkpcgb/qgrkpcgb/201104/t20110428_30327.html.
15. Damien Ma, "The Committee by the Numbers," MacroPolo. April 16, 2018, https://macropolo.org/analysis/the-committee-by-the-numbers/.
16. This is based on data from the Inter-Parliamentary Union, which can be accessed here: http://archive.ipu.org/wmn-e/world.htm.
17. Ibid. Accessed here: http://archive.ipu.org/wmn-e/classif.htm.
18. We could not find this data for five alternate members of the CC. Our figures represent average ages in March 2019 for the 203 full members and 167 alternate members for which we have data. Please note that official sources tend to provide only the month and year of birth, so we count all those born in March as having passed their birthday this year.

19. Daniel Bessner and David Austin Walsh, "America Has Become a Gerontocracy. We Must Change That," *The Guardian*, October 6, 2018, https://www.theguardian.com/commentisfree/2018/oct/06/congress-senate-house-age-problem.
20. "The Global Parliamentary Report," United Nations Development Programme, April 2, 2012, https://www.undp.org/content/undp/en/home/librarypage/democratic-governance/parliamentary_development/the-global-parliamentary-report.html.

US–China

CHAPTER 8

Reluctant Stakeholder: Why China's Highly Strategic Brand of Revisionism Is More Challenging Than Washington Thinks

Evan A. Feigenbaum

At the end of 2016, as Donald Trump prepared to take office as President, I penned an essay for *Foreign Affairs* magazine on "China and the World."[1] The editor, my friend Gideon Rose, had asked me to respond to two straightforward questions: Is China a "revisionist" power? And in particular, does not Beijing's championing of a new Asian Infrastructure Investment Bank (AIIB) demonstrate its revisionism?

Well, much has happened since I published that essay in December 2016.

For one thing, the Trump Administration has developed its *own* answer to these questions. In White House[2] and Defense Department strategy[3] documents, the Administration has made clear that it views China not just as a "revisionist" power but as the world's principal champion of alternative rules, principles, and structures.

In this telling, Beijing has eschewed the institutions and rules that have prevailed since World War II, especially those preferred by the

E. A. Feigenbaum (✉)
Chicago and Washington, DC, USA
e-mail: efeigenbaum@paulsoninstitute.org

D. Ma (ed.), *China's Economic Arrival*,
https://doi.org/10.1007/978-981-15-2275-8_8

United States. Instead, it aims to lock in a Sinocentric vision of the world through parallel institutions, disruptive bilateral initiatives, and a rewriting of global rules.

Some administration officials have gone further in their public statements. Take former Secretary of State Rex Tillerson. He displayed a reasonable grasp of history,[4] but absolutely zero sense of irony, when he praised the Monroe Doctrine in a speech about Latin America,[5] then warned the region to beware the "imperial" ambitions of you-know-who.

Treasury Secretary Stephen Mnuchin, meanwhile, has cautioned pretty much every country against taking China's money. Chinese infrastructure lending, he (correctly) notes, lacks transparency.[6] But Mnuchin extends that argument about transparency into something more like a rap sheet: take Beijing's money, he warns, and risk being trapped in a debilitating cycle of debt—something that has led to asset-stripping by Chinese practitioners of what the *National Defense Strategy* calls "predatory economics."[7] This, in turn, could undermine governance principles championed by the International Monetary Fund (IMF).

In recent weeks, the administration's nominee for Pacific Command, Admiral Philip Davidson, has taken that argument to its logical conclusion. In testimony to Congress, Davidson came pretty close to calling Chinese infrastructure plays a tool of anti-democratic subversion.[8]

In this changed context, it seems like a good time to take a long look back at my 2016 essay. I still see a lot more complexity than these many strategies, statements, and speeches do.

Here are six important things Washington is missing. Thinking through the implications of these could help the United States to compete more effectively.

It's Tough to Critique Another Country's Obvious Revisionism When You're a Revisionist Yourself

China *is* moving in some very troubling directions. But in the 16 months since I wrote my essay, the United States—and for that matter, some of its trans-Atlantic partners—has *also* changed in at least three notable ways:

First, while much of the pushback against Chinese activism has been framed as a conservative *defense* of prevailing rules and institutions, there is nothing either conservative or defensive about the political sentiment that now prevails in some Western capitals. Trump's Washington. Brexit London. A potential Five Star government in Rome. A Berlin that now has the far-right AfD as the third-largest party in the Bundestag. These signal not a doubling down on prevailing institutions, modes, and rules but an underlying desire by some governments—and many more in their electorates—to actually change them.

Second, the United States has long been the principal champion of trade multilateralism and, in recent years, of regional approaches to liberalization too. Now, the United States is moving briskly away from both of these, favoring instead a firm preference for bilateral agreements and managed trade. In fact, the politics of trade in Washington now raise serious questions about whether the United States can ever again undertake a large-scale multilateral deal.

Bluntly put, this has changed Washington's trade policy—and perceptions of and reactions to it—very considerably from 16 months ago. It is often noted that the administration has abandoned the Trans-Pacific Partnership (TPP) in a probably fruitless pursuit of bilateral agreements in Asia. But that isn't the only thing that has changed. Washington is also reemphasizing pre-WTO instruments (sensibly, in my view, but nonetheless to the chagrin of most of its partners). And it seeks to impose penalties and offer incentives in a mostly *bilateral*, not multilateral, context.

Third, this has meant a return to managed trade—a throwback resented by many and encapsulated, most recently, by the multiple separate bilateral negotiations that Washington has conducted with its allies for tariff exemptions. And here's the irony: the United States is pursuing throwback approaches with the very partners it seeks to enlist against Chinese rule-breaking. Take Japan: Tokyo shares American concerns about China but has seen the United States withdraw from TPP in favor of a managed approach to trade that looks eerily similar to the US–Japan structural impediments initiatives of the 1990s. Nor does Washington favor other approaches that its Japanese ally now champions.

China Is a Revisionist Power but Not a Revolutionary One

This distinction may sound too cute by half, but it is a distinction with a difference. China is emerging as a *disruptive* force on the international stage. For thirty years, it was encouraged to join international institutions and subscribe to their norms. Now, having joined them, it seeks, like most major powers, to leverage its seat at the top table to support its national interests.

But this is not even one iota surprising.

As China's military, economic, and financial power have grown, it has been patently obvious that Beijing would not accept all global institutions, rules, standards, and norms exactly as they are configured today. And importantly, this would be true *even without Xi Jinping in power.* China's sheer size, weight, and self-perception of its interests will invariably lead it to expect changes in the governance of international institutions and, in some cases, to their underlying rules.

Yet the proposition that China aims to construct a "parallel" order of competing institutions, rules, and initiatives to subvert, and perhaps even replace, the postwar international system both misstates and understates the challenge China *actually* poses.

It misstates the challenge because it lacks historical perspective and institutional memory. A "disruptive" China is not, after all, a "revolutionary" China. And we know this because we have seen *precisely* such a China in the very recent past.

Less than fifty years ago, in the 1960s, Mao Zedong's China actually *did* seek to overturn the architecture of the international system. Beijing opposed nearly every global institution. It promoted internal, often violent revolution against established governments from Bolivia to Borneo. It argued for an "anti-capitalist" order. When it entered the United Nations in 1971, the West's biggest fear was that Beijing would disrupt and undermine the organization. And China isolated nearly every aspect of its own economic and social systems from outside influences and global trends, restricting flows of goods, capital, people, technologies, and information almost completely.

Americans have largely forgotten what the world was like when China sought—and in many areas, achieved—a functional autarky. But today's China is, quite obviously, not *that* China. And in the case of the AIIB, a

China-backed institution has, in many ways, ended up aping and adapting practices from existing institutions.

But if many critics overstate what China is *not*, they also understate what China actually *is*—a stakeholder in existing institutions and rules but a habitually reluctant, seldom satisfied, and frequently ambivalent one, at best.

This means the challenge to Washington is far more complex than if China actually *did* seek to overturn the international order wholesale.

To put this pithily, China accepts most *forms* but not necessarily our preferred *norms*. And that disconnect between forms and norms means that Beijing's revisionism and demands for change often play out *within* the existing international framework.

This, in turn, means we risk misidentifying the problem.

China's strategy is actually one of *portfolio diversification*, not the replacement of institutions and systems. Beijing aims to give itself options—and by extension, leverage—not least to push for reform of these various groups and a larger role for itself and its preferred outcomes and standards.

To illustrate, look at the multilateral development banks: Beijing has not only joined but supports with financial muscle all of the prevailing development institutions, both globally and in Asia. It is the number-three shareholder in the Asian Development Bank—the very institution it is said to be "destabilizing" with its sponsorship of the AIIB. When China has endorsed new structures, such as the New Development Bank and BRICS contingency reserve arrangement, it has simultaneously made sizeable replenishment contributions to the IMF, where it now has nearly three times the voting weight of Canada, about a third more than Britain and France, and only a whisker less than Japan.[9] Beijing has joined regional development banks in Europe, Latin America, and Africa. It has transitioned from a net borrower to a net contributor in the International Development Association (IDA) and other institutions.

And then there is the AIIB, where China wields a veto—there, Beijing's "alternative" institution has struck up partnerships and cofinance arrangements with every other leading MDB, including the Islamic Development Bank, African Development Bank, Asian Development Bank, World Bank, and European Bank for Reconstruction and Development.

To put this somewhat pointedly, China *is* a revisionist power but one that is both highly strategic and carefully selective in its revisionism.

In the maritime domain, for example, it seeks to advance its territorial claims by challenging international law and customary practice. In the cyber domain, it is promoting a distinctive vision of cyber sovereignty. But in the majority of instances and institutions, Beijing pursues structural change by demanding changes to the *existing* framework.

And a more ambitious China cannot, by definition, be a "status quo" power, in any case. The same could be said of some other emerging powers. Merely by seeking a greater role, heftier voting weight, extra chairs, and expanded shares, Beijing is, by definition, attempting to force structural changes and achieve gains relative to the established powers, especially America's European partners.

China is no revolutionary, then, yet it is determined to gain leverage in almost every prevailing institution and rule-making body.

American Policy Did Not "Mistake" the Implications of China's Rise

Frankly, "portfolio diversification," as opposed to wholesale replacement, will make it harder for America to simply get its way. Washington needs strategy and foresight, above all. But in recent months, I've read three-dozen articles that claim America has compounded its own problem by "failing" to anticipate this Chinese challenge and, in effect, missing the boat on China's desire to undermine and replace the existing order.

Frankly, that, too, is ahistorical.

China's brand of revisionism is not at all surprising—first, because leveraging structures and rules to own advantage is among the most predictable behaviors of major powers, but second, because China's intensifying demands were not, in fact, unanticipated by prior administrations. The United States has seen precisely such a Chinese challenge coming. And in the decade of the 2000s, when I served in the George W. Bush Administration, I saw firsthand how Washington tried to get out in front of it.

Let me illustrate with some examples from my own experience:

In September 2005, I was responsible for East Asia on Secretary of State Condoleezza Rice's Policy Planning Staff. My then boss, Deputy Secretary of State Robert Zoellick, delivered an important conceptual speech that came to define much of the debate about China's global role in the ensuing decade, but which has sometimes been misconstrued or misinterpreted.[10]

Zoellick began his so-called "responsible stakeholder" speech by noting that US policy, through seven presidents from Richard Nixon to George W. Bush, had sought to "integrate" China into the international system. But with China having acceded to the World Trade Organization (WTO) in 2001, that process was largely complete. Structurally speaking, Zoellick argued, China already *was* "in." Beijing had joined most of the major institutions, and, on paper, subscribed to the major treaties and protocols from ozone depletion to chemical weapons.

Zoellick's conclusion was that American rhetoric about China lagged at least five years behind the new realities of Chinese power. So US policy, he argued, needed to change dramatically as a result.

The shift Zoellick advocated was to deemphasize *structure* and instead emphasize Beijing's *conduct and behavior*. The proper question for US policy, he implied, was no longer whether China was "in" or "out" of this or that institution or rule, but rather whether Beijing supported and sustained through its actions, even as it might demand to adapt, those aspects of the international system that had enabled its own success.[11]

Zoellick put this point pretty bluntly, deploying a now-famous catchphrase: "It is time to take our policy beyond opening doors to China's membership into the international system. We need to urge China to become a *responsible stakeholder* in that system."

From my vantage point, at least, the Bush Administration clearly sensed from its earliest days an impending challenge from Beijing. So it tried to get in front of, shape, and steer China's emerging energies.

One reason for this was that Washington faced a gathering problem with China in the mid-2000s: Beijing's power and capacity for action were growing, yet China was, in many areas, taking a big fat free ride as a *consumer* of the security and stability the United States was working to provide.

One way to think about this challenge is to turn Zoellick's catchphrase on its head. The logical opposite of a "responsible stakeholder" is an "irresponsible free rider." And since the administration had no interest whatsoever in encouraging China to be an irresponsible free rider, it made sense to encourage its logical opposite.

By late 2005, as President Bush swung into his second term, China was developing a truly global footprint for the first time since its revolutionary foreign policy of the 1960s. So Washington had every good reason to push Beijing to act as a stakeholder in the system it had joined, not continue to free ride on its benefits.

Operationally, the United States confronted specific examples of this challenge from Beijing nearly every day throughout the decade of the 2000s. And since I worked on quite a few of these, I saw how debilitating they could become at the ground level:

In 2001 and 2002, for instance, my boss on the Policy Planning Staff, Richard Haass, was dual-hatted as the US coordinator for Afghanistan policy. As a neighboring country that shared a continental border with Central Asia and was a member of the Six-Plus-Two group on Afghanistan, China derived security and counterterrorism benefits from the war against the Taliban and al Qaeda.

But while China made modest financial contributions at international donors' conferences in Tokyo and The Hague, it contributed little to the effort when weighed against its capacity and interests. And it tended to make its contributions unilaterally rather than in coordination with us and other donors.

But because Washington pressed, changes happened.[12] So where Beijing had made its Afghanistan pledges unilaterally, its initial pledges to Iraq, by contrast, were made multilaterally and in coordination with the United States and other donors, as was Beijing's participation in the process of Iraqi debt forgiveness.

By 2006, I had become the Deputy Assistant Secretary of State for Central Asia, the principal day-to-day official for the region. Among other challenges I inherited was the bitter taste left by China having most unhelpfully joined Moscow and fellow members of the Shanghai Cooperation Organization (SCO) in a 2005 statement that called for a "final timeline" to end coalition operations in Afghanistan.

From Washington's perspective,[13] this highlighted Beijing's propensity to mouth empty slogans while enjoying the benefits of a free ride on the security and stability America was spending blood and treasure to provide. In that instance, too, Washington sat on Beijing (and countries in Central Asia), urging them never again to repeat this statement—and, better yet, to step up to the plate with tangible or enhanced contributions to the international effort.

A third example from this period was Beijing's quixotic effort to "lock up" energy supplies through equity hydrocarbon investments in Africa and Central Asia by Chinese state-owned firms. China was hardly the first power to embrace neo-mercantilist energy investments overseas. But amid volatile global oil and gas markets, it held the potential to disrupt global stability—a point Zoellick specifically highlighted in his speech.

Domestically, China's Leninism Matters; Externally, Its Traditionalism May Matter More

Looking back on all this a decade later, this adjusted way of thinking about China still strikes me as ahead of trend.

For one thing, Zoellick's speech focused on China's global role *before* that role grew exponentially in the late 2000s and the decade of the 2010s. In that sense, he was prescient.

But China today is a changed country. It has more problems, but also a lot more capacity. Despite a growth slowdown and a crying need for structural reform, its $1 trillion economy upon entering the WTO in 2001 has become a $14 trillion behemoth (measured in nominal GDP). Its $220 billion in foreign exchange reserves in 2001 have ballooned over the same period to a staggering $3 trillion. Xi Jinping has injected a sharper edge and greater ambition to Chinese statecraft, not least through his advocacy of new institutions, such as the AIIB, and the massive "Belt and Road" infrastructure scheme.

In this context, US efforts to adapt—but also defend—the existing architecture are surely going to be more difficult than many in Washington presume:

One reason is that China rejects the trans-Atlantic preference for a liberal bias to the existing system but not "international order" per se. In other words, it subscribes to much of the existing order but not our desire to lock in a liberal bias.

It is often argued that China rejects these liberal norms internationally because it has an illiberal, Leninist government at home. But that is just one part of the story.

In fact, the Communist government's skepticism of the application of liberal ideas internationally reflects not just its *Leninism* but also its deep-seated foreign policy *traditionalism*. The roots of this lie squarely in the 1990s—fully two decades before Xi Jinping, a committed Leninist, took power.

Post-Cold War shifts, especially the NATO intervention in the Balkans, caused China and the West to diverge on many of the bread-and-butter issues of international relations: How should the international system be organized? Can states legitimately intervene militarily in another state—as for instance, the United States and NATO did through humanitarian interventions in the Balkans and elsewhere? What is the proper role of security alliances in a post-Cold War world? Does globalization erode the role of the state and, especially, of sovereignty? Who gets to decide how to interpret and apply international law?

On these questions, Beijing's preferences in the 1990s began to diverge sharply from the American view of international statecraft, especially in its post-Cold War variant. And one issue in particular shaped and defined these evolving Chinese preferences—Beijing's preoccupation with its territorial claims, especially to Taiwan.

When the United States intervened in the Balkans, Panama, and Haiti, Beijing's preoccupation with its own territorial claims hardened into a view of sovereignty and nonintervention that many in the United States and Europe view as antique. Likewise, when the United States relied on NATO in the Balkans, bypassing the UN Security Council where China (and Russia) could wield the veto, Beijing's inherent skepticism of alliances seemed to grow.

Much of China's revisionism, therefore, is aimed squarely at a trans-Atlantic version of international order. But on sovereignty and territoriality China is speaking the language of many other countries, particularly the "global south."

The second example of China's traditionalism is what I earlier termed "portfolio diversification."

The decade of the 2000s was an inflection point. By 2010, China had begun to embrace a handful of "parallel" structures, such as the SCO and the BRICS. These groups assembled members, such as China, Russia, and the Central Asian states, that lack a commitment to liberal values at home. But these countries are also suspicious of it as an organizing principle abroad. And in that particular aspect, they are joined by some democracies, including, I would argue, even democratic India, that do not view it as *the* singular organizing principle of international statecraft.

And yet ironically, even as Beijing embraced these parallel structures, its enthusiasm for the more traditional groups—groups that are core institutions of the liberal order—actually *grew*, not lessened.

China pursued bigger stakes in the World Bank and IMF at the 2009 Pittsburgh G20, and joined more of regional multilateral developments banks in Latin America and Africa. Beijing developed a $2 billion cofinancing fund with the Inter-American Development Bank and ramped up its role in UN peacekeeping operations.

As I argued in 2016 in *Foreign Affairs*, China's goals in shifting to this more diverse approach are presumably fourfold: to (1) hedge its commitment to existing groups and rules lest they turn against Beijing; (2) give

China leverage to demand faster and deeper reforms to existing structures; (3) "democratize" international governance by working with India and other emerging powers to establish groups not led by the G7 industrialized democracies; and (4) put Washington on notice that Beijing has the capacity and will to generate alternatives *if* its calls for reform and change are not respected.

The AIIB, in some sense, exemplifies this more diverse Chinese strategy.

The third example of Beijing's traditionalism is its frequent argument that institutions should reflect *current* power realities, not the legacies of decades past. It is obvious enough that China and India have risen while Belgium and the Netherlands have declined in relative terms. But here's the rub: enhancing China's role while reducing the "Western" footprint has significant implications for the effort to lock in a liberal bias within structures and rules.

The fact is, by reducing the European footprint to ensure that various groups better reflect the power realities of 2018 not 1948, they inevitably become less reliant on the trans-Atlantic powers.

As a result, Washington has faced a growing contradiction between its strong preference for liberalism and its growing need for functionalism—the more "Western" an institution, the more liberal it is but the less representative and thus potentially less functional it may be. The transition from the G7 to the G20, and the failure to adjust the membership of the International Energy Agency (IEA) (whose voting shares have been weighted to 1973 consumption) well illustrate this challenge.

China Has Leveraged Pan-Asian Ideas That Others Actually Invented First

So much for global institutions. Then, there is Asia, where the United States has withdrawn from TPP and rejected regional approaches *even* as efforts have been underway for decades to organize some of those approaches on a pan-Asian basis, excluding the United States.

China is not the only country to have been implicated in that effort. Asia has repeatedly flirted with preferential trade and financial arrangements, as well as regionally based regulations and standards, without American participation.

It has become fashionable to ascribe efforts to build pan-Asian groups to rising Chinese assertiveness—or, more precisely, to Chinese ambition. But once again, that captures just one part of a more complex story.

China's advocacy of pan-Asianism has been effective precisely *because* it draws off a deep well of sentiment and experience across Asia. The region boasts long traditions of pan-Asian ideas, ideologies, pacts, and negotiations—the subject of a Council on Foreign Relations monograph I coauthored with my friend, Bob Manning, in 2009.[14] And this was well underway before China is said to have become "assertive" in Asia, indeed when Xi Jinping himself, that great champion of assertiveness, had only recently been promoted up from the provinces.

Contemporary Asian regionalism—the desire to forge at least some cohesion out of the region's enormous diversity—has deep roots. It has found expression across Asia, in many countries, and over several decades.

Japan, for instance, is a close US ally, suspicious of the rise of Chinese power, and has a strong trans-Pacific identity. Still, Japan's bureaucracy has incubated a variety of pan-Asian ideas, especially with respect to monetary integration. Before there was an AIIB, there was Japan's proposal of an Asian Monetary Fund, which helped give rise to today's Chiang Mai Initiative of bilateral currency swaps among Southeast and Northeast Asian countries.

In the 1990s, the United States could squash such incipient regionalism. But relative power balances have changed considerably since then. Worse, the US withdrawal from TPP has fueled perceptions across Asia of American protectionism. Viewed through this frame, Beijing's proposal of the AIIB (and probably other ideas yet to come) cannot be so easily squashed since they lie squarely in a longer pan-Asian tradition.

American policymakers make much in speeches today about indebtedness to China and the potential for Beijing to exact a steep price in exchange for its loans. But the IMF itself was hardly popular in Asia not long ago.[15] Many in the region, especially in Southeast Asia, reacted badly when Washington refused to bail out Thailand in 1997, just three years after bailing out Mexico. And for many Asians, the most enduring image of the crisis is a photograph of IMF managing director Michel Camdessus standing, arms crossed over a seated Indonesian president Suharto, his head bowed, as he was compelled to sign onto the IMF's terms for financial support.[16]

The biggest takeaway is that when Washington absents itself (or merely shows disinterest in the region's concerns), Asians will grope for their *own* solutions.

This is precisely what happened with the TPP after American withdrawal. The United States frequently argues that Asia will pay a big price for failing to confront China. Actually, the United States stands to pay a far steeper price for creating, and then abetting, a vacuum. It is no surprise that the eleven remaining TPP parties completed the agreement without Washington: for all their tensions with one another, forging agreement on pan-Asian rules beats both "Chinese" rules and no rules.

Whining Isn't Competing

Finally, that brings us to the Belt and Road (BRI) infrastructure initiative that has become the principal target of Mr. Mnuchin's and Admiral Davidson's ire.

BRI is widely viewed as an attempt to foster dependence on China's economy, with potential strategic and even military effects. And there is something to that argument. Still, Beijing is succeeding, in part because it is borrowing and adapting ideas long advocated by others, *including the United States.*

Ironically, in the 2000s, the other foot wore the shoe. Instead of the United States condemning China's BRI, it was Beijing that bombastically condemned Washington as a "schemer."[17] America's "crime"? Daring to envision a "Greater Central Asia" and making efforts to connect Asia's subregions through infrastructure, policy coordination, and project finance.

This context strikes me as very important. The regrowth of economic connections across Asia's disparate subregions is a function of the choices, actions, and capabilities of many states, including Japan, South Korea, and India. It is not a Chinese invention, did not begin *only* in 2013, and did not spring from Xi Jinping like Athena from the head of Zeus. Indeed, China was part of this connectivity effort even before it launched the Belt and Road, breaking Russia's monopsony on Central Asian oil and gas with pipelines from Kazakhstan and Turkmenistan, an onshore production sharing agreement in Turkmenistan, and dozens of projects around the world.

Why do others' efforts matter? Well, the ADB and the World Bank, for instance, have undertaken longstanding efforts on roads and power lines in Asia. The ADB's CAREC program (which happens to include China) has been promoting six connectivity corridors—"linking the Mediterranean and East Asia"—for two decades.[18] Does the idea of "linking the Mediterranean and East Asia" sound anything like Beijing's sloganeering on behalf of the BRI? It does.

Here's another example from my own experience: The Bush Administration actually reorganized the State Department around a connectivity concept in 2005, when it moved the countries of Central Asia out of a westward-facing European bureau into an Asian-facing bureau that included India, Pakistan, and Afghanistan. During those years, Secretary of State Condoleezza Rice and her team developed a variety of US-backed ideas for regional infrastructure integration, most of them premised on leveraging the strengths of the international financial institutions and the ongoing efforts of many partners.

This included Japan, whose role remains notable—it has been Tokyo, not Beijing, which is playing the dominant role in project finance in India, for example, including building the Delhi–Mumbai Industrial Corridor, the Delhi Metro and the development of high-speed rail for Indian Railways.

Then there is the sheer "Asianization" of Central Asia, which owes as much to the retreat of Russian economic power and relative ebbing of Moscow's primacy as it does to the arrival of Chinese trade and capital.

What I'm trying to say is that the "challenge of China's new activism" is more complex than the BRI being some sort of binary counterpoint to the United States. Rather, we need to enlarge our framing of the strategic problem:

The United States risks being marginalized by an organic process through which numerous Asian states, including but not limited to China, are reintegrating East, Central, and South Asia through the direction of trade, capital flows, infrastructure, and new pan-Asian pacts and agreements. More often than not, this is happening without American involvement.

Gradually, but inexorably, the region is becoming more *Asian* than "Asia-Pacific," especially as Asian economies look to one another, not just the trans-Atlantic West, for new economic and financial arrangements; more continental than *sub*-continental, as East and South Asia become more closely intertwined; and, in its continental west, more Central *Asian* than *Eurasian*, as China develops its western regions and five former Soviet countries rediscover their Asian roots.

Insufficiently, in my view, the US response to this has mostly been to complain about the Belt and Road. Even without the Belt and Road, the United States was already increasingly out of the picture.

My own view is that Washington can and must do better.

For one thing, American policymakers need greater discretion and better judgment about when and where to pick their fights.[19] In the case of the AIIB, for example, the United States went to the mat, contesting a Chinese initiative in a functional area where existing structures were clearly insufficient and the United States itself offered no distinctive model. It turned China's proposal of a *multilateral* bank into a *bilateral* test of wills but without the leverage to stop Beijing from moving forward. Worse, Washington badly misread the sentiment of some of its allies.

Here are some final takeaways:

One, like Don Quixote tilting at windmills, it is futile for the United States to try to write China out of Asia's story. And this would be true of *any* China, not just Xi Jinping's assertive and nationalistic China.

One reason for this is cartographic: China borders every subregion of Asia Northeast, Southeast, Central, and South. The United States does not. Neither does any other big Asian player.

Another reason is financial: even if China cannot ultimately deploy the billions of state-backed project finance it has pledged to the Belt and Road, it can still drop plenty of meaningful money into countries all over Asia where the United States and its firms are largely invisible. To reject and battle against every instance of China's effort to foster connectivity, then, would require Washington to fight both geographic and economic gravity.

A more realistic way to counterbalance the spread of Chinese power, especially in Asia, is to be more successful at bolstering America's *own* power, presence, initiative, role, relationships, and arsenal of military, economic, and technological tools. And it can best do this in concert with other partners who have stepped into the vacuum created by US absence, disinterest, protectionism, and worse.

That is why the recent Trump Administration effort to coordinate infrastructure priorities among the United States and Japan and the United States, Japan, and India is so welcome. So, too, is a development finance reform bill making its way through Capitol Hill, which aims to make it easier for US firms to manage and mitigate risk in tough business environments.

To compete in geopolitics—as in sports, business, and life—one needs to actually compete. Washington has to outperform the Chinese competition, not just belittle and whine about it.

There is certainly a deep suspicion of Chinese intent across Asia today. But I have seen enough from every subregion of Asia to know that the United States will not get far by telling third countries that they should forestall deepening their economic relationships with China. For nearly every country, and especially the smaller ones, that is an impractical choice, and therefore will be rejected.

And that is not all. Trashing China's initiatives while failing to counter and compete with them signals other capitals that their countries are of little interest to the United States on their *own* terms. Their takeaway will surely be that the United States pays attention to them *only* in the context of its strategic competition with China. That is a poor message indeed.

The recent US approach, whether to BRI or to AIIB, risks inviting comparisons, both implicit and explicit, between what Washington is offering and what Beijing is offering. The United States is diplomatically challenged and commercially weak in around two-thirds of the Eurasian continental landmass—including many countries in Central Asia, South Asia, and mainland Southeast Asia. Sadly, then, the comparison will often benefit Beijing not Washington.

I have written elsewhere about how the United States could be more proactive in Asia, not reactive. But in responding to BRI, at least, it's important when designing US policies not to compare American apples to Chinese oranges. America isn't China. For instance, it doesn't have state-backed firms that it can leverage through billions channeled through state-backed policy banks.

So Washington should be better leveraging its uniquely *American* strengths—technology, innovation ecosystems, STEM education, connections to the global capital markets, best in class services and other firms, and so on.

It will be harder to deploy that leverage in the context of messages that say "America First." American business remains crucial, especially in East Asia. US companies have invested more than $200 billion into the ten ASEAN countries of Southeast Asia alone. But what is at stake is not just business but rules, norms, standards, and strategic momentum.

Ultimately, at the political level, Washington spends far too much time playing defense against Beijing. As Asia becomes more integrated, the United States will become progressively less relevant in many parts of the region—in Central Asia, in most of South Asia except India, and in mainland Southeast Asia, as noted above.

Within a generation, Americans could find their firms at a competitive disadvantage in a part of the world that will constitute as much as half of the global economy. Americans could become bystanders to the economic and strategic dynamics quickly reshaping this region.

The fact is, China is going to continue proposing initiatives like the Belt and Road. So the United States needs to get off its back foot and onto the initiative.

The United States can work with China but that needs to happen in the broader context of strategy and policy in Asia. And this includes leveraging the many initiatives and partnerships from Japan to Singapore that should also aim to promote economic expansion and connectivity. Ultimately, the best adaptation to China's new activism is a stronger offense, not perpetual defense.

Notes

1. Evan Feigenbaum, "China and the World: Dealing with a Reluctant Power," *Foreign Affairs*, January/February 2017, https://www.foreignaffairs.com/articles/china/2016-12-12/china-and-world.
2. National Security Strategy of the United States of America, December 2017, https://www.whitehouse.gov/wp-content/uploads/2017/12/NSS-Final-12-18-2017-0905.pdf.
3. Summary of the National Defense Strategy of United States of America, 2018, https://dod.defense.gov/Portals/1/Documents/pubs/2018-National-Defense-Strategy-Summary.pdf.
4. Hal Brands, "Tiller Was Sorta Right About The Monroe Doctrine," *Bloomberg*, February 6, 2018, https://www.bloomberg.com/opinion/articles/2018-02-06/tillerson-was-sorta-right-about-the-monroe-doctrine.
5. Robbie Gramer and Keith Johnson, "Tillerson Praises Monroe Doctrine, Warns Latin America of 'Imperial' Chinese Ambitions," *Foreign Policy*, February 2, 2018, https://foreignpolicy.com/2018/02/02/tillerson-praises-monroe-doctrine-warns-latin-america-off-imperial-chinese-ambitions-mexico-south-america-nafta-diplomacy-trump-trade-venezuela-maduro/.
6. Josh Zumbrun, "Mnuchin Calls for IMF to Increase Transparency of Surging Chinese Infrastructure Lending," *The Wall Street Journal*, April 20, 2018, https://www.wsj.com/articles/mnuchin-calls-for-

imf-to-increase-transparency-of-surging-chinese-infrastructure-lending-1524258618.

7. Summary of the National Defense Strategy of United States of America, 2018, https://dod.defense.gov/Portals/1/Documents/pubs/2018-National-Defense-Strategy-Summary.pdf.
8. "Advance Policy Questions for Admiral Philip Davidson, USN Expected Nominee for Commander, U.S. Pacific Command," April 17, 2018, https://www.armed-services.senate.gov/imo/media/doc/Davidson_APQs_04-17-18.pdf.
9. "IMF Members' Quotas and Voting Power, and IMF Board of Governors," International Monetary Fund, September 29, 2019, https://www.imf.org/external/np/sec/memdir/members.aspx.
10. Robert Zoellick, "Whither China: From Membership to Responsibility?" US Department of State Archives, September 21, 2005, https://2001-2009.state.gov/s/d/former/zoellick/rem/53682.htm.
11. "Deputy Secretary Zoellick Statement on Conclusion of the Second US-China Senior Dialogue," US Department of State Archives, December 8, 2005, https://2001-2009.state.gov/r/pa/prs/ps/2005/57822.htm.
12. Mitchell B. Reiss, "Challenges and Opportunities in a Changing Asia," Remarks to the Asia Foundation. Department of State Archives, May 14, 2004, https://2001-2009.state.gov/s/p/rem/32492.htm.
13. Evan A. Feigenbaum, "The Shanghai Cooperation Organization and the Future of Central Asia," The Nixon Center. Department of State Archives, September 6, 2007, https://2001-2009.state.gov/p/sca/rls/rm/2007/91858.htm.
14. Evan A. Feigenbaum and Robert Manning, "The United State in the New Asia," Council on Foreign Relations, October 2009, https://www.cfr.org/report/united-states-new-asia.
15. Enda Curran, "IMF Struggles to Shake Off Stigma 20 Years After Asia Crisis," *Bloomberg*, July 6, 2017, https://www.bloomberg.com/news/articles/2017-07-06/imf-struggles-to-shake-off-stigma-20-years-after-asia-crisis.
16. "Flashback: Camdesusu-Suharto Pic," International Political Economy Zone, September 4, 2007, https://ipezone.blogspot.com/2007/09/flashback-camdessus-suharto-pic.html.
17. "US Scheming for 'Great Central Asia' Strategy," *People's Daily*, August 4, 2006, http://en.people.cn/200608/03/eng20060803_289512.html.
18. "The CAREC Corridors—Linking the Mediterranean and East Asia," Asian Development Bank, November 27, 2017, https://www.adb.org/news/infographics/carec-corridors-linking-mediterranean-and-east-asia.
19. Evan A. Feigenbaum, "The New Asian Order: And How the United States Fits In," *Foreign Affairs*, February 2, 2015, https://www.foreignaffairs.com/articles/east-asia/2015-02-02/new-asian-order.

CHAPTER 9

For Company and for Country: Boeing and US–China Relations

Neil Thomas

When Henry Kissinger embarked on his secret mission in 1971 to lay the groundwork for President Richard Nixon's historic trip to China, he was shuttled from Islamabad to Beijing in a Boeing 707.[1] When Chinese President Xi Jinping arrived in Washington, DC in 2015 for a state visit, he stepped off a retrofitted Boeing 747 emblazoned with Air China insignia.

In those intervening 44 years, Boeing had been the preferred aircraft for every American and Chinese head of state between Nixon and Xi. In fact, every Chinese leader since Deng Xiaoping has visited Boeing's factories outside of Seattle.[2]

Boeing is hardly a nation-state, but perhaps no company exemplifies the complex and nuanced layers of the US–China relationship as much as this American multinational, the world's largest aerospace company.[3] From hiring a Chinese student as its first engineer in 1916 and cofounding China's first aircraft manufacturer in the 1930s, to the latest debates on trade and technology transfer, Boeing's story is a unique window onto

N. Thomas (✉)
Paulson Institute, Chicago, IL, USA
e-mail: nthomas@paulsoninstitute.org

D. Ma (ed.), *China's Economic Arrival*,
https://doi.org/10.1007/978-981-15-2275-8_9

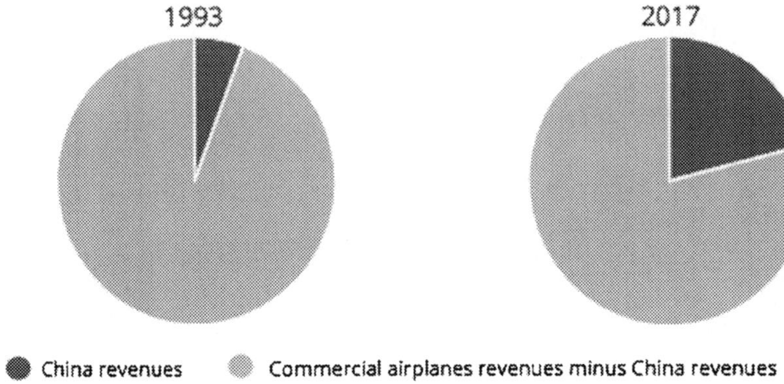

Fig. 9.1 Chinese market revenues grew to almost 20% of Boeing's Commercial Aircraft Revenues (*Note* Boeing's revenue from China is derived predominantly from sales of commercial airplanes. *Source* Company Reports)

the forces that have both fortified the bilateral relationship and might now pull it apart.[4]

As the Cold War ended, Boeing became a leading advocate of economic globalization. After all, the company has long been the United States' biggest exporter by dollar value, built supply chains around the world, and makes a product whose very purpose is to link distant corners of the globe.[5] It was only natural that Boeing would be fully invested in this international system that the United States was seen to lead—its business depended on globalization.

A significant part of globalization was integrating China into that international system. Boeing, as one of the earliest beneficiaries of the US–China rapprochement under Nixon, played a starring role both in prying open markets in China and in American debates on China's eventual accession to the World Trade Organization (WTO).

Assuming an outsized role in bilateral relations meant the company both reaped rewards and suffered consequences. Beijing has regularly played Boeing against Airbus, its European rival, by turning its market power into bargaining power during commercial negotiations.

Four decades since the formalization of US–China relations, China has grown to become Boeing's most important national market except the United States (see Fig. 9.1). But with plans for its own commercial jetliner, China is also the only country that could upset the global aviation duopoly that Boeing and Airbus have long enjoyed. This development is forcing Boeing to balance Chinese demands for technology transfer with protecting its bottom line and future prospects.

Yet Boeing's increased dependence on China is reciprocated by the country's continued dependence on the company's planes to fly not just its leaders but also hundreds of millions of Chinese citizens. Even as Beijing aspires to build a world-class commercial aviation industry, Boeing and Airbus still dominate.[6]

Irony would have it that for a company whose Chinese market entry was made possible by an American strategic pivot during the Cold War, Boeing's fortunes in China may now depend on whether the specter of a new economic winter becomes a reality.

Boeing's place in US–China relations shows how structural changes in the international system over the past five decades have affected the commercial calculus of a powerful multinational firm. Of course, Boeing was not the only actor affected by these sweeping changes. But understanding how this major player sought to adapt to the evolving environment yields valuable insights into commercial diplomacy, US–China politics, and how the future dynamics of globalization might be shaped.

The First Sale: Boeing and Cold War Strategy

When Nixon went to China in 1972, the American president "personally approved" a request from Chinese leaders to buy ten B707s, according to his interpreter Chas Freeman.[7] The White House's decision was motivated not simply by commercial considerations but also by Cold War maneuvering against the Soviet Union. This would not be the last time that Boeing had a hand in broader geopolitical machinations.

In the Nixon administration's view, the Boeing sale would weaken China's dependence on Soviet planes. Such a deal would signal to Moscow that Washington could help Beijing "become a strong, modern industrial state—on Russia's flank—much faster than she could without American aid."[8] Aligning Washington and Beijing against Moscow was a strategic imperative shared by Nixon and Mao, and this move trumped US concerns over technology transfers.[9]

While the Nixon administration dangled business opportunities as geopolitical leverage against the Soviet Union, China became the only Communist country except Yugoslavia to have US jetliners in its civilian fleet.[10] Perhaps *The New York Times* captured this sentiment best when its editorial board argued "the Chinese are entitled to buy products of advanced American technology even when...these products could have ancillary military significance."[11]

At the same time, the United States found an eager customer in China, whose civil aviation industry was in total disrepair. It was estimated that China's civil aviation fleet included only 350–500 planes based on Soviet designs, many of which were "obsolete and inefficient."[12] It was no surprise that American airline executives saw China as "one of the biggest untapped markets in the world for commercial aircraft."[13]

Sensing that international competitors were ready to pounce on the Chinese market, Boeing hastily dispatched a delegation to Beijing just two weeks after Nixon's visit. On September 9, 1972, two months after the White House granted Boeing an export permit, the company closed a deal with the Civil Aviation Administration of China (CAAC).[14]

The 125-page contract, which took five months of "most arduous" negotiations, stipulated that China would buy ten B707s, along with 40 Pratt & Whitney jet engines, for $150 million.[15] As part of that deal, Boeing agreed to train Chinese flight crews in Seattle and operate a flight training facility in Shanghai.[16] At the time, China suffered from severe shortages of qualified pilots, air-traffic controllers, and maintenance technicians. An observer wrote presciently that China's need for jets, parts, and technology meant this sale was "the beginning of what could be long-time dependence on the United States in this field."[17]

Boeing's first sale to the People's Republic of China came at a pivotal time for the US aviation industry. Military contracts were trailing off as the Vietnam War drew to a close, while commercial exports to developing countries began to flourish. Aviation industry exports more than doubled between 1970 and 1974 to $6.8 billion, and the superior efficiency of Boeing aircraft saw the company establish itself as the global industry leader.[18] From the 1970s onwards, Boeing gradually outcompeted other manufacturers and hastened the market exits of once iconic plane-makers such as Fokker, Lockheed, Hawker-Siddeley, and later McDonnell Douglas.[19]

Its rising dominance in commercial aircraft meant that Boeing was well-placed to capitalize on the opportunities that Nixon's opening to China afforded. Even before the normalization of diplomatic relations in 1979, China's enormous market and competitive exports created "a significant amount" of bilateral trade, which swelled from a mere $4.9

million in 1971 to $900 million in 1973.[20] Moreover, business contacts kept expanding through successive administrations, particularly after Deng Xiaoping initiated "reform and opening" in 1978.[21]

Aviation was a key pillar of this burgeoning trade. In December 1978 Boeing signed a second $156 million contract with China to deliver three B747 jumbo jets, which could fly nonstop between the United States and China.[22] By December 1980, Pan Am had started the first commercial flight service between the two countries since 1949.[23]

Businesses were more or less left to their own devices as they began forging ties with China. Although Nixon administration officials helped establish the US-China Business Council, of which Boeing was a founding member, and which today remains a prominent advocate for commercial engagement, the US government at the time largely stood in the back ground when it came to commercial relations.[24]

That's because presidents Nixon, Gerald Ford, and (eventually) Jimmy Carter mainly viewed relations with China through a strategic lens and took little interest in its internal governance. Nixon had told Mao in 1972, "What brings us together is a recognition of a new situation in the world and a recognition on our part that what is important is not a nation's internal political philosophy. What is important is its policy toward the rest of the world and toward us."[25] Kissinger, too, confessed to Mao that "Our interest in trade with China is not commercial. It is to establish a relationship that is necessary for the political relations we both have."[26]

Indeed, at this crucial turning point in bilateral relations, leading voices in US academia, business, and the media generally saw trade as an economic benefit and nonmilitary technology transfer as a good idea.[27]

Flying High: Boeing and Chinese Reforms in the 1980s

Boeing established its first (one-person) China office in 1980, and as economic growth took off that decade, the country emerged as "one of the last great frontiers for air travel."[28] Rising demand for aircraft seemed to validate Boeing's enthusiasm for China, whose large population and expansive geography made it especially suited to air travel (see Fig. 9.2).[29] But two other major factors also reinforced the company's focus on China: (1) a congenial US political environment and (2) rising competition from Airbus.

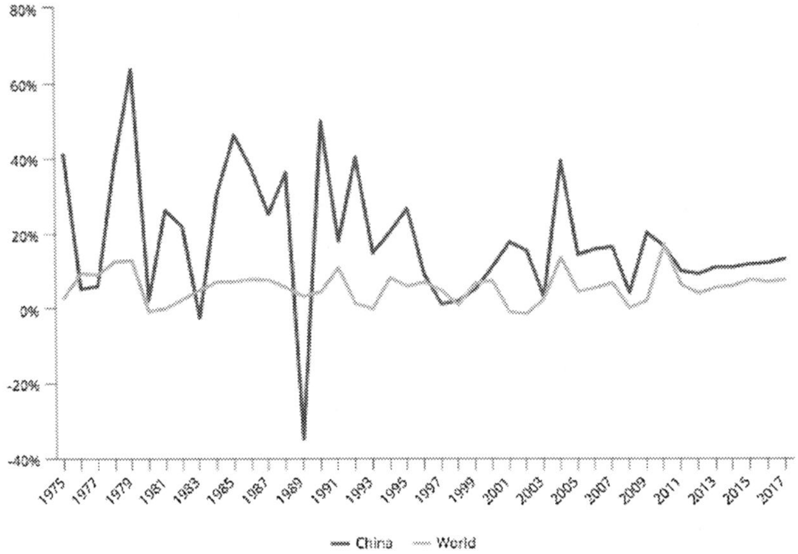

Fig. 9.2 Chinese air passenger volume has grown at more than three times the global average since 1975 (*Source* International Civil Aviation Organization)

As Cold War competition escalated at times under President Ronald Reagan, countering the Soviet Union dominated US strategic priorities. So, when it came to China policy, the Reagan administration basically continued the approach adopted by Nixon.[30] Like his predecessors, Reagan thought of China as a bulwark against Soviet power and therefore broadly supported China's economic modernization.[31] Reagan apparently admired the "free market spirit" of "so-called Communist China," and said that it was unnecessary "for us to impose our form of governments on some other country."[32]

In addition, Reagan granted China full Foreign Military Sales status, incorporated Chinese assistance into war plans against the Soviet Union, and more than doubled China's export credits.[33] When fielding complaints from US executives in Beijing in 1983, Reagan's Secretary of State George Shultz dismissively told them to "move to Japan or Western Europe."[34]

Part of the Solution

In this disobliging yet benign political environment, Boeing sought to deepen its ties in China. But that was easier said than done. China wanted more than simply imported aircraft—a prerequisite for continued market access was for the company to help China modernize its own aviation industry.

In the 1980s, China's aerospace sector was in shambles, as detailed in James Fallows' *China Airborne*.[35] The aviation regulator CAAC (equivalent to the US Federal Aviation Administration)—which also operated the national aviation monopoly—had enjoyed "a solidly built reputation for rudeness, inefficiency, and passenger discomfort."[36] Its dysfunctional supervision of China's skies had grave consequences: Chinese airlines had appalling safety records well into the 1990s and many planes were hijacked by Chinese who sought asylum in Taiwan, Japan, or South Korea.[37]

China had little experience running modern airlines, training commercial pilots, maintaining aircraft, or managing air-traffic control. Beijing recognized these deficiencies as threats to its development and began a series of reforms. In 1988, it dissolved the CAAC's airliner monopoly and created quasi-commercial state-owned airlines like Air China, China Eastern, and China Southern to introduce competition and improve performance.

Boeing supported these efforts by providing industry training, regulatory advice, and hundreds of millions of dollars in assistance to upgrade the safety of China's commercial aviation.[38] The results were remarkable: China transformed from having one of the worst safety records to having one of the best today (see Fig. 9.3).[39]

A Rising Threat

The competitive landscape fundamentally changed for Boeing, and particularly in the Chinese market, with the rise of Airbus in the 1980s. The European aviation consortium delivered its first jetliner to China in 1985, as part of a $150 million order for three A310 wide-body aircraft.[40] That same year, an Airbus subsidiary signed the group's first subcontracting agreement with the Xi'an Aviation Industrial Company to manufacture access doors for A300 and A310 planes.[41]

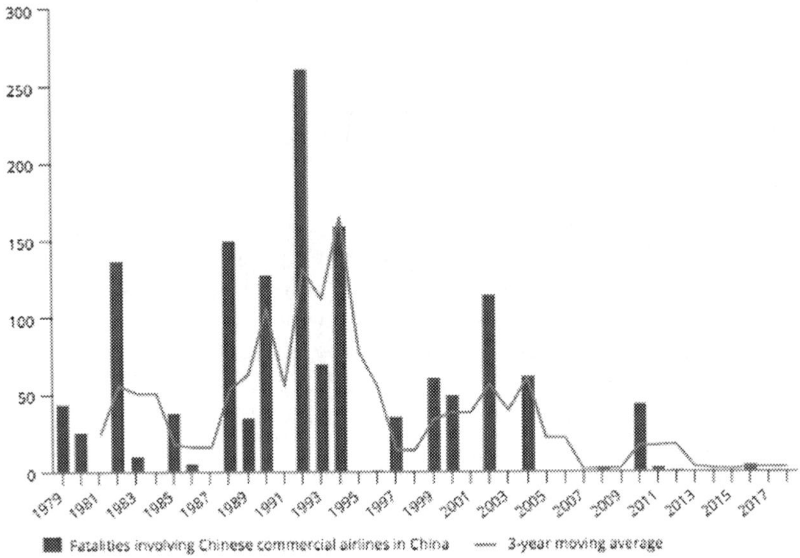

Fig. 9.3 Fatalities in China involving Chinese commercial airlines (*Source* Aviation Safety Network; ASN Aviation Safety Database)

Although Boeing had first-mover advantage in China, it was insufficient to deal with the advent of Airbus as a serious rival. That's because the creation of a global duopoly in passenger jetliners meant that Beijing now had a choice, which allowed the Chinese government to use its monopsony power to pit Boeing against Airbus in order to bargain for better prices, domestic production agreements, and limited technology transfer.[42] That's because Beijing effectively retained final approval powers for aircraft purchases by domestic carriers.[43]

With this newfound leverage, Beijing was happy to let foreign companies access its market, but only if an effort was made to impart their manufacturing knowledge. Deng was clear early on that China could not remain backward in technology if it hoped to become powerful.[44] And few sectors demand as much technological mastery as an "apex" industry like aviation, which involves not only assembling planes but also building engines, avionics, supply chains, and maintenance ecosystems. It is a highly complex operation that few have attempted, let alone conquered—meaning the economic rewards are enormous.

Indeed, industry observers noticed early that China "always preferred to build rather than buy."[45] As CAAC was busy spending over $2 billion on dozens of B737s, B757s, and B767s to upgrade a civilian fleet that still flew propeller planes on provincial routes, Beijing persuaded the American company to outsource production and transfer technology to state-owned factories.[46] But Boeing never gave the game away, transferring only modest, noncore technologies. Starting in 1980, the company signed contracts with Chinese suppliers for minor parts like vertical fins, horizontal stabilizers, trailing-edge ribs, and cargo doors.[47]

Beijing ultimately wanted to build a "Chinese Boeing"—an intention hidden in plain sight.[48] In May 1980, for example, a group of US industry representatives discovered the "Yun-10" project while visiting a Shanghai factory.[49] Built by the Shanghai Aviation Industrial Company, the 178-seater Yun-10 was a "virtual clone" of the B707s that China bought in 1972 and was powered by Pratt & Whitney engines that were ordered as "spare parts" for these planes.[50]

The reverse-engineered Yun-10 made its maiden flight in September 1980, and flew as far as Urumqi in Xinjiang in November 1983 before funding was cut in 1984.[51] Beijing sunk 537.7 million yuan into the plane's development, but only three prototypes were built.[52] The project failed because Chinese engineers did not really know how to make a commercially viable jetliner. For example, they struggled to pinpoint the Yun-10's center of gravity and built it out of steel not aluminum, making the plane far too heavy to be fuel-efficient.[53] (Today, the only surviving Yun-10 sits outside a state aviation facility in Shanghai.)

The hard lesson that Beijing took from the Yun-10 fiasco was that developing an indigenous aircraft industry would take a long time and a lot of experience. So, it doubled down on its strategy of leveraging competition to access its huge market to extract concessions from foreign producers.

None of this would have surprised Boeing, as it had encountered a similar aspirant to join the global aviation industry in Japan. Like China, Japan wanted its own passenger jets but, unlike China, it actually had the technological base to make such a goal seem feasible. Yet the fear in the 1980s that "Asian money" would turn the United States into a "techno-colony" led Congress to pass "extraordinary restrictions" on technology transfer to Japan and South Korea to protect the domestic industry.[54]

But Japan was also a future growth market for Boeing, so the company sought to bolster its competitive advantage without alienating potential customers. What Boeing did was to integrate Japanese manufacturers into its supply chain, so that powerful industries with considerable political influence in Japan had a stake in Boeing's success.

In 1990, Boeing even made the Japan Aircraft Development Corporation a minority risk-sharing partner in the production of the Boeing 777, a twin engine, wide-body jetliner that would become an industry standard.[55] While this strategy sapped momentum from the march of Japan's industrial policy, it also heralded a new era of truly globalized supply chains for Boeing—an issue that would later feature prominently as US–China politics heated up after 1989.[56]

Boeing and a "Long Decade" in US–China Relations from 1989 to 2001[57]

Before global supply chains and indigenous innovation became leading issues, bilateral economic relations in the 1990s were often dominated by contentious debates in Washington over Beijing's "most favored nation" (MFN) status, an issue that thrust Boeing into the limelight as a major force in US–China relations.

MFN status meant that the United States would give China trade advantages equal to the best that it gave any of its other trading partners—the vast majority of which already had MFN status. In practice, this status meant that a country avoided the punitive Smoot-Hawley tariffs imposed during the Great Depression.

President Carter first granted MFN status to China in 1980, with the backing of Congress and with the help of lobbying by Boeing.[58] But a kicker for China was that the US president had to renew MFN status each year for any "nonmarket economy" that restricted emigration, as stipulated in the Jackson-Vanik amendment to the 1974 Trade Act. While the president's decision could be overturned by Congress, Reagan renewed China's MFN status without controversy in the 1980s, despite the fact that China's cheap imports were accused of "killing the mushroom farmer" as early as 1982.[59]

But China's MFN status became a political lightning rod after the Tiananmen crackdown in June 1989. This tragedy was a watershed moment in American perceptions of China, and public opinion turned very negative almost overnight.[60] China's profile in American politics rose sharply, particularly with regard to democracy and human rights, and

Congress assumed a greater voice in bilateral relations by pressuring Beijing on political reforms.

Due to Tiananmen, Washington embargoed $700 million in arms sales to China, ended joint military planning and weapons development, and suspended trade and development assistance.[61] These new frictions drew Boeing deeper into the domestic politics of US foreign policy as the company had to work delicately with the administration to exempt a scheduled $200 million delivery of four B757s to China from military sanctions.[62]

The need for the US president to renew China's MFN status each year provided another means for Congress to punish China. Proponents argued that the United States should use denial of MFN status as "leverage" against Beijing because China wanted access to US markets, foreign investment, and "prestige meetings" with American officials.[63]

The George H. W. Bush administration, however, renewed China's MFN status every year and vetoed bills that attempted to revoke MFN or link it to China's progress on human rights issues.[64] Even though Democratic leaders in Congress and an "eclectic alliance of anti-Communists, human rights advocates, and protectionists" believed Bush's approach was wrong, they could never override his veto.[65]

Despite pushback, Bush adopted a policy of "engagement" with China that centered on strengthening linkages across the state, society, and economy.[66] He justified this approach to China on the belief that "…to influence China," it was not productive to isolate it.[67] Rather than seeking to limit bilateral trade and commercial linkages with China, which would hurt US companies and consumers, his administration saw Chinese entrepreneurs and private business as "the best long-term hope for political change."[68]

Bush also gave prominence to an argument that deeper economic ties with China would improve democracy and human rights. "No nation on Earth has discovered a way to import the world's goods and services while stopping foreign ideas at the border," he claimed.[69] It was an attractive argument that would help inform a bipartisan consensus on China policy for two decades.

New Era, New Paradigm

The growth of commercial ties with China had created business constituencies in the United States and other advanced economies that were invested in China's economic success.[70] For Boeing in particular, fierce competition from Airbus meant that it had to work overtime to preserve ties with its largest potential customer. But the American company saw its commercial horizons expand with the new global politics of the 1990s.

The fall of the Soviet Union and the dissipation of Japan's economic miracle ushered in a sense of euphoria in the United States, perhaps best captured in Francis Fukuyama's famous proclamation of the "End of History."[71] An executive at the US Chamber of Commerce aptly summarized the spirit of the times: "Now that the Cold War is over, it's economic policy that's most important. We won the war. Let's reap the benefits."[72]

Indeed, to the victor go the spoils, and superpower geopolitics yielded to the triumph of US-led economic globalization, which replaced anti-communism as a justification for America's outsized role in world affairs (see Fig. 9.4). Free trade agreements, emerging markets, and corporate interests naturally became more prominent in US foreign policy, as the international system was increasingly reorganized to promote transnational trade, finance, and investment.[73]

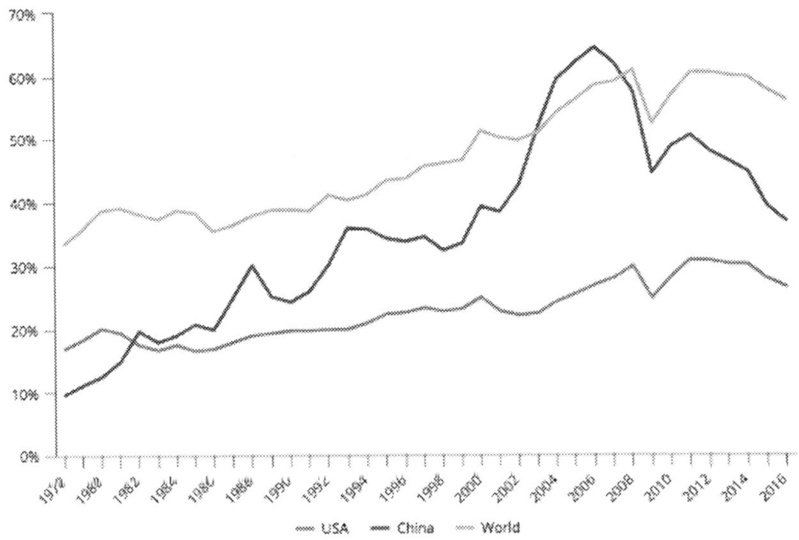

Fig. 9.4 Global trade expanded dramatically as % of GDP from 1992 to 2007 (*Source* World Bank)

As commercial linkages took center stage, multinationals like Boeing stood to benefit, particularly as a wave of democratization in Asia, Eastern Europe, and Latin America brought economic openings and business opportunities. But China was the most enticing emerging market, eyed by multinationals everywhere—especially after Deng rebooted the country's reform process with his celebrated "Southern Tour" of early 1992.

The Chinese market became even more strategically important to Boeing as a global economic recession in the early 1990s forced the company to slash production and reduce its workforce.[74] Amid the economic gloom, business held up in China, as Boeing received an aircraft order worth $9 billion in 1990 and delivered its 100th plane to China in 1992 and its 200th just two years later.[75] By 1993, China bought one-sixth of the planes Boeing sold.[76]

From "Coddling Dictators..."

Yet as Boeing's market share was expanding in China, domestic US politics was shifting with the arrival of Bill Clinton, the first post-Cold War president. While the fall of European communism turned American attention to economic globalization, it also ended the strategic rationale for engaging China as a counterbalance to the Soviet Union.

Democracy promotion and human rights dominated the China policy discourse during the 1992 presidential election campaign. Clinton embodied this change in approach when he criticized Bush for "coddling dictators from Beijing to Baghdad." He took office in 1993 promising to link approval of China's MFN status to its human rights record.[77]

When China's MFN renewal came up in May 1993, President Clinton issued Executive Order 12850 stipulating that renewal in 1994 would be conditional on China's promotion of free emigration, ending of prison-labor exports, and "overall, significant progress" on various human rights concerns.[78] This action also appeared to be taken in part to appease Senator George Mitchell and Representative Nancy Pelosi—the most prominent proponents of "linkage" between MFN status and human rights—so that they would shelve legislation that would bind the executive.[79]

That Clinton did not immediately revoke China's MFN status already reflected the immense pressure the business community could bring to bear on China policy. In what *The New York Times* described as "the most united display of corporate-lobbying muscle on a trade issue" since

NAFTA debates in 1992, nearly 300 large firms and 40 trade bodies wrote Clinton to urge him to maintain MFN.[80]

Beijing also understood this political dynamic in Washington and sought to buy US goods before the MFN deadline, including an $800 million purchase of 21 Boeing planes. Lawrence Clarkson, Boeing's vice president for international development, said that "We will lose orders and people will lose jobs" if Clinton ended China's MFN status.[81] That same year Clinton told Boeing employees that Asian countries "have gone from dominoes to dynamos."[82]

The battle over linking trade to human rights culminated when MFN was up for renewal in mid-1994. Boeing was reported to have "led the charge" in rallying multinationals to unite against linkage, making the case that, in addition to the danger of lost jobs and higher prices, commercial exchange was the best long-term strategy for political and economic liberalization in China.[83]

Clinton came to agree, particularly after China made it clear that it did not take his MFN threat seriously. Consequently, in May 1994, Clinton decided to renew China's MFN status and end his support for linkage despite no "overall, significant progress" on human rights—although Beijing granted exit visas to some families of dissidents and made gestures to curb prison labor.[84] At the same time, Clinton announced a new human rights policy for China that included increased funding for Chinese NGOs and more resources for Voice of America and Radio Free Asia.[85]

Clinton echoed the previous Bush administration when he argued that isolating China would do more harm than good to the US economy and multilateral security cooperation.[86] He embraced and expanded his forerunner's policy of "engagement" with China, which Clinton defined as "expanding our areas of cooperation with China while confronting our differences openly and respectfully."[87]

...To Selling America Inc. Around the World

Clinton may have abandoned the linkage policy, but MFN status remained a "focal point" in China policy debates of the 1990s.[88] The ballooning bilateral trade deficit, the 1995–1996 Taiwan Strait Crisis, the 1996 campaign finance controversy, China's intellectual property (IP) theft, and Chinese arms sales to Iran and Pakistan continued to feed opposition to MFN renewal.

Throughout this period, as anti-engagement constituencies consolidated, Boeing and numerous other US firms played a key role in persuading Congress to uphold China's MFN status.[89] Boeing was notable for being at the vanguard of "corporate foreign policy" and was considered by some observers to be the "most China-savvy" company in the country and "the quarterback" for these lobbying efforts.[90] A Senate staffer remarked that Boeing "put out the full-court press" for MFN on Capitol Hill.[91]

Aided by US businesses, the White House consistently defeated legislation to revoke MFN. Clinton's foreign policy had already reflected his domestic mantra of "It's the economy, stupid"—he established the National Economic Council to balance the influence of the National Security Council in the White House—but with the end of MFN linkage he now had more political space to champion business with China.

So Clinton empowered his Commerce Department, starting under the leadership of Ron Brown from 1993 to 1996, to spearhead an aggressive "commercial diplomacy" that was seen to markedly increase the US government's advocacy for American businesses abroad.[92] Brown even reportedly built a "war room" to identify international business opportunities that he wanted to win for US firms.[93] China was the centerpiece of this commercial diplomacy, as Commerce advocated on behalf of US firms, including Boeing, in meetings with top Chinese leaders.[94]

Fending off a Rival

A supportive position from the US government was important to Boeing as it faced off against its archrival Airbus in China. The European firm, dismissed for years by Boeing executives, became a peer competitor in the 1990s as it began to make aircraft of comparable quality that were more cost-effective than Boeing models (see Fig. 9.5).[95] Today the Boeing-Airbus duopoly accounts for 99% of orders for large jetliners and 90% of the global aircraft market by value.[96]

Airbus recorded more global orders than Boeing for the first time in 1995, and just five years later had achieved its ambitious goal of 50% global market share by the year 2000.[97] With regard to China, Boeing still accounted for over 70% of the country's commercial fleet in 1997, but it was starting to lose sales to Airbus.[98] In a post-ideological world, Boeing's competition with Airbus gained geopolitical significance.

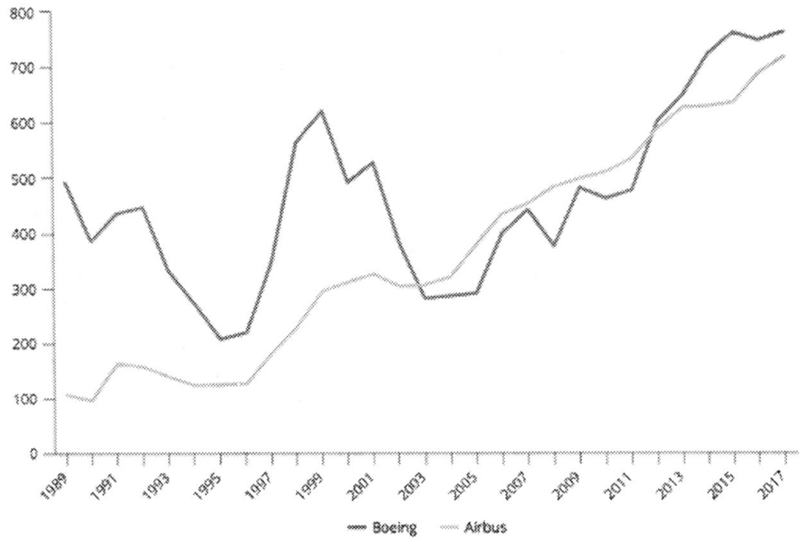

Fig. 9.5 Airbus closed the gap on Boeing in global jetliner deliveries (*Source* Company Reports)

From Beijing's vantage point, a duopoly was better than reliance on a price-setting monopolist.[99] And the central government made no secret about using its powers of final approval to play one company against the other to gain concessions on price and technology transfers.[100] The Boeing-Airbus competition became "downright bloody" because each deal had an enormous price tag and increased the possibility that an airline would develop a long-term dependence on a particular supplier (see Fig. 9.6).[101]

Beijing also ramped up its demands for the two companies to set up local production facilities. Consequently, both firms outsourced more production to China, a move that incurred political backlash for Boeing as it contributed to layoffs and sparked US union action.[102] Boeing defended its actions by arguing that even more jobs would be lost to Airbus if it did not agree to such outsourcing.[103] A Boeing executive lamented that "We don't do it to save money. We do it for the business."[104]

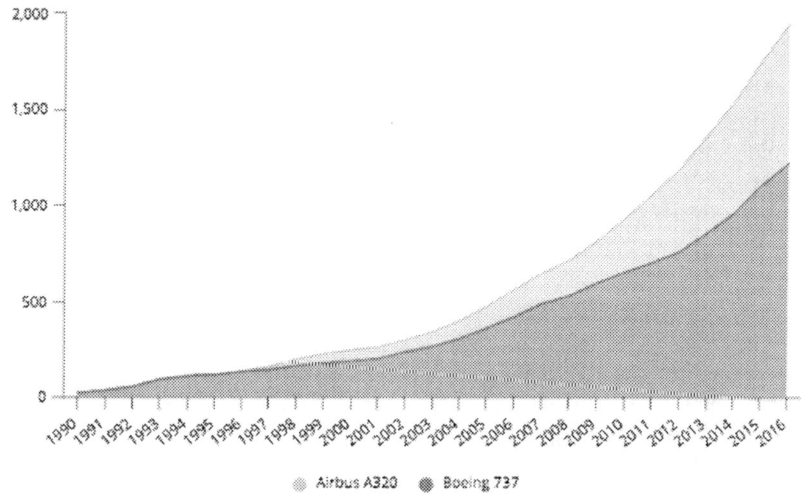

Fig. 9.6 Airbus supplies an increasing share of China's airplanes (*Note* Planes are often delivered several months or years after an order is placed. The Boeing 737 family of jetliners was introduced in 1968 and the Airbus A320 family in 1988. *Source* National Bureau of Statistics)

Finally, Boeing's rivalry with Airbus could be deployed by Beijing as diplomatic leverage. For example, Wu Yi, China's minister of foreign trade and economic cooperation, canceled a planned US visit in 1996 because Washington had sanctioned China for IP theft and the White House refused to grant her an audience with Clinton. Boeing had pushed for Wu's visit because she was expected to confirm $4 billion of aircraft purchases.[105]

Instead, the next month, Chinese premier Li Peng announced a $1.5 billion order for 30 Airbus jets on a state visit to France, a defeat for Boeing and a major breakthrough for the European consortium in China.[106] This was followed by the signing of a preliminary agreement between a Chinese state firm and an Airbus unit to codevelop a 100-seat regional jet for Asian markets.[107]

Boeing CEO Philip Condit described his company that year as "the designated hostage" in US–China relations: it was being used as a punching bag for diplomatic disputes.[108] Another company executive claimed that a high-level Chinese official told him: "Because your Government constantly chooses to kick us and harass us, many, many business opportunities that should go to the US have gone elsewhere."[109] Li Peng later admitted as much in public.[110]

The increasingly fierce competition between Boeing and Airbus, and China's ability to exploit this competition, had spillover effects for US foreign policy objectives. In 1997, when the United States cosponsored an annual United Nations Human Rights Conference resolution condemning China, the Clinton administration struggled to assemble a "unified position" with allies like Japan and the European Union that sought the same economic gains US multinationals had achieved in China.[111]

France's opposition to this resolution, which ultimately failed, prompted a Boeing vice president to quip, "When President Chirac arrives in Beijing in a few weeks, I am sure that he will be rewarded for that stance."[112] True to form, two weeks later, Airbus beat out Boeing on another $1.5 billion contract to sell 30 planes to China. Beijing subsequently confirmed that such deals "show a good relationship…between China and Europe."[113]

The WTO Accession

Intensifying global competition, combined with Beijing's ability to capitalize on commercial fissures for economic advantage, meant that Boeing and other American businesses with a stake in China hoped to change the game dramatically. That game changer was to get China into the WTO.

WTO membership would embed China in the global trade regime and provide a unifying theme for a Clinton administration that had been criticized for its "cacophony" of priorities on China policy.[114] From Boeing's perspective, this move would kill two birds with one stone. It would end the annual political brinksmanship over MFN renewal because the WTO requires members to grant MFN status to each other. And it would support China's economic growth, propelling demand for air travel and jetliners.

Chinese Premier Zhu Rongji led the charge in Beijing. As a staunch reformer and unabashed champion of China's WTO entry, Zhu thought that WTO rules could serve as a cudgel to force through stalled reforms and transform China's decaying state sector into a more market-based system. As far as Zhu was concerned, the WTO was the external pressure that China needed to defeat hardliners opposed to market liberalization.

For instance, to meet WTO requirements, China had to reduce over 7000 trade barriers and end formal demands for tech transfer.[115]

In November 1999, after years of bilateral negotiations, Clinton reached an agreement with Beijing to support China's entry into the WTO in exchange for lower tariffs and reduced barriers to trade and investment.[116] But now the White House had to sell the deal in Washington.

China did not need American approval to join the WTO, just a two-thirds vote of WTO members.[117] But if the United States did not grant China unconditional MFN status—often referred to as "permanent normal trade relations" (PNTR)—then China could still join the WTO but not give the United States the trade concessions it would offer to other WTO members.[118] In other words, the United States would shoot itself in the foot if it denied PNTR status to China.

To do so, Clinton needed Congress to repeal the Jackson-Vanik amendment, a vote that many thought would be a "close contest."[119] Not only did Congress show rising concern at Chinese military power and trade deficits, early signs of a backlash to globalization had appeared when protestors descended on Seattle during a WTO summit in November 1999.[120]

So the White House enlisted the business community, pro-trade Republicans, and sympathetic Democrats to launch "the most aggressive pro-trade lobbying effort" since NAFTA.[121] By this time China had become the United States' eleventh-largest export market and the second-largest recipient of foreign direct investment in the world.[122]

Boeing and other multinationals swung into action to argue for accession, leading pro-trade advocacies like the Business Coalition for US–China Trade, which boasted 1200 members.[123] The aviation giant ran an "all-out campaign"—modeled after its previous NAFTA lobbying—to mobilize its 10,000 suppliers (including a hot dog vendor) in 420 House districts to persuade their local representatives to support China's WTO bid.[124]

Clinton's arguments for PNTR were captured in a major speech on China policy in March 2000.[125] He said that a vote against PNTR would cost American exports and jobs, would make US firms less competitive in China, would push China away from the US-led order, and would reduce America's ability to press China toward more responsible international actions. American resistance would also have undermined efforts to build a "global" trading regime.[126]

Perhaps Clinton's best remembered argument, though, was that growth, trade, and economic freedom would foster political reform in China, as "The genie of freedom will not go back into the bottle." Such arguments, rooted in influential studies from the postwar heyday of modernization theory, resonated with pundits and policymakers in the 1990s.[127] After the democratization of South Korea and Taiwan, many concluded that "prosperity breaks down old controls and generates demands for improved political and social conditions."[128]

During debates about PNTR, versions of this argument were endorsed by voices as diverse as George W. Bush, Silicon Valley, House Republicans, Chinese dissidents, Hong Kong democrats, and Taiwan's president Chen Shui-bian.[129] Some activists were skeptical, but even Human Rights Watch praised Clinton's deal as "good for trade but also for human rights and the rule of law."[130]

The various arguments for PNTR worked—US businesses had emphasized economic benefits for Americans at least as much as political freedoms for Chinese—and Clinton's China bill was passed in the House in May 2000 and in the Senate by that September.[131] The president signed the bill into law on October 10, paving the way for China to officially join the WTO on December 11, 2001. This legislative victory was viewed as a "crowning foreign policy triumph" and a key aspect of Clinton's legacy.[132]

Boeing, too, considers this moment as part of its own legacy. Indeed, in its press releases, the company still touts that it "successfully promoted US approval of China's WTO accession and congressional approval of normal trade relations between the United States and China."[133]

Flying Solo: China Dreams of Its Own Jetliner in the 2000s

China's accession to the WTO proved to be a landmark event that catalyzed the country's extraordinary economic growth, which averaged over 10% annually in the 2000s. This growth was propelled by increased investment and robust exports, as China became the largest trading nation in the world. Rising incomes swelled demand for air travel, and the number of Chinese air passengers rose from 61.9 million in 2000 to more than half a billion in 2017 (see Fig. 9.7). China's global share of air passengers increased from 3.7% to 13.9% over the same period, while the US share dropped from 39.7% to 21.3%.[134]

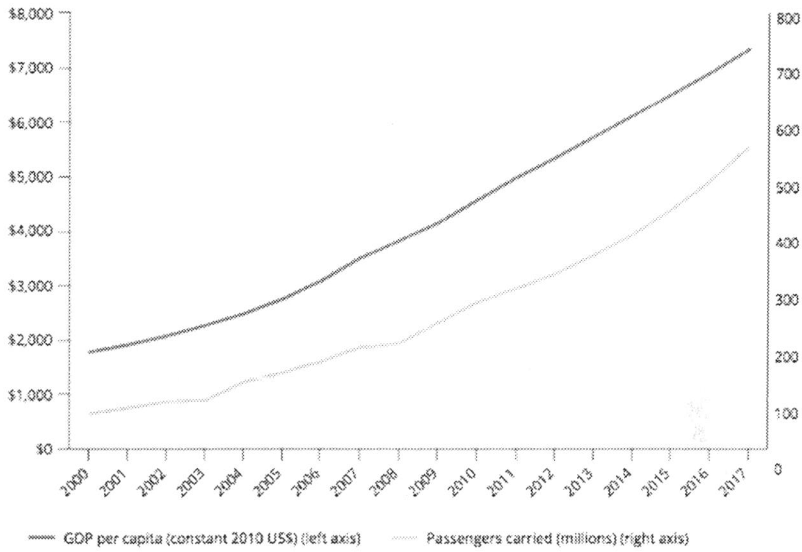

Fig. 9.7 As Chinese grew wealthier, they flew more (*Source* World Bank, International Civil Aviation Organization)

Growth in China helped cushion Boeing during downturns as the country began to fulfill its potential as the company's single most important market. The 9/11 terrorist attacks depressed air travel, and Boeing saw its profits contract 80% from 2001 to 2002, forcing it to lay off tens of thousands of workers.[135] When demand picked up again and Boeing moved lost jobs overseas, including work on the Boeing 787 to China, it only narrowly survived a major union strike vote.[136]

During the Global Financial Crisis of 2007–2010, which caused a dip in aircraft demand, China stood out as the world's only "dynamic aviation market," according to one Boeing executive.[137] The firm's Chinese market revenue grew tenfold from $1.2 billion in 1993 to $11.9 billion in 2017, or from 5.7% to 21% of Boeing's total revenue from commercial planes (see Fig. 9.8).

In the mid-2000s, Boeing still accounted for two-thirds of China's commercial aircraft, worth a total of $37 billion.[138] The firm even renamed its 7E7 the 787 because "in many Asian cultures the number eight represents good luck and prosperity."[139] Yet Boeing was still losing

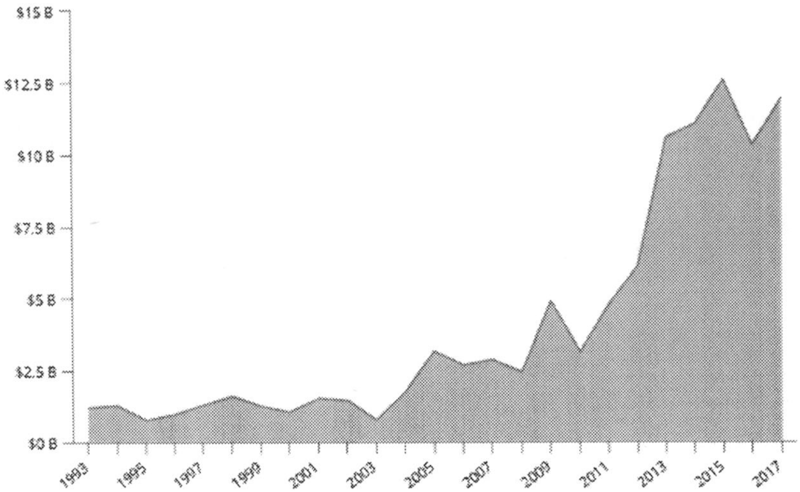

Fig. 9.8 Boeing's China revenue grew tenfold in 25 Years (*Source* Company Reports)

market share to Airbus. The European giant beat Boeing in global sales in eight of the ten years from 2001 to 2010, and in 2003, Airbus delivered more planes globally than Boeing for the first time.[140]

But Boeing's increasing dependence on China, alongside continued competition from Airbus, saw Beijing maintain if not strengthen its leverage in negotiating for aircraft purchases.[141] Boeing had little choice but to remain a high-profile participant in US commercial diplomacy to help fight its global "sales war" with Airbus, which was playing a similar game.[142]

Beijing, however, was gradually trying to change the game altogether. It never abandoned its dream of making a "Chinese Boeing" and decided it was time to up the pressure on foreign aerospace companies to help it realize this ambition.[143]

Disrupting the Duopoly?

China announced plans for its own commercial jetliner in 2006 and this goal has featured in Five-Year Plans ever since.[144] In 2008 Beijing reorganized the domestic aerospace industry to create the Commercial Aircraft

Corporation of China (COMAC), a Shanghai-based state-owned behemoth with assets of 54.4 billion yuan ($7.9 billion) as of 2016.[145] Its founding also coincided with the Global Financial Crisis, which made China more confident in its state-backed economic model.

COMAC was tasked with leading a commercial aviation program that centers around two main products: the ARJ21, a 75–90 seat regional jet similar to those produced by Brazil's Embraer or Canada's Bombardier, and the flagship C919, a 156–168 seat narrow-body jetliner intended to compete with the B737 and A320—the "workhorses" of air travel.[146]

Boeing and Airbus were asked to partner with COMAC and its subsidiaries to transfer some of their know-how. For each company, the calculus is basically a modified Prisoner's Dilemma: either resist Beijing and forfeit the Chinese market to the other firm, or both help COMAC become a more competitive player, when cartel-like cooperative resistance would be in the firms' best interests. Such difficult situations are not exclusive to Boeing or Airbus, though, as many American high-tech companies face the same dilemma. (For example, General Electric agreed in 2011 to share advanced avionics technology for the C919 with a Chinese SOE.)[147]

In general, Boeing has taken a more cautious approach than Airbus—which had to make up ground on its American rival—but both companies seem to have concluded that it is better to provide limited support to China's commercial aviation ambitions.

Airbus has moved quicker on this front, building an Engineering Center in Beijing to work with Chinese engineers on A350 models, opening its first A320 assembly plant outside Europe in Tianjin, and offering China an "industrial partnership" on its new double decker A380.[148]

Boeing, meanwhile, has awarded supply contracts worth billions of dollars to Chinese companies, established Manufacturing Innovation Centers in Beijing, Shenyang, and Xi'an, and opened a finishing plant for B737s near Shanghai in December 2018.[149]

However, like most aviation manufacturers, Boeing is acutely aware of the risks of technology transfer and has "jealously guarded" its competitive edge since it first awarded supplier contracts to China in the early 1980s.[150] Boeing's strategy for self-protection was put succinctly by a former Boeing CEO in the 1990s: "Obviously you don't tell someone everything you know…the trick is to give something away just as you are developing something better."[151] So, the firm transferred relatively dated technology and outsourced only simple parts like aircraft doors, aluminum structures, and cabin fittings.[152]

It is hard to assess the extent to which Boeing has helped COMAC. But the C919 had its maiden flight in May 2017 and is expected to enter commercial production in 2021.[153] COMAC claims it already has 785 orders, although these are nonbinding and over 90% are from domestic airlines.[154] The estimated price of a C919 is $50 million—just half that of the B737 and A320—but its inferior efficiency and lack of global support networks for fueling and maintenance mean it is far costlier to operate over the multi-decade lifecycle of a typical jetliner.[155]

Indeed, it is uncertain whether the C919 will ever become commercially viable on the scale of a Boeing or Airbus.[156] COMAC still lacks safety certifications from global aviation standards bodies and still relies on foreign suppliers for vital parts such as engines, avionics, and specialized materials. The unhappy reality for China is that the C919 is already one generation behind jetliner technology under development at Boeing and Airbus.[157]

Yet, while China has thus far failed to break into the jetliner market, the C919 is the most serious threat to the Boeing-Airbus duopoly in decades.[158] COMAC benefits from generous subsidies, favorable procurement policies, technology transfer, decades of basic research, and a growing pool of STEM talent. State support was important to the success of both Boeing and Airbus. Federal agencies and state authorities have doled out generous R&D grants, lucrative military contracts, and tax breaks to Boeing.[159] European governments played an even greater role in Airbus, showering the plane-maker with $22 billion in "illegal" subsidies and concessional launch loans.[160] Such lessons are not lost on China's economic planners.[161]

In 2011 Boeing's then CEO said the company has "opted to accept the reality of both partnering and competing with China."[162] This tension was on display when Xi Jinping visited a Boeing factory outside Seattle in September 2015. Xi witnessed the signing of both a deal by Chinese airliners to buy $38 billion worth of planes and a joint venture between Boeing and COMAC to establish a B737 finishing center in China.[163]

Many countries in Asia have tried and failed to foster a domestic aerospace industry, including Japan and South Korea.[164] When "Japan-bashing" peaked in the 1980s, some Americans predicted that they would now be flying in jetliners made by Mitsubishi (which has struggled to launch even a regional jet).[165] Boeing and Airbus seem to hope that COMAC will prove to be the Mitsubishi of today.

That bet is likely fair, as the aviation industry has enormous barriers to entry—not just in technical knowledge but also in the management systems that many industry observers believe are difficult to achieve in a nonmarket economy.[166] Even if COMAC masters today's technology, Boeing and Airbus may already be commercializing the technologies of tomorrow.

Yet, if any country can beat the odds, it's probably China. While past performance is no guarantee of future success, especially in aviation, China has a track record of leveraging foreign cooperation to establish domestic industries in high-end manufacturing.[167] Moreover, China's capacity for domestic innovation is rising, and if Boeing and Airbus are to maintain their edge, they will need to keep pushing the innovation frontier beyond China's reach.[168]

Back to the Future: Boeing and the US–China Trade War

Rising competition from China is a long-term concern for the United States. In the here and now, however, the most pressing geopolitical issue for Boeing is the rapidly deteriorating US–China economic relationship that it had worked hard to build in the 1990s. A seemingly dramatic shift in views among US policy elites and segments of the businesses community has rocked the bipartisan consensus on China that held since the Nixon administration.[169]

Rather than doubling down on engagement, an increasing number of policymaking elites argue that economic linkages with China have done more harm than good to the US economy, particularly with regard to manufacturing employment. In addition, certain manufacturing and technology firms suffer as a result of formidable competition from Chinese companies, IP violations, and Chinese regulatory barriers that make market entry challenging.

These groups and voices have found kindred spirits in the White House, which has embraced something of an anti-globalization agenda.[170] The current US administration is even relitigating China's WTO accession, arguing that Beijing has not liberalized its economy or society as much as was expected, and that this lack of progress means that past policy was a failure.[171]

In this contentious environment, China's aviation ambitions, too, have become an irritant in the bilateral relationship. The Section 301 report that the US Trade Representative issued to justify the ongoing US–China trade war raised concerns about forced technology transfer in the aerospace industry.[172] The administration has also charged Chinese entities with stealing industrial secrets from US aerospace manufacturers.[173] More important, China shows no sign of backing down from its commercial aviation program, as Beijing's industrial policy has clearly articulated a goal for the C919 to constitute 10% of the domestic market by 2025.[174]

A $1 Trillion Market

Boeing "is probably the American company with the most riding on a healthy relationship with Beijing," caught between its need to sell planes to China and its need to cooperate with the US government on commercial diplomacy.[175] The company now sends one-quarter of its planes to China, while Chinese suppliers are involved in every model in its commercial fleet.[176] Boeing projects that China will soon become its "largest commercial airplane customer" as the country is estimated to need 8090 planes worth $1.3 trillion between 2019 and 2038.[177]

Should the US–China trade war continue to escalate, Boeing is an obvious candidate for retaliation from Beijing.[178] It is not hard to imagine that Chinese airlines could be instructed to buy more planes from Airbus.[179] Boeing would also struggle to raise prices to absorb potential Chinese tariffs, because it would lose even more business to Airbus amid cutthroat price competition, putting both profits and jobs at risk (see Fig. 9.9).[180]

Fig. 9.9 A320s and B737s dominate China's commercial fleet as of 2016 (*Source* National Bureau of Statistics)

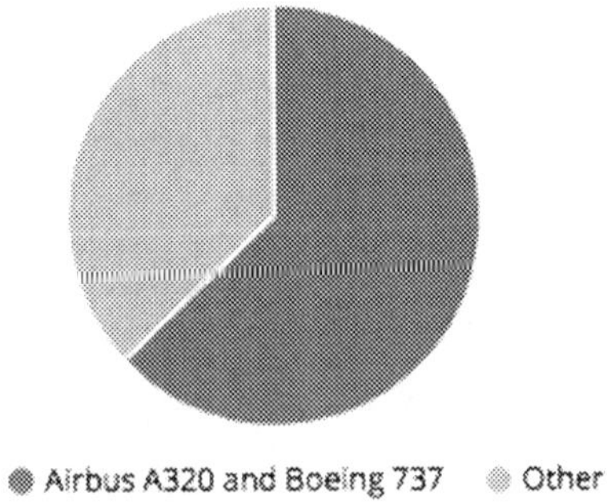

With so much at stake, Boeing will not be an idle spectator to the unwinding of US–China relations. It has taken a leaf out of its old playbook and embarked on a diplomatic offensive to ease bilateral tensions. After an early disagreement with the Trump administration over the cost of an Air Force One contract, then Boeing CEO Dennis Muilenburg accompanied the President on his state visit to China in November 2017, during which Boeing claimed a $37 billion order.[181] Possibly as a result, B737s also managed to be exempt from retaliatory tariffs imposed by Beijing in the US–China trade war, since China would not want to raise prices on such a vital import.[182] Yet Boeing has received no orders from China since 2017 and is still working actively to persuade both governments of trade's "mutual benefit."[183]

But the company soon ran into a problem far greater than the trade war. Two fatal crashes involving the B737 Max 8, in Indonesia in October 2018 and in Ethiopia in March 2019, were linked to faulty flight control systems on these latest Boeing aircraft. On the day of the Ethiopian crash, China, which at the time was receiving one-third of all 737 Max deliveries, became the first country to order a nationwide grounding of these planes. Other regulators in Asia and Europe quickly followed suit, eventually prompting the FAA to order its own grounding.[184]

In an industry that places safety above all else, the fallout from these accidents was immense. Boeing has worked overtime to resolve this safety issue but, as of late 2019, the 737 Max is yet to return to the skies. Reports suggested that the plane's engineering flaws stemmed from long-running problems with internal management and regulatory oversight.[185]

Given the competitive nature of the industry, this unsurprisingly resulted in Boeing losing out to Airbus on a $35 billion deal for 300 jetliner deliveries to China, accumulating almost 5,000 unfilled orders, and having to set aside $4.9 billion for compensation.[186] What remains uncertain is the extent to which this episode will narrow the company's advantage over emerging competitors like COMAC. Boeing is in the midst of negotiating a $30 billion order to China, and is contemplating a range of internal reforms, but the firm still faces an uphill battle to restore its reputation.[187]

Managing both the reputational risk from the 737 Max fallout and the political risk around feuding superpowers appears ever more important for Boeing, as its margin for error is getting smaller against Airbus, and potentially against COMAC too. As of August 2018, the two Western companies are neck-and-neck in China, with Boeing having 1670 planes

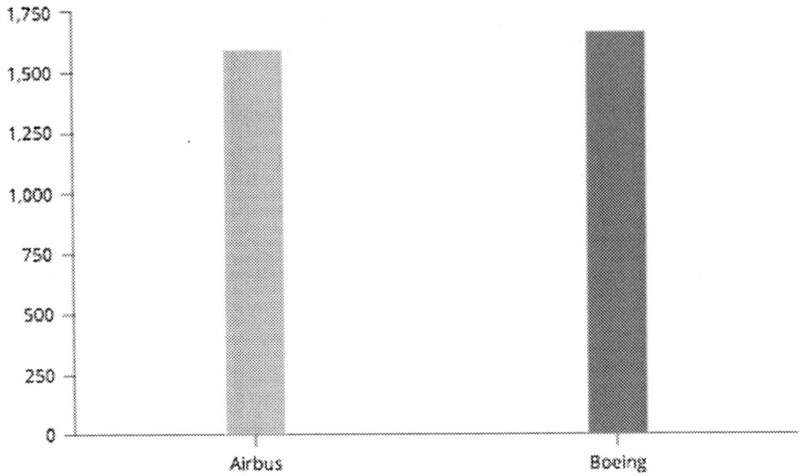

Fig. 9.10 Airbus and Boeing planes in China, August 2018 (*Source* CAPA Centre for Aviation)

in operation there compared to 1598 for Airbus (see Fig. 9.10).[188] Any further missteps could cause Boeing to fall behind and cede market share on a long-term basis.

Conclusion

China is now one of Boeing's most lucrative markets—it earned well over $100 billion of revenue there from 1993 to 2018. This success contributed to a US aircraft industry that is now worth $90 billion annually and sustains almost 500,000 jobs with an average salary north of $85,000.[189]

As a company whose relationship with China began even before Washington and Beijing established official diplomatic relations, Boeing has steered its China operations through the end of the Cold War, the Tiananmen crackdown, and the long road to China's WTO entry.

What the American multinational has to navigate now is how to pursue a deeper but more complicated relationship with a China whose capabilities have strengthened markedly. This precarious balance was reflected in Boeing's move to work with COMAC to open its first finishing plant in China. The light manufacturing facility, near Shanghai, will "finish" almost-ready planes that have been delivered to China.[190]

From Boeing's perspective, the strategic triangle between the United States, China, and the Soviet Union during the Cold War was replaced by a commercial triangle between Chinese authorities, American firms, and their competitors from other advanced economies. Global competition made it difficult for countries and companies to coordinate their approach to a China that acquired formidable market power and diplomatic leverage. To ensure that Boeing could compete in what has become a $1 trillion market, it had little choice but to work with Beijing. Because if it didn't, its rivals would.

This commercial logic led Boeing to become increasingly involved in US–China relations after 1989, a time when international business was ascendant in American foreign policy priorities and when Congressional activism and public opinion forced the White House to devote greater attention to democracy and human rights in China.

To protect its bottom line, the company played a leading role in advocating for China's MFN status and for WTO accession. This history suggests that the US business community was instrumental in helping successive White House administrations generate Congressional support to ensure that the basic premise of economic engagement with China held steady. But engagement was not an unalloyed success for all Americans. There were economic downsides and job losses that resulted from import substitution from China, although these were concentrated in specific manufacturing industries.[191]

Whether economic globalization, with China being the centerpiece, was ultimately a net gain or loss for the United States is at the heart of the current "reckoning" in US policy toward China. Critics level the charge that China hoodwinked Washington into accepting it into the WTO, but failed to deliver on political reforms. They also tend to blame multinationals for their complicity in moving production overseas.[192]

These criticisms are understandable but incomplete, and they credit the United States with inordinate power to shape Chinese economic and political behavior. Successive US administrations were over-optimistic about liberalization in China, but many China specialists also underestimated the resilience of the Chinese Party-state.[193] American politicians at the time used lofty rhetoric about democracy, but engagement was also about more prosaic matters.[194] It was often borne out of pragmatism and the pursuit of concrete interests to deliver economic benefits to Americans and to secure China's cooperation on a host of critical global issues.[195]

Simply blaming Beijing for America's various economic maladies may be politically satisfying but it can also be intellectually disingenuous. China's rise was just one, albeit significant, part of secular global trends. The United States, and firms like Boeing, partly shaped and participated in these trends, but did not themselves control overarching structural changes like economic globalization, transnational supply chains, and labor-displacing technological advances. The failure of domestic US policy to adapt to these forces, whether through better social policies or trade safeguards, exacerbated the fallout and resultant inequalities.[196]

But does Boeing's role in US–China relations offer any lessons for how to approach the current bilateral impasse? For Beijing, it seems ever more important to keep the US and European business community on its side, which may entail compromises and concessions on market access and technology transfer.[197] For Washington, to alter China's behavior across a range of economic practices will likely require both new incentives and coordinated pressure from an alliance of governments and businesses that spans China's main trade partners.

Boeing does owe part of its global success, including in China, to US commercial diplomacy. But ultimately, the company's success rested on its own product and capacity for innovation, which was nurtured for nearly a century in an open and competitive environment, but with a dose of smart support from the state.

Today, Boeing may still be able to keep its secrets from China, but it will likely have to work harder to sustain its reputation and run faster to stay ahead of the competition.

Notes

1. Xu Bailing, "Witnessing Moments of Top Secret," *China Daily*, February 18, 2002, http://www.chinadaily.com.cn/epaper/html/cd/2002/200202/20020218/20020218010_1.html.
2. "从邓小平到习近平 中国最高层访美为何总去波音?" *Ta Kung Pao*, September 23, 2015, http://news.takungpao.com/world/exclusive/2015-09/3180326.html.
3. "Boeing in Brief," Boeing company website, accessed February 2018, http://www.boeing.com/company/general-info/index.page.

4. Eve Dumovich, "The 1st … and the Best," *Boeing Frontiers* [*Challenge* pullout], December 2006, pp. 46–47, https://www.boeing.com/news/frontiers/archive/2006/december/ts_sf12.pdf; John Pomfret, *The Beautiful Country and the Middle Kingdom: America and China, 1776 to the Present* (Henry Holt and Company, 2016), pp. 214–218.
5. Christopher Drew, "Boeing Speaks in Trump Terms on Iran Deal: It's About Jobs," *The New York Times*, December 11, 2016, https://www.nytimes.com/2016/12/11/business/iran-boeing-airplane-billion-dollar-agreement.html.
6. Paulson Institute, "Flying High and Flying Blind: How One Chinese Buyout of a US Aviation Firm Soared While Another Crashed," *Paulson Papers on Investment*, January 2017, http://www.paulsoninstitute.org/wp-content/uploads/2017/01/PPI_Case-Study-Series_Aviation_English.pdf.
7. Stanley Holmes, "How Boeing Woos Beijing," *The Seattle Times*, May 26, 1996, http://community.seattletimes.nwsource.com/archive/?date=19960526&slug=2331332.
8. Harry Schwartz, "Nixon Tries Jetliner Diplomacy," *The New York Times*, July 9, 1972, https://www.nytimes.com/1972/07/09/archives/nixon-tries-jetliner-diplomacy-china.html.
9. Robert S. Ross, *Negotiating Cooperation: The United States and China, 1969–1989* (Stanford University Press, 1997).
10. Central Intelligence Agency, "China: Expanding Horizons for International Air Service," Intelligence Memorandum, Directorate of Intelligence, November 1972 [Approved for release: April 19, 2006], https://www.cia.gov/library/readingroom/docs/CIA-RDP85T00875R001700040047-5.pdf.
11. Editorial, "Jets for Peking," *The New York Times*, July 8, 1972, https://www.nytimes.com/1972/07/08/archives/jets-for-peking.html.
12. "Peking May Widen Air Links Abroad," *The New York Times*, January 26, 1971, https://www.nytimes.com/1971/01/26/archives/peking-may-widen-air-links-abroad-indicates-interest-in-lines-to.html.
13. Brendan James, "China Trade: Wary Hope," *The New York Times*, April 18, 1971, https://www.nytimes.com/1971/04/18/archives/china-trade-wary-hope-china-trade-wary-hope.html.
14. Holmes, "How Boeing Woos Beijing."
15. Richard Witkin, "Miller—Boeing's Man in Peking," *The New York Times*, September 18, 1972, https://www.nytimes.com/1972/09/18/archives/miller-boeings-man-in-peking-707-sale-involved-most-rigorous.html; Richard Witkin, "Boeing Expects 6-Million from Chinese in a Week," *The New York Times*, September 13, 1972, https://www.nytimes.com/1972/09/13/archives/boeing-expects-6million-from-

chinese-in-a-week-rest-of-125million.html; Reuters, "China Purchasing 10 Boeing Liners for $150-Million," *The New York Times*, September 11, 1972, https://www.nytimes.com/1972/09/11/archives/china-purchasing-10-boeing-liners-for-150million-china-purchasing.html.

16. Peter D. Weintraub, "...and Some Offices in Peking," *The New York Times*, January 4, 1976, https://www.nytimes.com/1976/01/04/archives/-and-some-offices-in-peking-companies-find-few-amenities-high-costs.html.
17. Schwartz, "Nixon Tries Jetliner Diplomacy."
18. John W. Finney, "Aerospace Outlook Brightens," *The New York Times*, January 5, 1975, https://www.nytimes.com/1975/01/05/archives/aerospace-outlook-brightens.html.
19. John Newhouse, *Boeing Versus Airbus: The Inside Story of the Greatest International Competition in Business* (Knopf, 2007).
20. Theodore Shabad, "China, in Aggressive Drive, Tops Soviet in Exports to U.S.," *The New York Times*, March 17, 1977, https://www.nytimes.com/1977/03/17/archives/china-in-agressive-drive-tops-soviet-in-exports-to-us.html; Clyde H. Farnsworth, "Curb Asked on Cotton from China," *The New York Times*, December 7, 1978, https://www.nytimes.com/1978/12/07/archives/curb-asked-on-cotton-from-china-talks-on-imports-meant-to-placate.html; Brendan Jones, "U.S. Study Sees Trade Increase with Pragmatic Post-Mao China," *The New York Times*, August 11, 1977, https://www.nytimes.com/1977/08/11/archives/us-study-sees-trade-increase-with-pragmatic-postmao-china-us-sees.html; Leslie Gelb, "Surging Trade with China," *The New York Times*, December 2, 1973, https://www.nytimes.com/1973/12/02/archives/surging-trade-with-china-surging-trade-with-china.html.
21. Editorial, "How Many Shirttails in China?" *The New York Times*, March 13, 1979, https://www.nytimes.com/1979/03/13/archives/how-many-shirttails-in-china.html.
22. Richard Witkin, "Boeing Gets 3-Jet Order from China," *The New York Times*, December 20, 1978, https://www.nytimes.com/1978/12/20/archives/boeing-gets-3jet-order-from-china-cost-156-million-pan-am-seeks-to.html.
23. "Arrival of U.S. Airliner Is China's First Since '49," *The New York Times*, December 8, 1980, https://timesmachine.nytimes.com/timesmachine/1980/12/08/111322437.pdf.
24. Ben Baden, "40 Years of US-China Commercial Relations," *China Business Review*, January 1, 2013, https://www.chinabusinessreview.com/40-years-of-us-china-commercial-relations/.

25. *Foreign Relations of the United States*, 1969–1976, Volume XVII, China, 1969–1972, ed. Steven E. Phillips (Washington: Government Printing Office, 2006), Document 194, https://history.state.gov/historicaldocuments/frus1969-76v17/d194.
26. *Foreign Relations of the United States*, 1969–1976, Volume XVIII, China, 1973–1976, ed. David P. Nickles (Washington: Government Printing Office, 2007), Document 12, https://history.state.gov/historicaldocuments/frus1969-76v18/d12.
27. James J. Nagle, "Trade Expansion with East Urged," *The New York Times*, September 11, 1972, https://www.nytimes.com/1972/09/11/archives/trade-expansion-with-east-urged-groups-from-six-western-nations.html; Editorial, "Progress with Peking," *The New York Times*, April 2, 1973, https://www.nytimes.com/1973/04/02/archives/progress-with-peking.html.
28. Sheryl WuDunn, "Selling Planes to China: High Stakes," *The New York Times*, May 1, 1989, https://www.nytimes.com/1989/05/01/business/international-report-selling-planes-to-china-high-stakes.html; Holmes, "How Boeing Woos Beijing."
29. James Fallows, *China Airborne* (Pantheon, 2012).
30. Ross, *Negotiating Cooperation*, Chs. 6–8.
31. Hal Brands, *Making the Unipolar Moment: U.S. Foreign Policy and the Rise of the Post-Cold War Order* (Cornell University Press, 2016), Ch. 4.
32. Hedrick Smith, "Reagan, in U.S., Says China Trip Advanced Ties," *The New York Times*, May 2, 1984, https://www.nytimes.com/1984/05/02/world/reagan-in-us-says-china-trip-advanced-ties.html.
33. Patrick Tyler, *A Great Wall: Six Presidents and China* (PublicAffairs, 1999), Ch. 6.
34. George P. Schultz, *Turmoil and Triumph: My Years as Secretary of State* (Scribner, 1993), Ch. 22.
35. Fallows, *China Airborne*.
36. James P. Sterba, "China's Airline, Casual at Home, Spruces Up for Its U.S. Service," *The New York Times*, January 8, 1981, https://www.nytimes.com/1981/01/08/world/china-s-airline-casual-at-home-spruces-up-for-its-us-service.html.
37. Nicholas D. Kristof, "Jet Crashes in China, Killing 141; 5th Serious Accident in 4 Months," *The New York Times*, November 25, 1992, https://www.nytimes.com/1992/11/25/world/jet-crashes-in-china-killing-141-5th-serious-accident-in-4-months.html; Sheryl WuDunn, "127 Killed in Jetliner Collision in China," *The New York Times*, October 3, 1990, https://www.nytimes.com/1990/10/03/world/127-killed-in-jetliner-collision-in-china.html.
38. Holmes, "How Boeing Woos Beijing."

39. Andy Pasztor, “How China Turned Around a Dismal Air-Safety Record,” *The Wall Street Journal*, October 10, 2007, https://www.wsj.com/articles/SB119198005864354292.
40. Press Release, “China Signs for 102 Airbus Aircraft,” Airbus company website, November 4, 2010, https://www.airbus.com/newsroom/press-releases/en/2010/11/china-signs-for-102-airbus-aircraft.html; “China’s Aircraft Market,” *The New York Times*, June 24, 1985, https://www.nytimes.com/1985/06/24/business/china-s-aircraft-market.html.
41. “Airbus Flies High in China,” *China Daily*, January 17, 2004, http://www.chinadaily.com.cn/en/doc/2004-01/17/content_299782.htm.
42. China Power Team, “How Is Commercial Aviation Propelling China’s Economic Development,” Center for Strategic and International Studies, September 26, 2018, https://chinapower.csis.org/china-commercial-aviation/.
43. “China’s Aircraft Market.”
44. Deng Xiaoping, “China Must Take Its Place in the Field of High Technology,” Remarks made while inspecting the electron-positron collider in Beijing, October 24, 1988, in *Selected Works of Deng Xiaoping*, Volume III (1982–1992) (Foreign Languages Press, 1994).
45. WuDunn, “Selling Planes to China.”
46. Ibid.; Christopher S. Wren, “China Moves to Buy a Modern Air Fleet,” *The New York Times*, November 24, 1982, https://www.nytimes.com/1982/11/24/business/china-moves-to-buy-a-modern-air-fleet.html.
47. “波音历史,” Boeing company website, http://www.boeing.cn/china/inchina/history/.
48. Sheryl WuDunn, “Civilian Shift for Chinese Plane Maker,” *The New York Times*, May 21, 1990, https://www.nytimes.com/1990/05/21/business/international-report-civilian-shift-for-chinese-plane-maker.html.
49. Fox Butterfield, “Chinese 707-Like Jet Doesn’t Fly,” *The New York Times*, May 17, 1980, https://timesmachine.nytimes.com/timesmachine/1980/05/17/111242161.pdf.
50. Jeffrey Lin and P.W. Singer, “China Has a New Jetliner—Here’s What That Means,” *Popular Science*, May 8, 2017, https://www.popsci.com/where-chinas-new-jetliner-fits-into-its-larger-aviation-future/; Richard A. Bitzinger, “Is China Leading the Rebirth of Asia’s Commercial Aircraft Industry,” *China Brief*, Jamestown Foundation, April 29, 2010, https://jamestown.org/program/is-china-leading-the-rebirth-of-asias-commercial-aircraft-industry/.
51. Dennis Wong, “Can ‘Made in China 2025’ Help Turn the Nation’s Domestic Aerospace Industry Into a World Leader?” *South China Morning Post*, October 30, 2018, https://multimedia.scmp.com/news/china/article/2170344/china-2025-aviation/index.html; AP, “China’s

First Jetliner Makes Long Test Flight," *The New York Times*, November 6, 1993, https://www.nytimes.com/1983/11/06/world/around-the-world-china-s-first-jetliner-makes-long-test-flight.html.

52. Chai Yinghui and Ye Wentian, "航空工业六十年: 从'运十'到'COMAC919'," *China Business Journal*, August 19, 2009, http://news.carnoc.com/list/144/144238.html.
53. Patrick E. Tyler, "Western Lifts for China's Air Plans," *The New York Times*, February 25, 1995, https://www.nytimes.com/1995/02/25/business/company-news-western-lift-for-china-s-air-plans.html.
54. David E. Sanger, "'Asian Money,' American Fears," *The New York Times*, January 5, 1997, https://www.nytimes.com/1997/01/05/weekinreview/asian-money-american-fears.html; David E. Sanger, "Overtures to Asia Pose Risk for U.S. Aerospace Industry," *The New York Times*, November 18, 1991, https://www.nytimes.com/1991/11/18/business/overtures-to-asia-pose-risk-for-us-aerospace-industry.html.
55. David E. Sanger, "Rousing a Sleeping Industrial Giant," *The New York Times*, May 20, 1990, https://www.nytimes.com/1990/05/20/business/rousing-a-sleeping-industrial-giant.html.
56. David E. Sanger and Steve Lohr, "A Search for Answers to Avoid the Layoffs," *The New York Times*, March 9, 1996, https://www.nytimes.com/1996/03/09/us/a-search-for-answers-to-avoid-the-layoffs.html.
57. The idea of a "long decade" is adapted from: Geremie R. Barmé, "The Pirouette of Time—After the Future in China," *China Heritage*, January 28, 2019, http://chinaheritage.net/journal/the-pirouette-of-time-after-the-future-in-china/.
58. "China Gets Favored Trade Status," *The New York Times*, January 25, 1980, https://timesmachine.nytimes.com/timesmachine/1980/01/25/111221083.pdf; Maureen Jenkins, "30 Years and Counting," *Boeing Frontiers*, December 2002–January 2003, https://www.boeing.com/news/frontiers/archive/2002/december/mainfeature.html.
59. "U.S. Continues Trade Benefit to Rumania, Hungary, China," *The New York Times*, June 3, 1987, https://www.nytimes.com/1987/06/03/world/us-continues-trade-benefit-to-rumania-hungary-china.html; "Mushroom Farmers Are Hurt as Imports From China Surge," *The New York Times*, December 2, 1982, https://www.nytimes.com/1982/12/02/business/mushroom-farmers-are-hurt-as-imports-from-china-surge.html.
60. Richard Madsen, *China and the American Dream: A Moral Inquiry* (University of California Press, 1995); "China," PollingReport.com, http://www.pollingreport.com/china.htm.
61. Gary Clyde Hufbauer et al., "Case 89-2: US v. China (1989–: Tiananmen Square Massacre, Human Rights)," Peterson Institute for International Economics, May 1, 2008, https://www.piie.

com/commentary/speeches-papers/case-89-2; Martin Tolchin, "House, Breaking with Bush, Votes China Sanctions," *The New York Times*, June 30, 1989, https://www.nytimes.com/1989/06/30/world/house-breaking-with-bush-votes-china-sanctions.html.
62. Michael R. Gordon, "U.S. Grants Boeing a Waiver to Sell Jetliners to China," *The New York Times*, July 8, 1989, https://www.nytimes.com/1989/07/08/business/us-grants-boeing-a-waiver-to-sell-jetliners-to-china.html.
63. Editorial, "Squandering Leverage on China," *The New York Times*, March 23, 1992, https://www.nytimes.com/1992/03/23/opinion/squandering-leverage-on-china.html.
64. Thomas L. Friedman, "Bush Seeks Trade Benefits for China," *The New York Times*, June 3, 1992, https://www.nytimes.com/1992/06/03/world/bush-seeks-trade-benefits-for-china.html; Michael Wines, "Bush, This Time in Election Year, Vetoes Trade Curbs Against China," *The New York Times*, September 29, 1992, https://www.nytimes.com/1992/09/29/world/bush-this-time-in-election-year-vetoes-trade-curbs-against-china.html/.
65. Keith Bradsher, "Senate Restricts Trade with China; Bush Veto Likely," *The New York Times*, July 24, 1991, https://www.nytimes.com/1991/07/24/world/senate-restricts-trade-with-china-bush-veto-likely.html; Clyde H. Farnsworth, "Congressional Attempt to Impose Higher Tariffs on China Collapses," *The New York Times*, October 20, 1990, https://www.nytimes.com/1990/10/20/world/congressional-attempt-to-impose-higher-tariffs-on-china-collapses.html.
66. Bill Bishop, "Jim Mann Details Why 'Engagement' with China Failed," *Axios*, December 15, 2018, https://www.axios.com/interview-james-mann-us-china-engagement-trade-8477691b-e353-41cd-8c8b-30ff9e48bd88.html.
67. Friedman, "Bush Seeks Trade Benefits for China."
68. Keith Bradsher, "A Hard Line from China on Trade," *The New York Times*, May 13, 1991, https://www.nytimes.com/1991/05/13/business/a-hard-line-from-china-on-trade.html.
69. George H.W. Bush, "Remarks at the Yale University Commencement Ceremony in New Haven, Connecticut," The American Presidency Project, UC Santa Barbara, May 27, 1991, https://www.presidency.ucsb.edu/documents/remarks-the-yale-university-commencement-ceremony-new-haven-connecticut.
70. R.W. Apple Jr., "Bush Withholding Normal Trade Ties from the Soviets," *The New York Times*, May 25, 1990, https://www.nytimes.com/1990/05/25/world/bush-withholding-normal-trade-ties-from-the-soviets.html.

71. Francis Fukuyama, "The End of History?" *The National Interest*, No. 16, Summer 1989, pp. 3–18.
72. Robert Dreyfuss, "The New China Lobby," *The American Prospect*, January–February 1997, https://prospect.org/article/new-china-lobby.
73. James Mann, *About Face: A History of America's Curious Relationship with China, from Nixon to Clinton* (Knopf, 1998), Chs. 12–16.
74. Lawrence M. Fisher, "Union Rejects Boeing Offer; Goes on Strike in Three States," *The New York Times*, October 7, 1995, https://www.nytimes.com/1995/10/07/us/union-rejects-boeing-offer-goes-on-strike-in-three-states.html.
75. Lawrence M. Fisher, "Boeing Sees Plane Orders Increasing," *The New York Times*, March 5, 1993, https://www.nytimes.com/1993/03/05/business/company-news-boeing-sees-plane-orders-increasing.html; Holmes, "How Boeing Woos Beijing."
76. David E. Sanger, "Mending Images with Pandas and Taking Home 747s," *The New York Times*, November 20, 1993, https://www.nytimes.com/1993/11/20/world/the-pacific-summit-mending-images-with-pandas-and-taking-home-747-s.html.
77. Nicholas D. Kristof, "China Worried by Clinton's Linking of Trade to Human Rights," *The New York Times*, October 9, 1992, https://www.nytimes.com/1992/10/09/world/china-worried-by-clinton-s-linking-of-trade-to-human-rights.html; Keith Bradsher, "Clinton Aides Propose Renewal of China's Favored Trade Status," *The New York Times*, May 25, 1993, https://www.nytimes.com/1993/05/25/world/clinton-aides-propose-renewal-of-china-s-favored-trade-status.html.
78. Bill Clinton, "Conditions for Renewal of Most-Favored-Nation Status for the People's Republic of China in 1994," Executive Order 12850, May 28, 1993, *Federal Register*, Vol. 58, No. 103, June 1, 1993, https://www.archives.gov/files/federal-register/executive-orders/pdf/12850.pdf; Daniel Southerl, "U.S., China Sign Prison Labor Pact," *The Washington Post*, August 8, 1992, https://www.washingtonpost.com/archive/business/1992/08/08/us-china-sign-prison-labor-pact/ee3e4ce8-cb71-4c92-8162-19813a20dac5/.
79. Mann, *About Face*, Chs. 15–16.
80. Keith Bradsher, "Pressure from Companies," *The New York Times*, May 13, 1993, https://www.nytimes.com/1993/05/13/world/pressure-from-companies.html.
81. Calvin Sims, "China Steps Up Spending to Keep U.S. Trade Status," *The New York Times*, May 7, 1993, https://www.nytimes.com/1993/05/07/business/china-steps-up-spending-to-keep-us-trade-status.html.
82. David E. Sanger, "Clinton Now Turns to Widening Trade Across the Pacific," *The New York Times*, November 19, 1993, https://www.

nytimes.com/1993/11/19/world/clinton-now-turns-to-widening-trade-across-the-pacific.html.

83. Edward A. Gargan, "Gauging the Consequences of Spurning China," *The New York Times*, March 21, 1994, https://www.nytimes.com/1994/03/21/business/gauging-the-consequences-of-spurning-china.html; Stephen Engelberg and Martin Tolbin, "Foreigners Find New Ally in U.S. Industry," *The New York Times*, November 2, 1993, https://www.nytimes.com/1993/11/02/us/foreigners-find-new-ally-in-us-industry.html; Peter Behr, "Major U.S. Companies Lobbying Clinton to Renew China's Trade Privileges," *The Washington Post*, May 6, 1994, https://www.washingtonpost.com/archive/politics/1994/05/06/major-us-companies-lobbying-clinton-to-renew-chinas-trade-privileges/f1003cd2-b169-4374-927a-e0032da889f5/.
84. Thomas L. Friedman, "U.S. Is to Maintain Trade Privileges for China's Goods; Clinton Votes for Business," *The New York Times*, May 27, 1994, https://www.nytimes.com/1994/05/27/world/us-is-to-maintain-trade-privileges-for-china-s-goods-clinton-votes-for-business.html.
85. Mann, *About Face*, Ch. 16.
86. Friedman, "U.S. Is to Maintain Trade Privileges for China's Goods"; David E. Sanger, "New Realism Wins the Day," *The New York Times*, September 20, 2000, https://www.nytimes.com/2000/09/20/world/opening-to-china-news-analysis-new-realism-wins-the-day.html; Peter Passell, "A Cold-War Trade Weapon Isn't Used on China and May Never Be," *The New York Times*, June 3, 1993, https://www.nytimes.com/1993/06/03/business/economic-scene-a-cold-war-trade-weapon-isn-t-used-on-china-and-may-never-be.html.
87. Bill Clinton, "Remarks by the President in Address on China and the National Interest," *Voice of America*, Washington, DC, October 24, 1997, https://1997-2001.state.gov/regions/eap/971024_clinton_china.html.
88. Stanley Holmes, "Boeing's Campaign to Protect a Market—Corporations Lobby to Save China Trade," *The Seattle Times*, May 27, 1996, http://community.seattletimes.nwsource.com/archive/?date=19960527&slug=2331446; Eric Schmitt, "House Defeats a Move to End China's Favored Trade Status," *The New York Times*, June 28, 1996, https://www.nytimes.com/1996/06/28/world/house-defeats-a-move-to-end-china-s-favored-trade-status.html.
89. Robert G. Kaiser and Steven Mufson, "'Blue Team' Draws a Hard Line on Beijing," *The Washington Post*, February 22, 2000, https://www.washingtonpost.com/wp-srv/WPcap/2000-02/22/004r-022200-idx.html; James V. Grimaldi and Stanley Holmes, "DNC Memo Refers to Boeing—Hints at Link to China Trade," *The Seattle Times*, March 22,

1997, http://community.seattletimes.nwsource.com/archive/?date=19970322&slug=2529988; David E. Sanger, "Two Roads to China: Nice, and Not so Nice," *The New York Times*, June 9, 1996, https://www.nytimes.com/1996/06/09/business/two-roads-to-china-nice-and-not-so-nice.html.

90. David E. Sanger, "A Giant in Jets and Foreign Policy," *The New York Times*, December 17, 1996, https://www.nytimes.com/1996/12/17/business/a-giant-in-jets-and-foreign-policy.html; Sanger, "Two Roads to China"; Dreyfuss, "The New China Lobby."
91. Holmes, "Boeing's Campaign to Protect a Market."
92. Richard W. Stevenson, "A Role as Nation's Chief Salesman Abroad," *The New York Times*, April 4, 1996, https://www.nytimes.com/1996/04/04/world/crash-in-the-balkans-the-policy-a-role-as-nation-s-chief-salesman-abroad.html; Robert S. Greenberger, "Daley Uses Caution to Promote U.S. Business Interests Overseas," *The Wall Street Journal*, April 8, 1997, https://www.wsj.com/articles/SB860456305456242000.
93. David E. Sanger, "At Commerce Dept., No More Flash a la Ron Brown," *The New York Times*, July 9, 1997, https://www.nytimes.com/1997/07/09/business/at-commerce-dept-no-more-flash-a-la-ron-brown.html.
94. Steven Erlanger and David E. Sanger, "On World Stage, Many Lessons for Clinton," *The New York Times*, July 29, 1996, https://www.nytimes.com/1996/07/29/us/on-world-stage-many-lessons-for-clinton.html; Laurence Zuckerman, "$1.6 Billion in Deals Can't Mask U.S. Disappointment," *The New York Times*, June 30, 1998, https://www.nytimes.com/1998/06/30/world/clinton-in-china-trade-1.6-billion-in-deals-can-t-mask-us-disappointment.html.
95. John Tagliabue, "Airbus Has Its Eye on Half of the Global Market," *The New York Times*, April 13, 1995, https://www.nytimes.com/1995/04/13/business/international-business-airbus-has-its-eye-on-half-of-the-global-market.html.
96. Kate Sprague, "Why the Airbus-Boeing Duopoly Dominate 99% of the Large Plane Market," *CNBC*, January 26, 2019, https://www.cnbc.com/2019/01/25/why-the-airbus-boeing-companies-dominate-99percent-of-the-large-plane-market.html.
97. Tagliabue, "Airbus Has Its Eye on Half of the Global Market"; "A WTO Ruling on Aircraft Subsidies Raises the Risk of a Tariff War," *The Economist*, May 10, 2018, https://www.economist.com/finance-and-economics/2018/05/19/a-wto-ruling-on-aircraft-subsidies-raises-the-risk-of-a-tariff-war.
98. Seth Faison, "New U.S. Muscle May Send China to Europeans Instead," *The New York Times*, December 17, 1996, https://www.nytimes.com/

1996/12/17/business/new-us-muscle-may-send-china-to-europeans-instead.html; Tyler, "Western Lift for China's Air Plans."

99. John Tagliabue, "Airbus Tries to Fly in a New Formation; Consortium's Chief Hopes a Revamping Could Aid Its Challenge to Boeing," *The New York Times*, May 2, 1996, https://www.nytimes.com/1996/05/02/business/international-business-airbus-tries-fly-new-formation-consortium-s-chief-hopes.html; Seth Faison, "China to Buy 30 Planes for $1.5 Billion from Airbus Industrie," *The New York Times*, May 16, 1997, https://www.nytimes.com/1997/05/16/business/china-to-buy-30-planes-for-1.5-billion-from-airbus-industrie.html.
100. Sanger and Lohr, "A Search for Answers to Avoid the Layoffs"; David E. Sanger, "Clinton Puts a Foot in the Opening Door of the Global Market," *The New York Times*, November 21, 1993, https://www.nytimes.com/1993/11/21/weekinreview/clinton-puts-a-foot-in-the-opening-door-of-the-global-market.html.
101. Adam Bryant, "The $1 Trillion Dogfight," *The New York Times*, March 23, 1997, https://www.nytimes.com/1997/03/23/business/the-1-trillion-dogfight.html.
102. Peter T. Kilborn, "Labor's New Leaders Visit Boeing Strike," *The New York Times*, November 13, 1995, https://www.nytimes.com/1995/11/13/us/labor-s-new-leaders-visit-boeing-strike.html; Lawrence M. Fisher, "Union Rejects Boeing Offer; Goes on Strike in Three States," *The New York Times*, October 7, 1995, https://www.nytimes.com/1995/10/07/us/union-rejects-boeing-offer-goes-on-strike-in-three-states.html; Sanger and Lohr, "A Search for Answers to Avoid the Layoffs."
103. Holmes, "How Boeing Woos Beijing."
104. Sanger, "Two Roads to China."
105. Holmes, "How Boeing Woos Beijing."
106. Craig R. Whitney, "China Awards Huge Jet Order to Europeans," *The New York Times*, April 11, 1996, https://www.nytimes.com/1996/04/11/world/china-awards-huge-jet-order-to-europeans.html.
107. Bloomberg Business News, "China and France Will Study Developing a 100-Seat Jet," *The New York Times*, April 12, 1996, https://www.nytimes.com/1996/04/12/business/international-business-china-and-france-will-study-developing-a-100-seat-jet.html.
108. Sanger, "Two Roads to China."
109. Ibid.
110. David E. Sanger, "U.S. Blames Allies for Undercutting Its China Policy," *The New York Times*, June 12, 1996, https://www.nytimes.com/1996/06/12/world/us-blames-allies-for-undercutting-its-china-policy.html.
111. Steven Erlanger, "China Protests U.S. Leaks on Contributions," *The New York Times*, March 29, 1997, https://www.nytimes.com/1997/03/29/us/china-protests-us-leaks-on-contributions.html; Jeffrey

E. Garten, "Opening the Door for Business in China," *Harvard Business Review*, May–June 1998, https://hbr.org/1998/05/opening-the-doors-for-business-in-china.

112. David E. Sanger, "Boeing and Other Concerns Lobby Congress for China," *The New York Times*, April 29, 1997, https://www.nytimes.com/1997/04/29/world/boeing-and-other-concerns-lobby-congress-for-china.html.
113. Faison, "China to Buy 30 Planes for $1.5 Billion from Airbus Industrie."
114. Steven Erlanger and David E. Sanger, "On World Stage, Many Lessons for Clinton," *The New York Times*, July 29, 1996, https://www.nytimes.com/1996/07/29/us/on-world-stage-many-lessons-for-clinton.html.
115. Joseph Fewsmith, "China and the WTO: The Politics Behind the Agreement," The National Bureau of Asian Research, November 1999, https://www.iatp.org/sites/default/files/China_and_the_WTO_The_Politics_Behind_the_Agre.htm.
116. David E. Sanger, "How Push by China and U.S. Business Won over Clinton," *The New York Times*, April 15, 1999, https://www.nytimes.com/1999/04/15/world/how-push-by-china-and-us-business-won-over-clinton.html; David E. Sanger, "A Deal That America Just Couldn't Refuse," *The New York Times*, November 16, 1999, https://www.nytimes.com/1999/11/16/world/the-trade-deal-the-strategy-a-deal-that-america-just-couldn-t-refuse.html.
117. Philip Levy, "Was Letting China into the WTO a Mistake?" *Foreign Affairs*, April 2, 2018, https://www.foreignaffairs.com/articles/china/2018-04-02/was-letting-china-wto-mistake; Craig S. Smith, "Wined, Dined, Wooed on Trade: Just 2 Lawmakers Travel to China," *The New York Times*, May 2, 2000, https://www.nytimes.com/2000/05/02/world/wined-dined-wooed-on-trade-just-2-lawmakers-travel-to-china.html; World Trade Organization, "Membership, Alliances and Bureaucracy," WTO official website, https://www.wto.org/english/thewto_e/whatis_e/tif_e/org3_e.htm.
118. David E. Sanger, "A China Trade Deal Is Now Up to Clinton," *The New York Times*, April 7, 1999, https://www.nytimes.com/1999/04/07/business/international-business-a-china-trade-deal-is-now-up-to-clinton.html.
119. Joseph Kahn, "White House Steps Up Efforts for China Trade Deal," *The New York Times*, January 11, 2000, https://www.nytimes.com/2000/01/11/business/international-business-white-house-steps-up-efforts-for-china-trade-deal.html.
120. Joseph Kahn, "Executives Make Trade with China a Moral Issue," *The New York Times*, February 13, 2000, https://www.nytimes.com/2000/02/13/us/executives-make-trade-with-china-a-moral-issue.html.

121. Kahn, "White House Steps Up Efforts for China Trade Deal"; Adam Clymer, "House Votes on China Trade: The Politics Was Local," *The New York Times*, May 27, 2000, https://www.nytimes.com/2000/05/27/world/house-vote-on-china-trade-the-politics-was-local.html.
122. Nicholas R. Lardy, "Issues in China's WTO Accession," Testimony before U.S.-China Security Review Commission, May 9, 2001, https://www.brookings.edu/testimonies/issues-in-chinas-wto-accession/.
123. Business Coalition for US-China Trade, Archived version of official website, https://web.archive.org/web/20000815061920/http:/business4chinatrade.org/.
124. Keith Bradsher, "Rallying Round the China Bill, Hungrily," *The New York Times*, May 21, 2000, https://www.nytimes.com/2000/05/21/business/rallying-round-the-china-bill-hungrily-rallying-round-the-china-bill-hungrily.html.
125. Bill Clinton, "Speech on China Trade Bill," School of Advanced International Studies, Johns Hopkins University, Washington, DC, March 9, 2000, http://movies2.nytimes.com/library/world/asia/030900clinton-china-text.html; Neil Thomas, "Matters of Record: Relitigating Engagement with China," *MacroPolo*, September 3, 2019, https://macropolo.org/analysis/china-us-engagement-policy/.
126. Levy, "Was Letting China into the WTO a Mistake?"
127. Bill Bradley, "Trade, the Real Engine of Democracy," *The New York Times*, May 25, 1994, https://www.nytimes.com/1994/05/25/opinion/trade-the-real-engine-of-democracy.html; Seymour Martin Lipset, "Some Social Requisites of Democracy: Economic Development and Political Legitimacy," *The American Political Science Review*, Vol. 53, No. 1, March 1959, pp. 69–105.
128. Jonathan Peterson, "New Openness Could Flower in Deal's Wake," *Los Angeles Times*, November 16, 1999, https://www.latimes.com/archives/la-xpm-1999-nov-16-mn-34078-story.html.
129. Alison Mitchell, "Bush, Invoking 3 Presidents, Casts 'Vote' for China Trade," *The New York Times*, May 18, 2000, https://www.nytimes.com/2000/05/18/world/china-trade-wrangle-bush-speech-bush-invoking-3-presidents-casts-vote-for-china.html; Lizette Alvarez, "High-Tech Companies Making Their First Big Push in Congress on a Trade Bill," *The New York Times*, May 18, 2000, https://www.nytimes.com/2000/05/18/world/china-trade-wrangle-silicon-lobby-high-tech-companies-making-their-first-big.html; Peterson, "New Openness Could Flower in Deal's Wake"; Clymer, "House Vote on China Trade"; Clinton, "Speech on China Trade Bill"; Eric Schmitt and Joseph Kahn, "The China Trade Vote: A Clinton Triumph; House, in 237-197 Vote, Approves Normal Trade Rights for China," *The New York Times*, May 25, 2000, https://www.nytimes.com/2000/05/25/world/china-trade-

vote-clinton-triumph-house-237-197-vote-approves-normal-trade-rights. html.

130. Sanger, "A Deal That America Just Couldn't Refuse"; Holmes, "Boeing's Campaign to Protect a Market."
131. For example, Business Coalition for U.S.-China Trade, "Not a Blank Check for China…A BIG Check for Americans!" https://web.archive.org/web/20000817054038/http:/www.business4chinatrade.org/relatives/18280.pdf; Clymer, "House Vote on China Trade"; Kahn, "Executives Make Trade with China a Moral Issue."
132. Schmitt and Kahn, "The China Trade Vote: A Clinton Triumph"; David E. Sanger, "President Views Success of China Trade Bill as His Foreign Policy Legacy," *The New York Times*, May 22, 2000, https://www.nytimes.com/2000/05/22/world/president-views-success-of-china-trade-bill-as-his-foreign-policy-legacy.html.
133. Boeing, "Boeing in China," Backgrounder, October 2018, https://www.boeing.com/resources/boeingdotcom/company/key_orgs/boeing-international/pdf/chinabackgrounder.pdf.
134. International Civil Aviation Organization, Civil Aviation Statistics of the World and ICAO staff estimates, "Air Transport, Passengers Carried," World Bank Open Data, https://data.worldbank.org/indicator/IS.AIR.PSGR.
135. Leslie Wayne, "Boeing Bets the House on Its 787 Dreamliner," *The New York Times*, May 7, 2006, https://www.nytimes.com/2006/05/07/business/yourmoney/07boeing.html; Micheline Maynard, "Boeing's Strong Results Alter Strike Dynamics," *The New York Times*, September 9, 2008, https://www.nytimes.com/2008/09/10/business/10boeing.html.
136. Steven Greenhouse, "Boeing Strike Vote Fails; Company Offer is in Effect," *The New York Times*, September 15, 2002, https://www.nytimes.com/2002/09/15/us/boeing-strike-vote-fails-company-offer-is-in-effect.html.
137. Fallows, *China Airborne*.
138. Mark Landler, "Raising the Bar in the Aircraft Wars," *The New York Times*, March 15, 2006, https://www.nytimes.com/2006/03/15/business/worldbusiness/raising-the-bar-in-the-aircraft-wars.html; Leslie Wayne, "Visiting Boeing, China's President Praises Planes and Trade," *The New York Times*, April 19, 2006, https://www.nytimes.com/2006/04/19/world/asia/19cnd-china.html.
139. "Lucky 8 Pays 60 in Boeing Deal," *The New York Times*, January 29, 2005, https://www.nytimes.com/2005/01/29/business/worldbusiness/lucky-8-pays-60-in-boeing-deal.html.
140. Tim Hepher, "The American Who Put a European Aircraft Maker into Orbit," *The New York Times*, February 12, 2011,

https://archive.nytimes.com/query.nytimes.com/gst/fullpage-9A02E2DE1739F931A25751C0A9679D8B63.html; Mark Landler, "Airbus Offers Look at Double-Decker Jet, a Challenger to 747's," *The New York Times*, May 8, 2004, https://www.nytimes.com/2004/05/08/business/airbus-offers-look-at-double-deck-jet-a-challenger-to-747-s.html.

141. Keith Bradsher, "China: Airlines Sign Boeing Contract," *The New York Times*, August 9, 2005, https://www.nytimes.com/2004/05/08/business/airbus-offers-look-at-double-deck-jet-a-challenger-to-747-s.html; Don Phillips and David Lague, "Airbus Jet Deal May Put on Assembly Line in China," *The New York Times*, December 6, 2005, https://www.nytimes.com/2005/12/06/business/worldbusiness/airbus-jet-deal-may-put-an-assembly-line-in-china.html.
142. Eric Lipton, Nicola Clark, and Andrew W. Lehren, "Diplomats Help Push Sales of Jetliners on the Global Market," *The New York Times*, January 2, 2011, https://www.nytimes.com/2011/01/03/business/03wikileaks-boeing.html.
143. Wayne Arnold, "Where the Appetite for Aircraft Is Big," *The New York Times*, November 28, 2006, https://www.nytimes.com/2006/11/28/business/worldbusiness/28asiaplanes.html.
144. "Lofty Ambitions," *The Economist*, February 8, 2007, https://www.economist.com/business/2007/02/08/lofty-ambitions; James Fallows, "Can China Escape the Low-Wage Trap?" *The New York Times*, May 26, 2012, https://www.nytimes.com/2012/05/27/opinion/sunday/can-china-escape-the-low-wage-trap.html.
145. Bitzinger, "Is China Leading the Rebirth of Asia's Commercial Aircraft Industry"; Keith Bradsher, "China's New Jetliner, the Comac C919, Takes Flight for First Time," *The New York Times*, May 5, 2017, https://www.nytimes.com/2017/05/05/business/china-airplane-boeing-airbus.html; "2018 年第 14 号公告：中国商用飞机有限责任公司 2016 年度财务收支等情况审计结果," National Audit Office of the People's Republic of China, June 20, 2018, http://www.audit.gov.cn/n5/n25/c123530/content.html.
146. Bitzinger, "Is China Leading the Rebirth of Asia's Commercial Aircraft Industry"; Bloomberg News, "Will 'Made in China' Threaten Boeing and Airbus," *Bloomberg*, May 4, 2017, https://www.bloomberg.com/news/articles/2017-05-03/will-made-in-china-threaten-boeing-and-airbus-quicktake-q-a.
147. Joy Dantong Ma, "From Windfalls to Pitfalls: Qualcomm's China Conundrum," *MacroPolo*, November 14, 2018, https://macropolo.org/analysis/from-windfalls-to-pitfalls-qualcomms-china-conundrum/; David Barboza, Christopher Drew, and Steve Lohr, "G.E. to Share Jet Technology with China in New Joint Venture," *The New York Times*,

January 17, 2011, https://www.nytimes.com/2011/01/18/business/global/18plane.html.

148. Mark Landler and Keith Bradsher, "Raising the Bar in the Aircraft Wars," *The New York Times*, March 15, 2006, https://www.nytimes.com/2006/03/15/business/worldbusiness/raising-the-bar-in-the-aircraft-wars.html; Keith Bradsher, "Airbus and China Select Assembly Plant Site," *The New York Times*, June 9, 2006, https://www.nytimes.com/2006/06/09/business/worldbusiness/09airbus.html; Peggy Hollinger and David Keohane, "Airbus Woos China with A380 Industrial Partnership Offer," *Financial Times*, January 8, 2018, https://www.ft.com/content/f67dd44e-f345-11e7-88f7-5465a6ce1a00.
149. Boeing, "Boeing in China"; Airbus, "Airbus in China," Airbus company website, https://www.airbus.com/company/worldwide-presence/china.html; Bloomberg News, "Boeing to Open its First 737 Plant in China Under Shadow of a Trade War," *Bloomberg*, December 13, 2018, https://www.bloomberg.com/amp/news/articles/2018-12-13/boeing-s-first-china-737-plant-to-open-in-shadow-of-trade-war.
150. Keith Crane et al., *The Effectiveness of China's Industrial Policies in Commercial Aviation Manufacturing* (RAND Corporation, 2014), https://www.rand.org/pubs/research_reports/RR245.html; Holmes, "How Boeing Woos Beijing."
151. Sanger, "Two Roads to China."
152. Richard Aboulafia, "A Reality Check on China's C919 Jetliner," *Forbes*, May 8, 2017, https://www.forbes.com/sites/richardaboulafia/2017/05/08/a-reality-check-on-chinas-c919-jetliner/#1eb6f9b1195f.
153. Bradsher, "China's New Jetliner."
154. Aboulafia, "A Reality Check on China's C919 Jetliner"; China Power Team, "How Is Commercial Aviation Propelling China's Economic Development."
155. Aboulafia, "A Reality Check on China's C919 Jetliner"; Reuters, "The COMAC C919 Jet, China's Answer to the Boeing 737, Now Just Needs to Sell," *Traveller*, April 26, 2017, http://www.traveller.com.au/the-comac-c919-jet-chinas-answer-to-the-boeing-737-now-just-needs-to-sell-gvrsce; Various, "The Power of Chinese Wings," *Zócalo*, May 13, 2012, https://www.zocalopublicsquare.org/2012/05/13/the-power-of-chinese-wings/ideas/up-for-discussion/.
156. Crane et al., *The Effectiveness of China's Industrial Policies in Commercial Aviation Manufacturing*.
157. Bradsher, "China's New Jetliner"; Thomas Duesterberg, "Can the Chinese Create a Competitive Commercial Aviation Industry?" The Aspen Institute, February 5, 2015, https://www.aspeninstitute.org/blog-posts/can-chinese-create-competitive-commercial-aviation-industry/.

158. Duesterberg, "Can the Chinese Create a Competitive Commercial Aviation Industry?"
159. Elizabeth Becker, "U.S. to Begin Trade Case over Airbus," *The New York Times*, May 31, 2005, https://www.nytimes.com/2005/05/31/business/worldbusiness/us-to-begin-trade-case-over-airbus.html; John Cassidy, "Enter the Dragon," *The New Yorker*, December 13, 2010, https://www.newyorker.com/magazine/2010/12/13/enter-the-dragon; "A WTO Ruling on Aircraft Subsidies Raises the Risk of a Tariff War."
160. Christopher Drew and Nicola Clark, "W.T.O. Affirms Ruling of Improper Airbus Aid," *The New York Times*, March 23, 2010, https://www.nytimes.com/2010/03/24/business/global/24subsidy.html.
161. Neil Thomas, "Change of Plans: Making Market Capitalism Safe for China," *MacroPolo*, December 30, 2018, https://macropolo.org/analysis/change-of-plans-making-market-capitalism-safe-for-china/.
162. Barboza, Drew, and Lohr, "G.E. to Share Jet Technology with China in New Joint Venture."
163. Dominic Gates, "Boeing Chief Defends China 737 Center, Unveils 300 Jet Orders," *The Seattle Times*, September 23, 2015, https://www.seattletimes.com/business/boeing-aerospace/boeing-agrees-to-open-737-center-in-china-inks-300-new-jet-orders/; Boeing, "Boeing in China."
164. Bitzinger, "Is China Leading the Rebirth of Asia's Commercial Aircraft Industry."
165. Sanger, "'Asian Money,' American Fears"; Victoria Bryan and Jamie Freed, "After Delays, Japan's Regional Jet Faces Dogfight with Industry Giants," *Reuters*, July 17, 2018, https://www.reuters.com/article/us-britain-airshow-mrj/after-delays-japans-regional-jet-faces-dogfight-with-industry-giants-idUSKBN1K71IW.
166. Lee Hudson Teslik, "China's Motor Vehicle and Aerospace Industries," Council on Foreign Relations, October 5, 2007, https://www.cfr.org/backgrounder/chinas-motor-vehicle-and-aerospace-industries; Amanda Lee, "China's Aviation Industry Has a Steep Climb to 'Made in China 2025' Goals," *South China Morning Post*, October 29, 2018, https://www.scmp.com/business/article/2170746/chinas-aviation-industry-has-steep-climb-made-china-2025-goals; Bradley Perrett, "Global Market Opens for C919 as EASA Works on Certification," *Aviation Week & Space Technology*, April 28, 2017, https://aviationweek.com/new-civil-aircraft/global-market-opens-c919-easa-works-certification; Fallows, *China Airborne*.
167. Crane et al., *The Effectiveness of China's Industrial Policies in Commercial Aviation Manufacturing*.

168. UBS, "The 3D Revolution Takes Off in China," *The Wall Street Journal*, undated, https://partners.wsj.com/ubs/invest-in-china/printing-planes/?campID=DS-CTNT2018-GLOBAL-ENG-BAN-WSJ-NA-NATCONT-PP-HTML5-ANY-RM-WSJ-TL-FP-STD-BRD; Chad J.R. Ohlandt, "Implications of China's Aerospace Industrial Policies," Testimony before the U.S.-China Economic and Security Review Commission, April 27, 2016, https://www.rand.org/pubs/testimonies/CT456.html.
169. "China Should Worry Less About Old Enemies, More About Ex-Friends," *The Economist*, December 15, 2018, https://www.economist.com/china/2018/12/15/china-should-worry-less-about-old-enemies-more-about-ex-friends.
170. Donald J. Trump, "Inaugural Address," Washington, DC, January 20, 2017, https://www.whitehouse.gov/briefings-statements/the-inaugural-address/.
171. Lesley Wroughton, "Trump Administration Says U.S. Mistakenly Backed China WTO Accession in 2001," *Reuters*, January 20, 2018, https://www.reuters.com/article/us-usa-trade-china/trump-administration-says-u-s-mistakenly-backed-china-wto-accession-in-2001-idUSKBN1F82U1.
172. United States Trade Representative, "Findings of the Investigation into China's Acts, Policies, and Practices Related to Technology Transfer, Intellectual Property, and Innovation Under Section 301 of the Trade Act of 1974," March 22, 2018, https://ustr.gov/sites/default/files/Section%20301%20FINAL.PDF.
173. "American Accuses China of Stealing Aerospace Trade Secrets," *The Economist*, November 5, 2018, https://www.economist.com/gulliver/2018/11/05/america-accuses-china-of-stealing-aerospace-trade-secrets; Lingling Wei and Bob Davis, "How China Systematically Pries Technology from U.S. Companies," *The Wall Street Journal*, September 26, 2018, https://www.wsj.com/articles/how-china-systematically-pries-technology-from-u-s-companies-1537972066.
174. Bradsher, "China's New Jetliner"; Keith Bradsher and Paul Mozur, "China's Plan to Build Its Own High-Tech Industries Worries Western Businesses," *The New York Times*, March 7, 2017, https://www.nytimes.com/2017/03/07/business/china-trade-manufacturing-europe.html.
175. Natalie Kitroeff, "Tariff Impact Colors a Key House Race in Boeing Country," *The New York Times*, May 3, 2018, https://www.nytimes.com/2017/03/07/business/china-trade-manufacturing-europe.html.
176. Ibid.; Boeing, "Boeing in China."
177. Boeing, "Boeing in China"; Boeing, "Commercial Market Outlook, 2019–2038," https://www.boeing.com/commercial/market/commercial-market-outlook/.

178. Bradsher and Mozur, "China's Plan to Build Its Own High-Tech Industries Worries Western Businesses."
179. Keith Bradsher, "In China-U.S. Trade War, Trump Would Have Weapons," *The New York Times*, November 10, 2016, https://www.nytimes.com/2016/11/11/business/international/trump-china-us-trade-war.html; Bloomberg News, "Is This Chinese Love-In with Boeing About to End?" *Bloomberg*, October 19, 2018, https://www.bloomberg.com/news/articles/2018-10-19/chinese-boeing-client-said-to-be-in-airbus-talks-amid-trade-war.
180. Kirk Johnson, "Trump Talk Rattles Aerospace Industry, Up and Down Supply Chain," *The New York Times*, February 23, 2017, https://www.nytimes.com/2017/02/23/us/trump-talk-rattles-aerospace-industry-up-and-down-supply-chain.html; Airbus, "Airbus in China."
181. Natalie Kitroeff, "Boeing May Become a Target in a Trade War over Trump's Tariffs," *The New York Times*, March 14, 2018, https://www.nytimes.com/2018/03/14/business/economy/boeing-tariffs-china.html; Keith Bradsher and Ana Swanson, "Trump's Visit to China: More Business Deals Than Trade Pacts," *The New York Times*, November 7, 2017, https://www.nytimes.com/2017/11/07/business/trump-china-trade.html; Keith Bradsher, "Trump Promotes Deals in China, but Hints at Long Trade Fight Ahead," *The New York Times*, November 8, 2017, https://www.nytimes.com/2017/11/09/business/donald-trump-china-trade-xi-jinping.html.
182. Natalie Kitroeff and Ben Casselman, "In Sparing Consumers Tariff Burden, Trump Hit Manufacturing," *The New York Times*, April 4, 2018, https://www.nytimes.com/2018/04/04/business/economy/trade-impact.html.
183. Danny Lee, "Aircraft Maker Boeing Says It Is Playing Peacemaker in US-China Trade War and Committed to Chinese Investments," *South China Morning Post*, October 27, 2018, https://www.scmp.com/news/hong-kong/transport/article/2170509/aircraft-maker-boeing-says-it-playing-peacemaker-us-china; Eric M. Johnson, "Boeing CEO Eyes Major Aircraft Order Under Any U.S.-China Trade Deal," *Reuters*, August 27, 2019, https://www.reuters.com/article/us-usa-trade-boeing-ceo-exclusive/exclusive-boeing-ceo-eyes-major-aircraft-order-under-any-u-s-china-trade-deal-idUSKCN1VH2J2.
184. Gerry Shih, "China's Ban on the Boeing 737 Max Inspires Others, Ramps Up Pressure on U.S. Regulator," *The Washington Post*, March 12, 2019, https://www.washingtonpost.com/world/asia_pacific/chinas-ban-on-the-boeing-737-max-inspires-others-and-ramps-up-pressure-on-the-faa/2019/03/12/4d4bf2b0-44a3-11e9-90f0-0ccfeec87a61_story.html.

185. Dominic Gates, "With Close Industry Ties, FAA Safety Chief Pushed More Delegation of Oversight to Boeing," *The Seattle Times*, April 14, 2019, https://www.seattletimes.com/business/boeing-aerospace/with-close-industry-ties-faa-safety-chief-pushed-more-delegation-of-oversight-to-boeing/; Peter Robison, "Former Boeing Engineers Say Relentless Cost-Cutting Sacrificed Safety," *Bloomberg Businessweek*, May 8, 2019, https://www.bloomberg.com/news/features/2019-05-09/former-boeing-engineers-say-relentless-cost-cutting-sacrificed-safety.
186. "Boeing's Troubles Cost the Aerospace Industry $4bn a Quarter," *The Economist*, August 22, 2019, https://www.economist.com/business/2019/08/22/boeings-troubles-cost-the-aerospace-industry-4bn-a-quarter; Chris Isidore and Rene Marsh, "Yet Another Boeing Plane has a Problem," *CNN*, September 11, 2019, https://www.cnn.com/2019/09/10/business/boeing-777x-safety-test/index.html; Orange Wang, "Airbus, Boeing and Comac See Blue Skies Ahead for China's Aircraft Market," *South China Morning Post*, September 23, 2019, https://www.scmp.com/economy/china-economy/article/3029876/airbus-boeing-and-comac-see-blue-skies-ahead-chinas-aircraft.
187. *Bloomberg News*, "Boeing is in Talks for a Megadeal That the Trade War Could Derail," *Bloomberg*, June 5, 2019, https://www.bloomberg.com/news/articles/2019-06-05/boeing-in-talks-for-china-megadeal-that-trade-war-could-derail; Julie Johnsson, "Boeing Warns U.S.-China Spat Raises New Risk for 787 Dreamliner," *Bloomberg*, September 11, 2019, https://www.bloomberg.com/news/articles/2019-09-11/boeing-warns-u-s-china-spat-raises-new-risk-for-787-dreamliner; David Gelles and Natalie Kitroeff, "Boeing Board to Call for Safety Changes After 737 Max Crashes," *The New York Times*, September 15, 2019, https://www.nytimes.com/2019/09/15/business/boeing-safety-737-max.html.
188. *Bloomberg News*, "Boeing to Open Its First 737 Plant in China Under Shadow of a Trade War."
189. Deloitte, MIT, and Datawheel, "Aircraft & Parts Manufacturing," Data USA, https://datausa.io/profile/naics/33641M1/#io.
190. *Bloomberg News*, "Boeing to Open Its First 737 Plant in China Under Shadow of a Trade War."
191. David H. Autor, David Dorn, and Gordon H. Hanson, "The China Shock: Learning from Labor-Market Adjustment to Large Changes in Trade," NBER Working Paper No 21906, January 2016, https://www.nber.org/papers/w21906.
192. Bob Davis, "When the World Opened the Gates of China," *The Wall Street Journal*, July 27, 2018, https://www.wsj.com/articles/when-the-world-opened-the-gates-of-china-1532701482.

193. Andrew Nathan, "Authoritarian Resilience," *Journal of Democracy*, Vol. 14, No. 1, January 2003, pp. 6–17; Nicholas D. Kristof, "It's China Against the World, with a Great Deal at Stake," *The New York Times*, November 29, 1992, https://www.nytimes.com/1992/11/29/weekinreview/the-world-it-s-china-against-the-world-with-a-great-deal-at-stake.html.
194. R.W. Apple Jr., "Clinton Concedes China Policy Hasn't Helped Much on Rights," *The New York Times*, January 29, 1997, https://www.nytimes.com/1997/01/29/world/clinton-concedes-china-policy-hasn-t-helped-much-on-rights.html.
195. Scott Lincicome, "A Failure to Adjust," *The Bulwark*, January 15, 2019, https://thebulwark.com/a-failure-to-adjust/.
196. Jun Mai, "Former Top US Trade Negotiator Charlene Barshefsky Says China Deviated From Its Commitments, Paving Way for Trade War," *South China Morning Post*, January 1, 2019, https://www.scmp.com/news/china/diplomacy/article/2180216/former-top-us-trade-negotiator-charlene-barshefsky-says-china.
197. "China Scrambles To Sustain Its Trade Truce with America," *The Economist*, December 22, 2018, https://www.economist.com/finance-and-economics/2018/12/22/china-scrambles-to-sustain-its-trade-truce-with-america.

CHAPTER 10

Conclusion

Damien Ma

In recent debates about China's future, there has been a notable tendency toward fatalism. For many observers and commentators, the "new era" of today's China is the "end of history" in the country: what is now must always and forever be. Such a view, as the Harvard scholar Julian Gewirtz has noted, seems to have been cemented after Xi's elimination of presidential term limits in March 2018.

Yet who could have predicted that Deng Xiaoping's "reform and opening" would follow the 20 years of chaos and violence under Mao Zedong? So too should we remain wary of narratives that extrapolate linearly from the present, as if China's future is somehow entirely path-dependent.

These narratives take hold because too often "China" is used as an abstract idea to win policy fights or to expose America's own inadequacies. Op-ed pages regularly feature columns about China's supposed leadership in some arena and how America needs to wake up to the challenge or risk falling behind. China has become the all-weather "Sputnik moment" that America needs to jolt it out of its complacency and rise to the challenge. But such narratives rarely reflect the complexities of the world's second-largest economy and most populous country.

D. Ma (✉)
Paulson Institute, Chicago, IL, USA
e-mail: dma@paulsoninstitute.org

D. Ma (ed.), *China's Economic Arrival*,
https://doi.org/10.1007/978-981-15-2275-8_10

The current US–China technology competition exemplifies this tendency. In the course of just a few years, China suddenly transformed from the tortoise to the hare in the race. The decades-long narrative of a nondemocratic China incapable of innovation has been swiftly replaced with that of an authoritarian tech goliath capable of exporting Orwellian techno-dystopia throughout the world.

But neither narrative maps that closely onto reality. China always had both technological ambition and capabilities—it had sent its first satellite to space in 1970, in the midst of the Cultural Revolution—but today it is also not the unstoppable juggernaut in every technological sphere that some seem to believe. As this volume has shown, China has focused on technological catch-up for many decades, pouring state capital into developing talent, infrastructure, and research and development. Much investment was wasted, but much met with success. None of it took place overnight, however.

What China has mastered is the ability to rapidly deploy the present, but it has not invented the future. This convergence with current technological advancements can be seen in areas such as 5G. Mobile technology has been incubating for decades in Western economies, and China's main advantage is in the deployment and scaling of such technology, which would allow its standards to gain global market share. For US companies, it is not a matter of being a technological laggard, but a matter of neglecting to invest in 5G, having focused on the previous 3G and 4G standards.

A similar situation unfolded with AI—supposedly another front in the contest for technological supremacy—which is an old technology that was pioneered in America decades ago. China did not invent AI, but by making it a national priority, it invested in the academic talent and technical capabilities needed to make many AI applications a practical reality. Now that computing power, semiconductors, and data have caught up, China has the AI scientists who can implement these technologies, whether it is in the private or public sector.

These nuances matter, because US–China competition is not a blunt head-to-head race, but rather a complex interdependency in which both countries have strengths and vulnerabilities. China's main advantage continues to be its impressive ability to commercialize and scale existing technology. Where America falters is not in its technological leadership, but in its inability to define national priorities and its vitiated capacity to scale quickly. Yet instead of devising solutions to drive and nurture American development, Washington has largely resorted to trying to slow China down.

Neither strategy is sufficient by itself. And while fundamental technological breakthroughs are rare and unpredictable, they tend to be propelled by outside-the-box thinking, diversity of ideas, and universalizing appeal. China still lags far behind the United States on all three fronts. In fact, with only a handful of exceptions, Chinese companies are mainly interested in innovating within its domestic market, having had little success in globalizing their innovations.

Such gaps between reality and perception are not confined to technology. On the economy, the usual battles between bulls and bears have metastasized into more extreme polarization: China's economy is either teetering on the edge of collapse or it is a triumph of a state capitalist model that will be exported to developing nations.

But these debates hover at 30,000 feet and miss the trees. Accumulating enormous debt in the decade after the financial crisis was a major risk for the Chinese economy, but Beijing seemed to have gotten a grip on the problem when it began to deleverage in earnest a few years ago. Policymakers clamped down on the shadow banking system and then moved to gradually dispose of nonperforming loans, all the while withholding credit to curtail wasteful investments.

Combined, these efforts were meant to force a reset from the countercyclical stimulus that served as the default position of Chinese economic policymaking. Beijing pumped credit into the system, got immediate growth, and accumulated waste—rinse and repeat. A reckoning had to come at some point, and it arrived under the Xi administration, which is far more tolerant of austerity than was anticipated.

In fact, most of Xi's major priorities have not been conducive to near-term growth—everything from the anti-corruption campaign that began under his tenure to the environmental crackdown and regulatory screws imposed on the financial system. Whether it is corruption in the political system or the economy, this is an administration intent on mopping up the excesses.

This new environment required a psychological adjustment as well, namely a downplaying of the headline GDP growth target that has been central to Chinese economic policy for decades. Yet the Xi administration has gradually watered down its political importance, particularly after its adoption of a new "principal contradiction" in 2018 that laid the groundwork for a post-growth development platform. As a result, some provinces have abandoned the target altogether. The profound impact this shift will have on the Chinese growth model over the long term should not be underestimated.

Yet these dynamics within China have yet to change the conventional wisdom that Beijing has an itchy trigger finger for stimulus. Market observers still wonder when Beijing will supercharge growth again and remain skeptical that the government will let the economy slow for the sake of long-term structural adjustment. Yet if the "GDP obsession" has actually fallen out of favor, then old frameworks centered around that fixation are no longer so useful.

A tendency to consult old frameworks is unsurprising: to understand the present, we often look to the past. This inclination is particularly pronounced when it comes to the current moment in US–China relations. Whether present tensions are characterized as a "Cool War" or the "New Cold War," such analogies can be risky when applied haphazardly. That's because they imply policy responses from a bygone era to deal with new and different challenges.

Indeed, the evolution of this bilateral relationship is often best viewed from the ground up, through institutions, organizations, and companies. Like Boeing, for example, the aviation giant has had a front-row seat to forty years of change in China, during which the country transformed from an insular society to an international powerhouse. Accordingly, the firm had to vie for market share and to protect itself from Chinese demands for technology—in a word, to adjust.

Boeing is only one company, but its experience makes tangible what engagement actually means and what severing ties would entail. Without internalizing these realities from the bottom-up, "decoupling" remains an appealing abstraction that ignores potentially devastating and counterproductive costs.

As this volume has shown, the American debate on US–China relations needs more "China"—not a crude and blurred caricature but a nuanced portrait of America's most formidable competitor in sharp relief. Untangling something as complex as China's arrival—a once-in-a-century disruption that affects labor markets and global governance to commodity prices and climate change—is never easy and may not even be appealing.

But then again, all great power rises have been disruptive. The United States' own ascent in the twentieth century was no exception. That process was far from quiescent—if anything, America was so disruptive that it ended up creating a system from scratch to replace the one that produced two successive, catastrophic world wars.

The global system remains one predicated on economic complementarity and openness: America provided a "default setting"—rules, standards, ideology—from which all countries could borrow and attempt to advance themselves within these parameters. This "open source code" also fundamentally benefitted American interests, because it was the first time a global superpower offered a blueprint for governing the world with principles and rules, not merely through territorial claims and warships. Far from perfect, that system nonetheless defined modernity for an entire century, largely kept the peace, and generated unprecedented global prosperity.

It lifted all boats, including that of China. So why would China seek the demise of a system in which it was one of the largest beneficiaries? Moreover, Beijing has no alternative vision of a Chinese-led global system to offer. But China is clearly dissatisfied with some features of the current system, and with its growing capabilities and influence, it wants to modify those features to better serve its own interests. That desire should come as no surprise.

But renegotiating the status quo—especially if a new equilibrium requires America to cede some of its preeminent position—was never going to be simple. And it will likely involve collateral damage, especially when this dynamic involves two countries that constitute 40% of the global economy. What will ultimately determine China's conduct and behavior, however, will be driven as much by what happens inside the country as US responses to Beijing's moves.

This volume serves that purpose, not by merely peeking behind the curtains but by diving deep inside China's development, its political economy, and its organizations. I hope the collection has exposed readers to a China that is different from what they may have imagined. It isn't some abstract "Frankenstein" bent on overturning the world or able to outmaneuver America at every turn. But it is an ambitious and challenging country, alternately projecting aspiration and insecurity in a bid to assume a status it feels is deserved of a great power.

When asked what he thought about the French Revolution, Chinese Premier Zhou Enlai famously quipped "it's too soon to tell." The impact of China's arrival, however, is already evident and reverberating in both profound and prosaic ways. A generation of Americans will have grown up amid a geopolitical reality in which China was always a global power and in which a brewing contest between the world's number one and number two seems a *fait accompli*.

As both observers of, and participants in, this tectonic shift, we hope that we are doing our part in confronting the realities that will inform the future. After all, the best kind of history is the one you take part in shaping.